# Personal Memoirs
## of John H. Brinton

## Shawnee Classics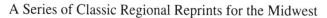

A Series of Classic Regional Reprints for the Midwest

**"Black Jack"**
John A. Logan and Southern Illinois
    in the Civil War Era
*James Pickett Jones*

**The Outlaws of Cave-in-Rock**
*Otto A. Rothert*

**A Woman's Story of Pioneer Illinois**
*Christiana Holmes Tillson*
*Edited by Milo Milton Quaife*

**Army Life of an Illinois Soldier**
Including a Day-by-Day Record of
    Sherman's March to the Sea
*Charles W. Wills*

# PERSONAL MEMOIRS
# OF JOHN H. BRINTON
## CIVIL WAR SURGEON,
## 1861–1865

FOREWORD BY JOHN Y. SIMON
PREFACE BY JOHN S. HALLER, JR.

SOUTHERN ILLINOIS
UNIVERSITY PRESS

CARBONDALE AND EDWARDSVILLE

Foreword by John Y. Simon
and Preface by John S. Haller, Jr.,
copyright © 1996 by the Board of Trustees,
Southern Illinois University

99 98 97 96      4 3 2 1

The publisher would like to thank Morris Library, Southern
Illinois University at Carbondale, for providing the copy of the
original edition of John H. Brinton's *Personal Memoirs* from
which this reprint was made.

Library of Congress Cataloging-in-Publication Data

Brinton, John H. (John Hill), 1832–1907.
    Personal memoirs of John H. Brinton, Civil War Surgeon,
    1861–1865 / foreword by John Y. Simon; preface by John S.
Haller, Jr.
        p.  cm. — (Shawnee classics)
    Originally published as Personal memoirs of John H.
    Brinton, major and surgeon U. S. V., 1861–1865. New York:
    Neale Pub. Co., 1914.
    Includes index.
    1. Brinton, John H. (John Hill), 1832–1907. 2. United
States—History—Civil War, 1861–1865—Medical care.
3. United States—History—Civil War, 1861–1865—Personal
narratives. 4. Physicians—United States—Biography. I. Title.
II. Series.
E621.R75    1996
973.7'75'092—dc20
[B]                                           95-49078
ISBN 0-8093-2044-4 (paper: alk. paper)        CIP

# CONTENTS

limb—Sidelights on the alcohol problem—A cure for whiskey tapping—The varied uses of cherry brandy—Vicissitudes of the museum.

# FOREWORD

One year into the Civil War, Dr. John H. Brinton, an extremely well-trained and capable surgeon, received orders to report to Washington. He soon found himself immersed in the preparation of a medical and surgical history of the war and in the establishment of the Army Medical Museum. Ultimately, both enterprises immensely benefited medical science, in large part through Brinton's organizational and intellectual ability. Nonetheless, one must wonder why a man of unusual surgical knowledge and skill transferred from battlefield to desk duty in the midst of a sanguinary civil war.

The assignment may have reflected Brinton's efforts to obtain promotion. By passing the examination for surgeon with distinction early in the war, Brinton achieved the status of brigade surgeon, ranking fourth on the list of appointments. Those ranking first and second received promotion to medical inspector. When Congress abolished the rank of brigade surgeon, those lower on the list were virtually demoted to ordinary surgeons. Although service in Washington brought access to influential supporters, Brinton resigned at the close of the war with the same rank at which he entered.

Brinton pointed out that the surgeon ranked second among brigade surgeons, Frank H. Hamilton, was a brother-in-law of the chairman of the Senate Committee on Military Affairs. Brinton conceded that Hamilton was, in addition, a professor of surgery and the author of a medical text. And Brinton was hardly in a convincing position to imply that others benefited from family connections. He received his original appointment at nearly the same time that his first cousin, George Brinton McClellan, received a call to reorganize and train the disorderly troops who had streamed back to Washington after the disastrous battle of Bull Run. The general's father was a pillar of both the social and medical establishments in Philadelphia, and his mother was a Brinton, a family that presumably ranked with the McClellans or the marriage would never have taken place.

Brinton profited from his cousin's prominence in the early years of the war but paid for it later. Removed from command by President Lincoln in November 1862, McClellan drifted into Democratic politics and eventually ran against Lincoln in the 1864 election. Brinton's *Personal Memoirs* record remarkably little about his cousin save an absurd story that McClellan refused to advance after the battle of Antietam because of orders received from General-in-Chief Henry W. Halleck. Assigned to visit the battlefield at the time, Brinton had heard grumbling about McClellan's failure to pursue the enemy, which he discounted later on the basis of information from a recent patient, General Ruggles, presumably George D. Ruggles, who had served on McClellan's staff during the Antietam campaign. On October 6, 1862, Halleck had telegraphed to McClellan that "The President directs that you cross the Potomac and give battle to the enemy or drive him south. . . . the Secretary of War [Edwin M. Stanton] and the General-in-Chief fully concur with the President in these instructions."[1] McClellan had already written to his wife that he had "insisted that Stanton shall be removed & that Halleck shall give way to me as Comdr in Chief. I will *not* serve under him—for he is an incompetent fool—in no way fit for the important place he holds."[2] Had Halleck given the orders reported by Ruggles, McClellan would not necessarily have obeyed; nor did McClellan ever need exhortations for caution. Brinton had formed his own

---

1. *The War of the Rebellion: A Compilation of the Official Records of the Union and Confederate Armies* (Washington, 1880–1901), series I, vol. xix, part 2, 10–11.
2. *The Civil War Papers of George B. McClellan: Selected Correspondence, 1860–1865,* edited by Stephen W. Sears (New York: Ticknor and Fields, 1989), 473.

poor opinion of Halleck in May 1862 on the basis of close acquaintance with him as his physician. Brinton believed that Halleck
was "overestimated," lacked energy, and was so fond of wine
that he was often drowsy after dinner. Brinton dismissed Halleck's
chief of staff, George W. Cullum, as a "Miss Nancy." In Washington, Brinton reported to Surgeon General William A.
Hammond, an energetic medical reformer favored by General
McClellan. Hammond's skill kept him in office until August 1864,
when his career collapsed amid a vindictive court-martial. One
month later, with the presidential campaign in full swing, Brinton
was sent westward from Washington, completing his wartime
service under General William S. Rosecrans, another commander
of diminished reputation. In answer to Brinton's question about
his exile from Washington, a fellow military surgeon reminded
him of McClellan's middle name. Despite nascent professional-
ism in medicine in postwar America, Brinton secured support for
his application for a professorship of anatomy from generals such
as Grant, Sheridan, and Rosecrans and mentioned none from
Cousin George.

Brinton's acceptance of late-nineteenth-century gossip
about his cousin is an exception in memoirs that are otherwise
remarkable for accuracy and frankness. McClellan plays a minor
role in an account that is chiefly valuable as a medical memoir
and as an intimate portrait of Ulysses S. Grant early in his Civil
War career. Grant assumed command at Cairo on September 4,
1861; Brinton arrived on September 13. Grant had already re-
sponded to Confederate violation of Kentucky neutrality by occupying Paducah, but his first battle lay ahead. Brinton found a
quiet and unassuming man smoking a pipe—he could not yet
afford cigars—and soon recognized a commander with mysterious strength of intellect and character. Brinton describes Grant
with enough perceptive insight and admiration to arouse suspi-
cions that his opinions benefit from hindsight. But Brinton quotes
from his own wartime correspondence, notably a letter of March
2, 1862, to Dr. J. M. DaCosta (Brinton's future brother-in-law)
written soon after the fall of Fort Donelson, assuring him that

"our General is a good soldier and prompt. He means what he says, and says what he means. He is not afraid of responsibility."

In return, Brinton received Grant's favor. Grant put Brinton in the place of the former medical director, sent to Washington to obtain more support from the surgeon general. Surgeon General Clement Finley then complained that Grant "substitutes an inexperienced Medical Officer for the performance of very important duties."[3] In his report of the battle of Belmont, fought on November 7, Grant wrote that Brinton "was on the field during the entire engagement and displayed great ability and efficiency in providing for the wounded and organizing the Medical Corps."[4] Brinton even convinced an incredulous Grant that the enemy was sending reinforcements across the Mississippi River in time for Grant to prepare to meet this unexpected threat. Brinton left for Washington in May 1862, carrying a letter from Grant to his congressional patron, Elihu B. Washburne, explaining that "as we have lived together most of the time for the last six months our acquaintance is more than transient, it has become intimate." Again writing to Washburne a few months later, Grant referred to Brinton as "an honor to his profession and to the service both for his moral worth and attainments in and out of his profession. Although yet but a young man you will find that Dr. Brinton has won for himself . . . a reputation attained by but few in the country, of any age, and by none others as young as himself." So close was the relationship between general and surgeon that Grant later counted upon the assistance of Brinton's mother in finding the Grant family a house to rent in Philadelphia.[5]

Brinton was still under thirty when he left Grant's com-

---

3. *The Papers of Ulysses S. Grant,* edited by John Y. Simon, 20 vols. to date (Carbondale: Southern Illinois University Press, 1967– ), 3:75.
4. *The Papers of Ulysses S. Grant,* 3:143. Brinton's reports of the battles of Belmont and Fort Donelson are in *The Medical and Surgical History of the War of the Rebellion* (Washington, 1870), part I, appendix, 18–22, 24–33.
5. *The Papers of Ulysses S. Grant,* 12:77.

mand. The *Personal Memoirs,* written when Brinton was twice
that age, sometimes reflect the crusty opinions of the eminent
surgeon that he had become. He persistently complained about
"this female nurse business" that brought him women "helpless,
irritable and unhappy," too often the "fussy female, intent on
notoriety and glorying in her good works." More creditably, he
had sent for nuns from Indiana who "adapted themselves admirably to their new duties." Yet Brinton's upper-class Protestant
biases erupted in all-too-frequent instances of anti-Semitism,
something that became epidemic in the western armies and culminated in Grant's disastrously misconceived orders expelling all
Jews from his department. Had he remained longer with Grant,
Brinton might have been one of the few to applaud Grant's blun-
der. His comments about hospitals for black troops possess a
singularly offensive tone.

Upon completing the manuscript in 1891, Brinton intended
to send it out for binding rather than for publication. He had
written his story for his family, not for the public. He died in
1907, seven years before publication of his *Personal Memoirs.* Why
the Brinton family chose the Neale Publishing Company, which
specialized in Confederate reminiscences, remains a mystery. Like
many other Neale books, Brinton's *Personal Memoirs* has become
scarce and costly. Less puzzling was the choice of S. Weir Mitchell
to write an "Introductory Note." An eminent physician also respected as a poet and novelist, Mitchell dominated social and
literary society in Philadelphia. Edward T. Stuart, also of Philadelphia, "a high authority on the Civil War," received credit for
help in editing and annotating the manuscript. Stuart's annota-
tions too frequently either belabor the obvious or exude pedan-
tic irrelevancy. Whoever transcribed the manuscript for printing
apparently had difficulty with Brinton's handwriting, a problem
resulting in many mishandled proper names.[6]

It is possible to disapprove of aspects of Brinton and of the

---

6. Examples include: "Walker and Stemble" for Walke and Stembel
(71); "I. P. Hawkins" for J. P. Hawkins (108); "Hiller" for Hillyer (128);

book that chronicled his Civil War experiences while acknowledging that history would be the poorer without the *Personal Memoirs*. The young Philadelphia surgeon, unexpectedly sent so far from home, brought to the western armies a fresh perspective on campaigns that doomed the Confederacy. As Grant rose to military prominence, many witnesses observed him closely, but Brinton first knew him in relative obscurity. Trained in the precise craft of surgery, Brinton recorded his experience accurately and dispassionately. Grant told Brinton that "the art of war is simple enough; find out where your enemy is, get at him as soon as you can, and strike him as hard as you can, and keep moving on." The surgeon better understood Grant's military style than did many professional soldiers. One of very few who had ever seen Grant tearful, Brinton left us an appraisal of his close friend that has lasting significance and appeal.

JOHN Y. SIMON

---

"Clarkesville" for Clarksville (143); "Ogelsby" for Oglesby (148); "Thorn" for Thom (165); "Folten" for Totten (224); "McCullough" for McCulloch (260); "Gerault" for Gerolt (260); "Chiselin" for Ghiselin (296); "Grane" for Crane (313); "Jenny" for Jenney (331); "Hewitt" for Hewit (passim).

# PREFACE

The reprinting of John Hill Brinton's *Personal Memoirs* comes as a welcome addition to the literature on the Civil War. Almost thirty years have passed since I first read these memoirs as part of a graduate readings course. I had the good fortune at the time of finding a copy in a used bookstore in Riverdale, a small community adjacent to the University of Maryland at College Park, that catered to those of us who purchase books out of habit, love for the written word, and perhaps a desire to complete our own personal canon. Somewhere, over the years and in the course of five different moves, I misplaced the book. Perhaps it was never really lost but found its way to the shelf of another used bookstore where it was discovered by a less fickle owner.

My first reading of *Personal Memoirs* was to learn more about Ulysses S. Grant who, having just received his brigadier general's commission, had befriended Brinton in the early days of the war when Brinton served in the Department of the West. I had little concern for Brinton himself except for the military men he knew and the impressions he kept of them. Besides Grant for whom he served as medical director, Brinton had the opportunity to meet and observe many of the Union's top military, including Philip H. Sheridan, John C. Frémont, Henry W. Halleck, William A. Hammond, D. C. Buell, John A. Rawlins, James Birdseye McPherson, C. F. Smith, John A. McClernand, William S. Rosecrans, and Brinton's first cousin, George B. McClellan. That Brinton had been commissioned by Lincoln as a major and brigade surgeon of volunteers in August 1861 seemed only incidental to these more important associations.

My latest reading of *Personal Memoirs* came as a joyful surprise, almost as if the first had never occurred. Now I noticed

Brinton's observations on the poor state of health and medicine in the Union army and the questionable quality of medical training he found among the surgeons. Unlike most American physicians at the time of the Civil War, Brinton was well educated. He was not, however, well prepared for the work before him, since the Civil War made painfully clear to all the defects of the American system of medical education. A Philadelphian by birth (May 21, 1832), he followed a very classical education, studying first under Samuel Crawford and then at the Classical Institute. Following this preparatory education, he entered the University of Pennsylvania in 1848, receiving his A.B. in 1850 and his A.M. in 1852. The same year he obtained the A.M., Brinton took the M.D. degree from Jefferson Medical College in Philadelphia, followed by a year of postgraduate clinical training in Paris and Vienna.

Jefferson Medical College, whose parent institution was Jefferson College in Canonsburg, Pennsylvania (near Pittsburgh, 320 miles southwest of Philadelphia), was not unlike most university-affiliated medical schools of the day in that the college was physically separated from its mother insitution, had full responsibility for its financial operations, and had little formal relationship except for student transfers and the conferring of degrees. Opening in 1825, it touted such medical names as Daniel Drake and J. K. Mitchell in theory and practice; Franklin Bache in chemistry; W. P. C. Barton and R. M. Huston in materia medica; Nathan R. Smith and Joseph Pancoast in anatomy; Francis S. Beattie and Charles D. Meigs in midwifery; George McClellan in surgery; and Robley Dunglison in institutes and medical jurisprudence. In 1838, the legislature granted the college its own independent charter.

At the time of Brinton's medical schooling, didactic education at Jefferson consisted of two four-month terms, with the second term a repetition of the first, no gradation of studies, no written examinations, and only a short oral quiz at the completion of the term. Although the college lacked hospital facilities in its early years (due to the control that the University of Pennsylvania had over Pennsylvania Hospital and the Philadelphia General Hospital), it did operate an infirmary or out-patient department until owning its own hospital in 1847. By the time Brinton had become a student, the problem of clinical experience had thus been overcome. As in other medical colleges, the curriculum consisted of seven subject areas: anatomy; physiology and pathology; materia medica, therapeutics, and pharmacy; chemistry and medical jurisprudence; theory and practice of medicine; principles and practice of surgery; and obstetrics and diseases of women and children.

Through much of the nineteenth century, a clear distinction separated students who attended liberal arts colleges from those who enrolled in professional schools. The former were required to meet a broad array of subject prerequisites, while applicants to professional schools could usually matriculate following completion of just about any English secondary school course or, as was often the case, entering directly from grammar school after some form of apprenticeship. Essentially, the criterion for admission to medical school was the ability to pay the tuition and fees. Three years in apprenticeship was the standard condition for receiving the M.D. degree and most medical schools were satisfied with only a grammar school education for applicants. (By 1904, only four medical colleges—Johns Hopkins, Harvard, Western Reserve, and Rush—required any education beyond high school, and in 1914, only 23.5 percent of the graduates of regular medical schools had earned an A.B. or a B.S. degree.) In contrast, Brinton's education seems highly unusual if not exceptional, placing him among a very select group of young men fortunate enough to have received a college education prior to medical studies.

Equally remarkable was Brinton's postgraduate training in Paris and Vienna. Here again, he found himself among an elite group of young doctors who not only benefited from the Paris clinical school that made the hospital the focal point of medical education, but who also tasted the beginnings of German laboratory medicine. In Paris, his medical study took on new meaning as Pierre Louis (1787–1872) and other clinical teachers demonstrated the importance of observation and, through it, the possibility of disease identification on the basis of extensive clinical and postmortem examinations. The work of Louis and that of Gabriel Andral (1799–1876), Jean-Baptiste Bouillaud (1796–1881), Pierre Adolphe Piorry (1794–1876), and Armand Trousseau (1801–67) dominated this period in French medicine. Louis's application of the numerical (statistical) method became the means by which the newer school of clinicians refuted the speculative rationalism and biases of traditional medicine. Through his numerical method and its application to the different branches of medical science, Louis and his disciples were able to better understand the natural history of disease and demonstrate the relative superiority or weakness of one method of treatment over another—factors that weighed heavily in the war and postwar years.

Returning to Philadelphia after a year of postgraduate work, Brinton entered general practice and became a demonstrator and, later, a lecturer in operative surgery at Jefferson Medical College, from 1853 to 1861. In 1854, he edited *The Science and Art of Surgery*, consisting of the lectures of Sir John Eric Erichsen (1818–96), professor of surgery at University College and, later, surgeon extraordinary to Queen Victoria. Brinton was convinced the book would become a useful reference to both students and practitioners. The text was supplemented by illustrations that Brinton prepared.[1]

In 1861, Brinton was appointed professor of principles and practice of surgery at Jefferson, an indication of a long-term commitment to the school and to the Philadelphia area. But the American Civil War became an all-consuming passion, captivating the collective conscience in ways that few wars have done

---

1. John Eric Erichsen, *Science and Art of Surgery. Being a Treatise on Surgical Injuries, Diseases, and Operations* (Philadelphia: Blanchard and Lea, 1854).

before or since. As Brinton observed, from the moment of the firing on Fort Sumter, "the spirit of the North changed, discussion ceased, political arguments were at an end, and almost absolute unanimity prevailed, the only question was how best to establish the supremacy of the Government, and how to vindicate its authority. . . ." Feeling a certain restlessness at home from "not doing [his] full duty," Brinton applied for and received a commission in the brigade of volunteer surgeons attached to the General Medical Staff and served under the direction of the surgeon general. To be eligible for such a commission, he was required to take a written examination to validate his diploma. In the absence of state or national examining boards, the diploma had become the license to practice. Considering that most doctors of Brinton's age group were educated in proprietary schools through didactic teaching, not clinical experience (hospital training was sometimes optional but was never a central part of the educational program), it is not surprising that the quality of candidates for surgeon's appointments was meager at best. From 1841 to 1849, only 55 out of 170 applicants managed to pass the Army Medical Board examinations. According to Dr. H. L. Heiskell, the acting surgeon general at the time, the most striking causes for failure were "insufficient preparatory education, a hurried course of pupilage, want of proficiency in practical anatomy, in pathology and in clinical medicine."[2] Even in the period between 1888 and 1909, of the 1,512 candidates applying for the army medical corps, 72 percent failed the examinations.[3]

Once commissioned, Brinton's early duties consisted of serving as president of the Medical Examining Board in Washington.

---

2. Quoted in "Requirements of the U. S. Army and Navy Boards of Medical Examiners," *Transactions*, American Medical Association, 2 (1849), 315.

3. Abraham Flexner, *Medical Education in the United States and Canada: A Report to the Carnegie Foundation for the Advancement of Teaching* (New York: Carnegie Foundation, 1910), 170.

This responsibility involved meeting daily with the board to examine candidates. "Some were well prepared; some were not," Brinton recalled, and "quite a number failed to pass, until finally we were indirectly informed by the Secretary of War [Stanton] . . . that he wanted more doctors." Faced with the secretary's threat to shut down the board, Brinton and the other examiners lowered their standards to ensure the needed numbers of surgeons for the war effort. One self-educated candidate for an appointment as brigade surgeon explained to the board that he could do "almost anything, from scalping an Indian, up and down." Although found singularly deficient in formal education, the man was assigned duty in Kansas where Brinton hoped he would do the least amount of damage.

With his commission as brigade surgeon, Brinton was assigned to Major General Frémont's headquarters at St. Louis, far removed from his preferred choice, which was under the command of McClellan in the Army of the Potomac. Despite this initial disappointment and a distinct feeling of being surrounded by men not his social equal, Brinton had the good fortune of meeting Grant and beginning a friendship and an association that lasted though the war. The experience changed Brinton's opinion of his assignment; he recognized that western life and western men suited him. "I was among the men who were day by day making the nation's history," he observed, "and who were destined to become the heroes of the war."

It was there in the western theater that Brinton also discovered the patriotic "Mrs. Brundages," women sanitarians who insinuated themselves into the war effort. For these self-proclaimed busybodies, Brinton showed little respect, describing them as "clamorous for [their] little wants," faultfinding, and "helpless, irritable and unhappy . . . each one with an enamelled leather bag between her feet, waiting to be sent somewhere, anywhere!" Brinton was not alone in his feelings. Along with many other officials, he disliked these do-gooders who deliberately ignored the military's chain of command. Like the U.S. Sanitary Commission, they were viewed by the military with contempt and were treated as "Lincoln's fifth wheel," meaning they were as useful as a fifth wheel on a coach.

One of the early difficulties encountered by the Union army was the scarcity of trained doctors. Faced with a problem of supply and demand, the Union resorted to "contract physicians," many of whom were charlatans or men who had been "long out of practice, if indeed they ever had any." Brinton decried these impostors as products of western proprietary colleges and hoped to resolve the problem by encouraging a "better class" of physicians from the east, especially graduates of schools in the larger cities. Presumably, Brinton was referring to those who had served as house pupils or resident physicians in urban hospitals or who had supplemented their meager course of medical lectures with European study. But the scarcity of good physicians continued to plague the west, and to Brinton's regret, proprietary schools continued to produce inferior doctors for decades following the war.

Brinton was a keen observer of character. He recalled an Illinois surgeon who, being at a loss as to how to perform an amputation, asked for instructions on how it should be done. Once shown, he "at once took rank as an experienced surgeon." Later, on hearing from hospital stewards of a "great surgeon" working in one of the rear field hospitals, Brinton found this same man busy at work on the second floor of a country house with amputated arms and legs littering the floor, a pool of blood beneath the operating table, and the room "ghastly beyond all limits of surgical propriety." Given the fact that amputation was the standard treatment for severe wounds to the limbs, that doctors considered "laudable pus" a natural part of the healing process, and that potent purgatives and emetics were the mainstays of traditional therapies, it is no wonder that the Civil War was such a medical and human tragedy.

Brinton sheds light on the work of Jonathan Letterman, who replaced the regimental medical service with a divisional service supported by a corps ambulance service and who started the collection of shot and shell and unusual specimens of morbid anatomy (both medical and surgical) for Surgeon General William A. Hammond's proposed Army Medical Museum in Washington. As early as June 1862, Hammond directed Brinton, then in charge of surgical records, to collect specimens for a museum and to prepare a surgical history of the war. No doubt his experience in Paris gave grist for this project, providing him the basis for his system of wound classification in his July 1, 1863, "Consolidated Statement of Gunshot Wounds." Brinton truly enjoyed being curator of the Army Medical Museum, founded in May 1862 (now the Armed Forces Institute of Pathology). "My whole heart was in the Museum," he wrote, "and I felt that if the medical officers in the field, and those in charge of hospitals, could only be fairly interested, its growth would be rapid, and the future good of such a grand national cabinet would be immense." He collected specimens of mutilated limbs and gross anatomy at the battlefields and field hospitals (sometimes digging them out of trenches where they were buried), packed them in kegs of alcohol, whiskey, or salt and water, and then shipped the specimens to Washington where they were cleaned, tagged, and preserved under the care of the museum curator. Brinton hoped the collection would serve to instruct future generations of military surgeons. Of course, there was a light side to this ghoulish work. The museum became a virtual warehouse for all forms of confiscated alcohol—from champagne to whiskey—which were used in preserving and transporting specimens. In order to prevent an attractive barrel of whiskey from dropping out of sight during transport, museum officials found it advantageous to add tartar emetic (antimony) to the barrel, which induced nausea and vomiting in the thief but did not detract from the preservative value of the alcohol.

In the course of his work on the multivolume *Medical and Surgical History of the War of the Rebellion (1861–1865),* a title that greatly vexed the South, Brinton sought to develop a system for classifying gunshot wounds that would be consistent from the field hospital to division, corps, and general hospital.[4] Explaining the problem to General Muir of the British Service, Brinton learned of the British method of tagging each wounded man with a descripton of the wound; the tag would accompany the soldier during his transportation and, in the event of death, became the basis of the medical bureau's statistical file. Brinton adopted the system and distributed descriptive tags to each of the medical directors requesting that they put them to use. To his disappointment, the system failed because medical officers found themselves overworked by the large numbers of wounded and were unable to take the time to establish a registration system. In place of Brinton's system, a board of officers in 1863 adopted a modified form of registers for each hospital.

Brinton provides interesting commentary on some of the medical etiquette of the Civil War, that is, the occasional passing within enemy lines of medical supplies from the opposing army and the neutralization of personnel caring for the wounded. These latter actions, largely made possible because of personal acquaintanceships that existed between and among military officers before the war, were eventually codified by representatives of eleven governments who signed the Convention of Geneva on August 22, 1864.

In September 1864, Brinton was relieved from duty in the Surgeon General's Office, a decision that removed him from the preparation of the *Medical and Surgical History of the War of the Rebellion* and that, he surmised, resulted from his friendship with the recently cashiered Hammond, from his blood ties to McClellan (who was then being talked about as a potential presi-

---

4. Surgeon-General's Office, *The Medical and Surgical History of the War of the Rebellion (1861–1865). Prepared, in Accordance with the Acts of Congress, Under the Direction of Surgeon General, Joseph K. Barnes, United States Army* (Washington: Government Printing Office, 1870–88).

dential candidate), and from his being perceived as an enemy of the new surgeon general, Joseph K. Barnes. Banished to St. Louis, he served on General Rosecrans's staff and found duty in Nashville as Superintendent and Director of General Hospitals. While there, he gave lectures on the surgical history of the war, taking special notice of the flight of projectiles and the character of the wounds they produced at points of entrance and exit. In February 1865, he resigned his commission and returned to his home and family in Philadelphia and to his former work at Jefferson, eventually replacing Samuel D. Gross in 1882 as professor of the practice of surgery and clinical surgery. From 1882 until his death, he held the position of professor of bacteriology and clinical surgery.

Brinton was a member of the Academy of Natural Sciences of Philadelphia, the Philadelphia Surgical Club, and the American Surgical Association, and he was one of the founding members of the Pathological Society of Philadelphia. Besides his editing of Erichsen's surgical lectures and his contributions to the surgical history of the war, he gave a major address to the graduating class of the Army Medical School in Washington, D.C., in 1896 and was coauthor with John Hampton Porter of an unpublished manuscript, housed in the National Library of Medicine, entitled *History of the Organization of the Medical Department of the U.S. Army.* He died of a cerebral hemorrhage March 18, 1907.

JOHN S. HALLER, JR.

# Personal Memoirs
## of John H. Brinton

# INTRODUCTORY NOTE

The College of Physicians of Philadelphia, the oldest medical society in America, had, during the War of the Rebellion and up to 1866, an average of 186 fellows. Of these, fifty held commissions in the regular or volunteer service, and seven in the navy.

Among those early commissioned, in 1861, was John Hill Brinton, the author of the present memoirs. His story does not relate how much of growing surgical practice and successful teaching he gave up to serve a great cause. Neither he nor others as faithful and as distinguished, expected or received the honors which fell to officers of the line. No statue celebrates, no commemorative tablet records their services. These men, who were not less busy in the camps than in battle, suffered by wounds, disease, and prisons as, and in like proportion with, other officers, although technically regarded as non-combatants.

In the front rank of this remarkable list of surgeons, whose only records are their permanent contributions to the art of the surgery of war, was the man who tells here his story of the war, as seen from the position of one who was the close friend of General Grant throughout that great soldier's life. The trials, risks, and triumphs of a remarkable army career as a surgeon are here related in a simple, direct way, and cast interesting side lights on many of the generals, and even on the campaigns the writer saw.

Soldiers from private to commander-in-chief have

related their personal stories of the great war, but the physicians who served have nowhere as adequately told their side of unrewarded peril and service as is done in the notable record of which I am privileged to say these introductory words.

John H. Brinton was born in Philadelphia, May 21, 1832. He was graduated from the University of Pennsylvania in 1850 (from which institution he received the degree of LL.D. in 1901), and in medicine from the Jefferson College in 1852. Commissioned Brigade Surgeon, U. S. Volunteers, in August, 1861, he became under General Grant at Cairo his trusted medical director. He died on March 8, 1907.

He may be left to relate the story of his army life, of his connection with the Surgical and Medical History of the War, and of his creation of the Army Medical Museum.

His later life as the competent successor in the chair of surgery of Professor S. D. Gross, and his career in surgical practice, will be elsewhere told, but I cannot close this brief statement without a word of what he was in other relations, a man with whose friendship I was honored for two-thirds of my life. His straightforward ways, his perfect rectitude in every social relation, a certain kindliness and simpleness, won for him the esteem and affection of the many whom he honored with his friendship, while his unswerving fidelity to every duty, large or small, was an example of what my profession may make of a man who brought to it all that is best in the way of the character of a well-bred gentleman.

S. WEIR MITCHELL.

# INTRODUCTION

My dear Children:—

My book is finished; the illustrations have been collected; I have everything ready to go to the bookbinders, —and now I ask myself why I have written all this. The question is hard to answer, at all events, truthfully and completely. It may be that I want you to know something about the War.—No, that is not it; it is not the War, for that no doubt you can find in the books and histories which are being written, and which will be written. It is rather, I think, that I want you to know something about *myself*, and what and whom I saw, and what I was doing during those four years, which formed so prominent a part of the lives of the men of that day. For you must know that *then*, the War, to all of us, was *everything*, it was all in all. The past was forgotten; the future we scarcely dared to think of; it was all then the grim present, in which everyone tried to do his best, and in which almost every gentleman felt it his duty to take his share. Like the rest, I went out, and strangely enough happened to see more of the great men of the War than often falls to the lot of a medical man. In fact my "details of duty" were always with the generals, the great generals of the day, and in high places, and I was thus placed in daily intercourse with men who were earning for themselves illustrious names. One of these, whom I counted my friend, afterwards became one of our nation's greatest men,—in fact he was growing great when I knew him, making for himself, and for his country, history, accomplishing great deeds, and bringing about great results by the simple plan of doing each day's duty as well as he knew how, leaving to the Future the summing up of his work and trusting to the judgment of his countrymen. You will guess that I am speaking of General Grant.

Then too, with Sheridan and Rosecrans, I was on terms of friendship and lived in intimacy; and so with McPherson, whom I loved, and all four of whom I attended professionally. President Lincoln I knew slightly, and visited at the White House, and Secretary of War Stanton, and Generals Halleck, Thomas and Meade I knew well, and many others whose names you may meet in these pages. General George B. McClellan, as you know, was my first cousin, named, perhaps, after my father, as well as after his own.

To the next generation the "War of the Great Rebellion" will be almost as far away as that of the Revolution, or the French War of '57, or the Civil War of England, or the Punic Wars. Yet the War of 1861-1865, the "Scorpion War," the "War between the States," the "Civil War," "The Rebellion," when fought to a close, accomplished the preservation of our country, in which you, my descendants, will, I hope, be privileged long to live and do your duty.

Now let me say one more word of myself, and confess one more reason for the writing of these pages. You remember that the great Mr. Pickwick (never forget him) on a memorable occasion said,—"He (Mr. Pickwick) would not deny that he was influenced by human passions and human feelings, possibly, by human weaknesses." Now, My Dears, like that great man I, too, plead guilty to human passions and feelings and weaknesses. I confess to you that I wish to be kindly thought of by those of my blood who may follow me, even though I shall never know them, and that I want you to feel that I love you all dearly, born and unborn.

Occasionally I have (and I like to have) queer fancies, and one of these is that some day these lines and this book may fall into some fair hands, and that she reading may say to herself, "He was a nice kindly old fellow, this ancestor of mine, I wish I could know him." She will not know me, but I shall see her and know her, if there be, as I believe there must be, both knowledge and vision in a disembodied spirit from another sphere. Even now I fancy I can see her in the future, a dark haired girl, lounging on a sofa, half dreaming over my pages. I imagine I can almost trace her features, and touch her dress, and know its colors. My Dear, try and believe that as you may be, when you read this, I see you now, in the bright month of June, 1891, Sunday the 14th.

J. H. BRINTON.

June 14, 1891.

# Personal Memoirs of John H. Brinton

## CHAPTER I

### THE OUTBREAK OF THE WAR

The war began, with the flash of the first gun fired on Fort Sumter, in Charleston Harbor, S. C., on Friday, the 12th day of April, 1861. From that moment the spirit of the North changed, discussion ceased, political arguments were at an end, and almost absolute unanimity prevailed, the only question was how best to establish the supremacy of the Government, and how to vindicate its authority; in short, the problem was how to preserve the unity and majesty of the Nation, and how soonest to trample out the doctrines of disintegration and "secession."

I well remember walking down Chestnut Street, in front of the Continental Hotel, with my cousin Brinton Coxe, just after the attack on Fort Sumter was authentically announced on the bulletin boards. The effect on the people was instantaneous and indescribable. For the time, or rather at the instant, "mere party lines," as Mr. Coxe expressed it, "ceased to exist,—for the North had become a Nation, determined to fight for its existence, and resolved to accomplish its salvation."

The North now prepared for war; for the first time

15

it realized that the sword was the only umpire, and that on it, must the life of a nation depend. Then came the first call for troops, the proclamation of President Lincoln, and the disastrous battle of Bull Run, on the 21st of July, 1861. Business of every kind, at all events the businesses of Peace, were disturbed. The spirit of war, or the spirit of patriotism, call it which you will, seemed to seize upon all. Men became fierce-minded, and the most respectable and quiet-spirited persons were thus affected. Drill companies were formed, and the mildest individuals, earnestly, industriously and conscientiously practiced the manual. At one time a strange rumor was circulated that the Southern people were about to march on Pennsylvania, with the intention of sacking Philadelphia. Our citizens rushed to arms, and every man, young and old, purchased a pistol,—a revolver if he could, if not, a pistol of some description to defend his altar and his hearth-stone. Everybody bought, and I can hardly keep from laughing, as I recall the solemnity with which the subject was discussed by solemn men in my profession, and how advice was eagerly sought and given, as to where to procure fire-arms. Pistols went up in price,—one could hardly obtain them; for a day or two the supply was exhausted. I remember purchasing one, a discreditable looking affair with a white handle. As I walked away from the shop, I met Dr. John Forsyth Meigs, who had just purchased one for himself. He was preëminently a man of peace, a doctor for children and infants, but the spirit of war had seized him too. My pistol, I afterwards exchanged for the navy pattern of Colt's revolver, which I carried through the war, and which I never discharged, except at a mark. Once I aimed it at a man who was about to shoot me, but I will tell you of this later. That pistol saved my life, I think, so I do not regret the eleven dollars I paid for it.

In response to the call for "three months men," military companies were hastily formed and mustered in. Young men everywhere hastened to offer themselves to the Government, and it soon came about, that every young fellow you met was on his way to active service. They went in every capacity, as company officer, staff officer, quarter master, pay master, commissary of subsistence, and in fact, in whatever position or grade they could obtain appointments.

I remember very distinctly in these early days of the war, meeting on one occasion at the corner of Tenth and Spruce Streets, a young Friend, a very pearl of neatness, and a man well known in social life. He was carefully picking his way across the muddy street, mentally absorbed in preserving the cleanliness of his boots. Looking up, he saw me, and called out, "Dr. Brinton, will you kindly stop one moment. I want to ask you a question. Perhaps you can give me some information. Can you tell me what a 'commissary of subsistence' is? I have just been appointed one, and I have not an idea as to the duty of that officer. Can you tell me anything about it?" This gentleman, then so ignorant, afterwards greatly distinguished himself in that branch of the service.

Like the rest of the men of my age, I soon began to feel restless at home. I felt that I was not doing my full duty; that home was now no place for me. Yet as an only son, upon whom rested the business cares of the family, I dreaded to speak to my dear Mother on the subject. She may have guessed my feelings; at all events she spoke first; and one evening she surprised me by saying to me, "My dear son, do you not think that you ought to be out with the army, doing what share you can for the country?" When I expressed my great desire to go, she added "that she was glad of it, as she had almost felt grieved that I had not gone before." So the way was made easy for me to enter the service.

I naturally determined to go in my professional capacity, and I therefore decided to enter the Corps of "brigade surgeons," a grade of medical officers created by an act of Congress, approved July 22nd, 1861. By a later act of Congress, approved July 2nd, 1862, brigade surgeons were thereafter to be known as "surgeons of volunteers," and were attached to the General Medical Staff, under the direction of the Surgeon General.

In order to be eligible to the position of brigade surgeon, it was necessary to pass an examination before a board of medical officers of the regular army, and, on their favorable report, to receive the appointment with the approval of the Senate. On the 18th of June, 1861, I made application to the Surgeon General for permission to present myself for examination for the grade of brigade surgeon about to be created, for although the act creating that grade had not yet been passed, it was well known that it would be passed, and all preparations were made to fill promptly the future positions. In a few days, I received a reply from the Surgeon General, dated June 20th, 1861, directing me to apply to the Secretary of War for the necessary permit. This I did, and having received the requisite authorization, I went to Washington, for my examination, on or about July 3rd, 1861. I was not kept long in waiting, the examination which was chiefly a written one was not very rigid, and at its conclusion I was informed that the result was satisfactory, and that I might return home and await my commission.

During this, my first visit to Washington, I stopped at Willard's Hotel, on Pennsylvania Avenue, near the treasury building. The city was crowded, the hotels filled to overflowing. People of all sorts were rushing busily about, and the weather was very warm. Active preparations for the coming war were being made on all sides. At the same time there appeared to be a lack of confidence. Matters were apparently in a chaotic state: the sympathy for the North was not strong or widespread,—on the contrary the sympathy of many of those who lived in Washington was directed towards the South. It seemed to be generally expected, if indeed not wished for, that the southern states would win, and succeed in their attempt to withdraw from the union, and thus overthrow the national government. Exaggerated accounts of the organization, discipline, and forward state of preparation of the southern states came from every quarter, and the names of their political and military leaders were on many lips. Against this chilling state of despondency, and unbelief in the stability of our Government, the administration was stoutly struggling, as but few Washingtonians trusted the President, or expected that any good would come through such a "Nazarene." His jestures, manners, mode of speech, and deportment, were ridiculed, and few, if any, could believe that a great man stood in their midst. Disaffection stalked everywhere, and a sense of isolation had apparently crept over those who administered, and those who believed, in the national government. The incidents of the hour, too, were disheartening. Of one of these I was a witness.

It had been announced that on the afternoon of the

4th of July, the President, surrounded by his cabinet, would publicly hoist the flag of the United States on a high flagpole, planted in the grounds in the rear of the White House. The hour arrived, and a large crowd had gathered to witness the ceremony. The day had been warm, and in the afternoon a heavy shower of rain had set in. The President and his suite stood under a tent, or *marquée,* which surrounded the base of the flagpole. By the side of the pole, an opening had been made in the canvas roof, intended to be sufficiently large to allow the great flag of the stars and stripes to be hoisted through it. As soon as the usual speeches were concluded, President Lincoln, grasping the halyards, pulled them vigorously. Up went the flag. It was a tight fit, but by sheer strength, the President hoisted it through the opening, and it slowly rose above the tent roof. According to every poetic and patriotic inspiration, it should have unfurled and fluttered in the breeze. This it did not do. The heavy rain caused it to dangle, and hang limp, and, what was worse, a projecting nail caught in the "union," and as the flag went wearily up, a strip of blue bunting, charged with eleven white stars, was ripped out, and fell helplessly downwards to the roof. But the President could see nothing of this, and feeling the resistance, tugged away all the more manfully, until the torn strip was freed and was dragged upwards, hanging from the body of the flag. The eleven stars, the emblems of the eleven seceding states, thus torn from their "Union Firmament" seemed, in very truth, a sorry omen to those who stood anxiously watching. For my own part, I turned away shuddering, almost overcome by a superstitious horror and fear. I saw all this take place, but I am not aware that any newspaper notice or publicity was given to the occurrence.

On that same evening, I returned home, and in a few days learned from a private source that I had passed my examination satisfactorily, and in proper time would be commissioned. Mr. Thomas A. Scott was acting Secretary of War, and Mr. Leslie, who was a friend, and an assistant, of Mr. Scott, was a relative or connection of my friend, Dr. William Thomson, from whom I learned the little secret of my commission before it was fairly due. It is the history of all courts, royal and republican, that very many feet tread up and down the back stairs.

The month of July dragged slowly on, and everywhere, throughout the North and the South, troops were being mustered in. On April 14th, President Lincoln issued his call for 75,000 volunteers; early in May more than 200,000 had been called for; and immediately after the battle of Bull Run in Virginia, Congress ordered a call for 500,000 more. At the same time, Congress made an appropriation of $500,000,000 to meet the expense of the Army and Navy.

And now, let me tell you something about the Battle of Bull Run, which was fought on July 21st, 1861. For some weeks the Confederate Generals had been busily collecting their forces, and had massed them at Bull Run (I use the common name), thus directly threatening Washington. The troops of the United States had meanwhile been hurried on from the North, and were stationed at and near Washington, prepared to attack the Southern army. Early on the morning of the 21st of July (Sunday) the Federal forces moved forward, and encountered the Confederates near what was known as the Stone Bridge, at Manassas, or Bull Run. A sharp fight took place which ended in a panic-stricken, dis-graceful retreat of the United States Army back to Washington, with a loss of four or five hundred killed, and twelve or fifteen hundred wounded.* As usually happened in a rout of this kind, the defeated parties spread the most exaggerated account of the number and bravery of their foes, and the entire country was soon ringing with the terrible stories of the fierce Virginia Cavalry, "The Black Horse Cavalry," as they were styled, and the prowess of the Southern forces.

General Winfield Scott was at this time in command of the army of the United States with the rank of Lieutenant General. His original entry into service was in 1808, as captain of light artillery. He was a Vir-ginian, and appointed from his native state, and was at this time, therefore, very old, but was looked upon, both in and out of the army, as a good soldier, and enjoyed a high reputation due to his conduct of the Mexican war. He doubtless was in his time a good soldier, though very fond of military ostentation, for which he was sometimes nicknamed "old fuss and feathers." His plans for the advance of the Union army would seem to have been well laid, but his troops were new levies, and his orders were imperfectly carried out. On ac-count of his advanced age, General Scott remained in Washington, and did not participate in the active move-ments of the army.

I am afraid that some of the troops of the North behaved in this battle in a rather shabby manner, and it may be that if the Southern generals had pushed

*Federal losses were 460 killed and 1,124 wounded; the Confed-erate losses were 387 killed and 1,582 wounded. Total number of troops engaged, Federal 30,000 and 43 guns; Confederate 18,500 and 55 guns.

boldly on to Washington, they might have taken the capital.* Fortunately, they did not do so, but halted where they were, fearing to advance. So the army was safe in Washington, and immediate steps were taken to protect the capital from an attack. Earthworks and forts were hastily erected, cannon were planted, and fresh troops were called for, and hurried down from the northern states. I nearly went to Washington at this time, for on the night following the battle of Bull Run, an order was sent to Philadelphia to hasten forward any soldiers who might be available for immediate service. A regiment, the 28th Pennsylvania Volunteers, was being recruited at this time by Colonel John W. Geary † (who, after the war, was elected Governor of Pennsylvania), of which Hector Tyndale was Major. A surgeon was wanted for the regiment and Major Tyndale applied to Prof. Joseph Pancoast for the name of some medical man who would volunteer in that capacity. My name was suggested, and accordingly Major Tyndale rang me up in the middle of the night to know whether I would accept the position. I told him that I expected an appointment from Washington, but that in the emergency I would go with his regiment. He told me to be ready to start the next day and I promised to do so. On the morrow, it was found that the regiment was not sufficiently armed to be of service, and

* However, Gen. Joseph E. Johnston, the Confederate, states "Our army was more disorganized by victory than that of the United States by defeat." E. T. S.

This and subsequent footnotes bearing the same initials are from the pen of Edward T. Stuart, Esq., of Philadelphia, a high authority on the Civil War, who also very kindly rendered valuable assistance in the editing of the original manuscript.—Ed.

† Commonly called "the Marshal Ney of the Army of the Potomac." E. T. S.

orders were issued from Washington to delay starting
for a day or two until proper and sufficient arms could
be furnished. In the meantime, I received, as I have
already stated, an indirect communication from the war
department, informing me of my appointment as brigade
surgeon. Under the circumstances, I determined to
await my commission at home, and transferred my appointment as surgeon of Colonel Geary's regiment to
Dr. Ernest Goodman, who went out with this command and remained with it, doing good service, until
much later in the war when he entered the staff corps
of surgeons of volunteers. My commission as brigade
surgeon, issued on August 8, 1861, to bear date from
August 3rd, reached me in the latter days of that month.

The news of the Battle of Bull Run created a deep
sensation throughout the north. For the first time, it was
realized that we were entering upon war in dead earnest, and that our southern foes intended to fight to
the best of their ability. It became only too plain that
the work we had undertaken was a most serious one,
and that the resources of the loyal portion of the country
would be severely taxed. No one could doubt that the
war would be a long one; how long, no one could tell.*
A few enthusiasts believed that the government would
crush, "stamp out," as it was phrased, the rebellion, in
a little while, but the more thoughtful realized the terrible earnestness of the South, and recognized the military ability of their leaders and generals.

And here I must tell you, that when the wave of
secession rolled over the South, carrying with it all

*Gen. Winfield Scott declared that conquest of the South might be
achieved "in two or three years, by a young and able general,—a
Wolfe, a Desaix, a Hoche, with 300,000 disciplined men kept up to
that number." E. T. S.

doubting souls, few, very few, remained loyal citizens, and these dared not speak, but could only cling in silence to their opinions. Before the war, the South was largely represented in our army, the profession of arms was attractive to those from that section, and their young men sought more eagerly than those of the North, a West Point education and a commission in the regular service. So when the lines were strictly drawn, and secession was fairly entered upon, the officers of the old army generally went with their respective states. It happened, therefore, that in organizing the army of the confederate states, it was well supplied with trained officers, who had received a military education. Many of the officers of the old army of the United States left it with regret. They remained in it until their states had formally seceded, when they resigned their commissions, and followed their state flags. Having once entered upon their new positions, they fought bravely and well, and sustained the cause of secession until it fell from absolute exhaustion.

The immediate effect of the battle of Bull Run was to elate the spirit of the South and to create a corresponding condition of depression in the North. In Philadelphia, many took a most gloomy view of the situation; thus, I remember a thoughtful, cool-headed man (the late Prof. Joseph Pancoast) at that time saying to me, "Doctor, no one can tell how all this will end; it will surely last ten years or more; and possibly neither you nor I may live to see the end of it."

Yet there were some who could see farther into the bank of the war-cloud. I can hear now the words of my Mother, and see the earnest expression of her face, as she came to my room door, early on the morning after the defeat at Bull Run, and told me the result,—

that our troops had been put to flight, and that the rebels were triumphant. "It is far better," she said, "that it should be so, my son, for the war will go on now until the end shall be reached, and the curse of slavery wiped away. If our troops had won, it could not have been so, but now the war must go on. It will cost more lives, but the end will be more sure." She was indeed right in her judgment.

Now that I was sure of my appointment, I busied myself in making ready for my future service, concerning which my ideas were very vague. Where it would be, or what it would be, I could not tell, but I pictured to myself all sorts of hardships, and so waited anxiously to know how my military life would begin. Before very long, the list of brigade surgeons was published, and I was well satisfied in my grade, being fourth on the list, the first four names standing thus:

George H. Lyman, of Massachusetts.

Frank H. Hamilton, of New York.

Henry S. Hewitt, of Connecticut, appointed from New York.

J. H. Brinton, of Pennsylvania.

Dr. Hamilton had been a professor in New York, and was a brother-in-law of the chairman of the Senate Committee on Military Affairs; Dr. Hamilton was distinguished as a professor of surgery, and the author of a treatise on "Fractures and Dislocations," and Dr. Hewitt had been an ex-assistant surgeon U. S. A., who had entered the corps of brigade surgeons—so I had no reason to be dissatisfied.

I may add that on the 11th of June, 1862, Dr. Lyman was made a medical inspector with the rank of Colonel, and on the 9th of February, 1863, Dr. Hamilton was promoted to the same rank. For the rest of the war,

Dr. Hewitt was the Senior "surgeon of volunteers," and I was second. After a short western experience of a most friendly nature, we two concluded that it was not well for us to be placed in the same command. By keeping apart, both of us thus secured the full value of our leading positions in the corps of surgeons of volunteers.

Although my appointment as given in the army register dates from August 3rd, 1861, my commission did not reach me until the end of August. The interval I occupied in making my final preparations. I had to bring my teachings to a close, and to care for the preservation of my anatomical possessions. The former was easily done as the southern students had ceased to come north, and those who had been here had returned to their homes. As for the northern students, for the most part, they were hurrying off to the war in different capacities. Then, too, I had to arrange to leave the affairs of our family estate in such a condition that they could be administered by my mother in my absence, and moreover, to procure my outfit, consisting of my uniform, blankets, and all the accoutrements for "man and horse."

Above all, I must think of my future steed, and diligently I sought him. Particularly do I recall a very black, broken kneed animal offered to me by a quite respectable gentleman. The horse had considerable action, with a very arched neck. In the innocence of my heart, I think I would have bought him, had not my good friend, honest John Ellis, whose stable was in the rear of our house, kindly whispered to me "Let him alone"; I did so, and in doing so probably saved myself a broken neck.

And then I tried, too, a quite fierce animal, also black, with very large feet. They said he was up to my weight. I think he was, for as I recall him, I feel sure that he would have proved a most serviceable beast in a brewer's dray. Good horses were just then greatly sought in Philadelphia, so fortunately I waited. My uniform I purchased at Hughes and Müller; tailors in Chestnut Street. It was very satisfactory, and the reinforcement of the breeches for riding was stupendous. When I afterwards came to wear these reinforced breeches, I felt as if a quilt had been placed between myself and the saddle.

My blankets, I recollect, were deep blue, well dyed, and of extraordinary size. I bought them at a wholesale store in Market Street below 9th. I heard of the place from Arthur McClellan, who was fitting up at this time, for his brother's * staff. These blankets proved to be excellent, and I used them until after the battle of Shiloh, when I was ordered east. Then I parted with them, expecting easily to find their counterparts. But alas! when I reached Washington, I found that the reign of shoddy had begun, and in vain might I search the loyal cities for a pair of honest blankets.

My saddle and horse equipments, I bought of Lacey & Phillips, the leading harness makers of the city. The saddle, of capacious size, was of the "McClellan" pattern, in which the rider sat much as a two-pronged fork would straddle a round stick. He could not readily fall off, and yet it could not be said that he had anything of a seat. This saddle, I afterwards exchanged for a "Jennifer" saddle, modeled after one designed by Captain Nolan of the 13th Hussars of the British Army, who was conspicuous in the Crimean War and who was the "some one who blundered" in the charge of the light brigade at Balaklava.

* Major-General George Brinton McClellan.

During all this time of waiting, I was impatiently anxious as to where I would be ordered. I hoped to be assigned to the Army of the Potomac, to the command of which my cousin, George B. McClellan, was appointed July 27th, 1861, and I learned afterwards that General McCall, a personal friend, whom I had known at the Academy of Natural Sciences, and also General Franklin, had both been good enough to express a wish that I might be assigned to duty with them. I had yet to learn the lesson that, to a soldier, especially in times of active service, it should not matter what his detail of duty may be. A riper experience and the counsel of men old in the service, before long taught me that the surest, and most often the greatest success, is obtained by prompt and cheerful obedience to orders; and that in military life, it is utterly useless to attempt to arrange matters to suit one's comfort or personal convenience. Chance, or rather let me say providence, so orders events, and so baffles human plans, that, as an old officer once told me, "It often happened that orders sought for, ended in regrets."

You can understand, that dreaming nothing of all this, I was quite annoyed to receive this my first order:

[SPECIAL ORDERS—No. 238]

War Department, Adjutant General's Office,
Washington, September 4, 1861.

3. The following Brigade Surgeons are assigned to duty as noted below, and will report accordingly: Surgeon J. H. Brinton, to Maj. Gen'l. J. C. Fremont, U. S. A., Commanding Dept. of the West.

By Order
(Signed)   L. THOMAS,
Adjutant General.

Surg. Brinton.

General Fremont's Headquarters were at this time at St. Louis, and with a heavy heart I set out to report to him.  St. Louis seemed to me then to be very far away, and the accounts which had then reached us from the west of events past, and threatening to happen, were of a most unromantic and blood-curdling character.

# CHAPTER II

I remember, as it were only yesterday, my final packing up, my leaving home, and the good-bye to all at the old house, 1423 Spruce Street. Even now, as I think of it, it seems as if I were going over it again. I see my dear Mother and my sisters, and I hear the "God bless you, my son," and the quiet leave taking, as I turned away to the carriage in waiting to take me to the depot of the Pennsylvania Railroad, which was then at 11th and Market Streets, where the Bingham House now stands. My luggage was a sole leather trunk, with a big canvas cover, under which were nicely strapped my blankets, and on the outside, my buffalo robe and gum blanket. I was in fatigue uniform, a blue sack coat with brass buttons, and major's straps, blue trousers with gold cord down the side, a "regular army" falling cap, with a gold wreath, and a glazed cover, very different indeed from the smart French kepi, which afterwards came into vogue, but which I never fancied, and never wore.

I took to the regular army from the start; I had seen considerable of the medical staff of the old army, as Dr. J. M. DaCosta and I had for years been preparing young doctors for the army, and young assistant surgeons for their passing examination after five years of service. With my general acquaintance with the medical

31

staff, therefore, I had absorbed some of their traditions, and a good many of their prejudices. But I am not yet quite out of Philadelphia. Dr. DaCosta and my cousin Brinton Coxe, accompanied me to the railroad station and saw me off, by the night train, which left at 11 o'clock. Sleeping berths of a very inferior pattern had just been introduced, and I considered myself very fortunate to procure an upper single berth. But I confess, that grown man as I was, and twenty-nine years of age, I felt very lonely upon departing, although anxious to join the army.

I left Philadelphia, as nearly as I can remember, on the night of Monday, the ninth of September, 1861. After a considerable delay, I reached St. Louis very tired early on the morning of the 12th, and went to the Planters House, at that time the fashionable hotel of the city. The hotel swarmed with officers, contractors, and others busied with military affairs. I found St. Louis in a strange state; it was, I believe, under martial law, and preparations for war were being carried forward on all sides. The streets swarmed with soldiers, mostly Germans, and the hotels were crowded with money-making people, not a few of whom were Jews. A large number of the inhabitants, they said some fifty or sixty thousand, had already left the city, and I did not wonder, for there was everywhere a feeling of insecurity.

After breakfast on the 12th of September, I put on my uniform frock coat, and started to report to General Fremont at his headquarters. But I could not get near him, as he was busily engaged in making a political speech from the steps or balcony of the building. The impression I received from the first, of this somewhat noted person, was not a very favorable one. He was a man of middle age, in major general's uniform. He was surrounded by a queer crowd of foreigners, Germans, Hungarians and mixed nationalities, much over-uniformed, and rejoicing in gold belts and breast sashes unknown to our service. There was much jabbering and gesticulation, and the scene was most un-American. I was told that General Fremont had gathered around himself a host of adventurers, who seemed to look upon him as an autocrat, and to be forgetful of the existence of a national government. At the time I was in St. Louis, he was busy creating strange offices, and filling them with strange appointees. The selection of Fremont as the commandant of the western district was, I suppose, based upon political grounds. He was believed to control the German settlement in Missouri, an element which had remained loyal to the Union, and in fact had preserved the state of Missouri for the Union; so looking back, after this long interval, perhaps the selection was not so bad after all, although certainly Fremont was little of a real soldier.

After listening to the General's speech, and the applause which followed it, I pushed my way through the middle of the crowd of civilians and soldiers, and reached the office of the adjutant general, Major Chauncy Mc-Keever, to whom I reported, and who treated me with the greatest courtesy and kindness. I am sure that he must have realized how young a soldier I was—how green in fact—and I know that he gave me some good advice, for which I was very grateful at the time, and which I did not forget. Among other things he informed me that the sooner I took myself away from St. Louis, and its mongrel soldiers, the better it would be for me, and added that I would receive my orders that afternoon, which I did, when I found that I was directed to proceed, without delay, to Cairo, Illinois, there to report to the Medical Director, Surgeon Simons, U. S. A.

That afternoon, having dined at the Planters' House, I took a walk through the streets of St. Louis, and I remember quite well passing in front of a German regiment drawn up in line. As I stopped on the sidewalk to look at them, I was thunderstruck to have the whole regiment present arms to me. At first, I could not take it in. But there was no mistake,—they were presenting arms to me; so I gravely raised my regular army cap, made the best salute I could in turn, and sauntered off, just as if I had been accustomed to that sort of thing all my life. However I can assure you that I had never, in my whole experience, felt quite so foolish before. The thing seemed to me to be little less than a swindle on my part. I was conscious of perpetrating some sort of deception. I suppose that it must have been due to the extremely military appearance of my uniform, and most of all, perhaps, to my cap, which had already begun to assume a truly military swagger.

My orders directed me to Cairo, Illinois, to report there to the medical director. I cannot at this time recall very much of the journey down, except that I went by rail, and arrived at Cairo very late in the night of the 14th of September. The train stopped on the levee, immediately in front of the St. Charles' Hotel, the only hotel of any size in Cairo. I was shown to my room—that is to say, I found myself entitled to one-third of a very dirty, dark, horrid sort of a chamber, containing two little beds, not double beds, and yet not single beds. It seemed that I was entitled to one-half of either of these beds, that is to say, if I were able to move the occupant of whichever I might select, away from the middle of the bed. A wretched, flickering, dirty gas light was burning, and I had an excellent chance to study the two sleepers, and to select which one, if either, was to be preferred. As far as I could determine, it was an even thing, for both were very dirty. Each of them had wrapped himself up in all the clothes of the bed, and each snored and grunted harmoniously with the other, as my movements startled him. I was not accustomed to that kind of thing, and even now as I recall that night, I laugh to myself to think how very wretched I was. A homesick feeling came over me, which I have not forgotten to this day. The more I looked at the lovely sleepers, the less I liked them, and so I made up my mind to disturb neither of them, but to wrap myself up in my blanket shawl, and to sleep on the very dirty floor. This I did, and dozed off, feeling that never was there so dirty a floor, nor so miserable a soldier as myself. I tell you all this, because as you will find before long, I learned quite bravely how to rough it, but just at that time I was, to use the western language of the day "a featherbed fellow." In the morning, I was early enough off the floor, and having breakfasted, I started to report to Dr. Simons. I found him eventually in the third story of Safford's Bank, the headquarters of the general commanding the district of Cairo, as it was designated at that time. Dr. Simons, who was a full surgeon in the regular army, was from South Carolina and dated his commission from July, 1839. He had been through the Mexican war and regarded himself as a typical soldier. He was full of old war remembrances and had much to tell of General Scott, and all the old army worthies. His wife, as he himself told me, was a Baltimore lady, the daughter, I think, of a gentleman whose leanings were to the United States government. Dr. Simons, from this cause, or possibly from native loyalty, had adhered to the old army and had not seceded with his state. Yet I could see that he felt lonely; he was parted from all of his old associates, and he could not bring himself to any intimate companionship with the new men, with whom the new war brought him in contact. He had no medical confidant, no one to whom he could talk, and I saw at once that we probably would become good friends.

In fact, Dr. Simons, who was a great talker, wanted some one to listen to him, and assist him in his professional work. I do not think he was very fond of this latter; he seemed to me to be more an army man than an army surgeon. However, he was kind to me and immediately assigned me to some work in connection with the medical director's office. I had to prescribe for a great many sick, and I know that I did direct a vast quantity of Dover's powders.

Dr. Simons advised me to leave the St. Charles Hotel at once, and to take boarding at the house in which he was staying, over Safford's Bank, stating that the headquarters were located there. By this he meant that the general and the staff boarded in the house, and I then found out that the lower story, the back offices in fact, or a part of them, were occupied by Brigadier General U. S. Grant, U. S. V., as headquarters. I was at once introduced to the general, who, I believed, had only a few days previous received his brigadier general's commission.

Of the many who have written of him, made speeches about him, applauded him, and flattered him, few, very few are left who saw him, and watched him, and studied him, as I did. From the very first, he attracted me, and I felt very soon, and indeed at the time of the battle of Belmont, Mo., wrote home, that the man had come who would finish this war, should he have the chance.

I first saw General Grant at the dinner table, when I was introduced to him by Dr. Simons, receiving from him a friendly nod. On the same evening I went into the bank. Behind the counter, the general and his assistant adjutant general, Jno. A. Rawlins, or Captain Rawlins, as he was then, were seated at a little round table. I fancy that I wanted to write a letter home, for I remember that the general very kindly asked me to sit down, and continued his work with Rawlins. I had then a good opportunity to observe him, and I did so very closely. He was then a very different looking man from the General Grant, or the President of after days. As I first saw him, he was a very short, small, rather spare man with full beard and moustache. His beard was a little long, very much longer than he afterwards wore it, unkempt and irregular, and of a sandy, tawny shade. His hair matched his beard, and at a first glance he seemed to be a very ordinary sort of a man, indeed one below the average in most respects. But as I sat and watched him then, and many an hour afterwards, I found that his face grew upon me. His eyes were gentle with a kind expression, and thoughtful. He did not as a rule, speak a great deal. At that time he seemed to be turning matters over in his mind, and to be very much occupied indeed with the work of the hour. He did nothing carelessly, but worked slowly, every now and then stopping and taking his pipe out of his mouth.

But this reminds me, that I have not yet spoken of his pipe. The man in after days became so thoroughly identified with the cigar, that people could scarcely believe that he was once an assiduous smoker of the pipe. Well, the pipe which he first used was a meerschaum with a curved stem eight or ten inches long, which allowed the pipe to hang down. He smoked steadily and slowly and evidently greatly enjoyed his tobacco.

The day after my arrival at Cairo was Sunday, when I expected I should have comparative leisure, but I found myself busier than ever, Dr. Simons assuring me most earnestly, that "in wartime there were no Sundays or holidays." Two days later I was ordered to St. Louis, with a cargo of sick soldiers, under the following order, in General Grant's own handwriting.

[SPECIAL ORDER]

Headquarters Dist. S. E. Missouri,
Cairo, Sept. 16, 1861.

"In consequence of the lack of capacity of the hospitals at this Post, to hold the sick unfit to remain in camp, Brigadier Surgeon Brinton will proceed by boat this evening to St. Louis, in charge of such sick as may be put under his charge by the Medical Director of the post. On his arrival at St. Louis, Dr. Brinton will report to the Medical Director of the Department of the West, Dr. DeCamp. Upon being relieved of his sick, he will return to this Post without delay. A list of the sick, so disposed of, together with the company and regiment to which they belong, will be furnished to this office, in order that the General commanding may cause to be made out, and furnish to the proper Medical Officer in St. Louis, a descriptive role of them."

By order of BRIG. GENL. GRANT,
Commanding.

JOHN A. RAWLINS,
Capt. and A. A. Genl.

I greatly enjoyed this trip up the Mississippi. I had never before been on a western river steamer, and then, too, I was in authority, official authority, for the first time in my life. It was all so new to me. The poor sick wretches under my command were ready to do what I ordered. The associations, for the time being, with the officers of the boat, the captain of the steamer consulting with me as to when and where we would stop and the pilot inviting me into his den, far up by the "texas" (that is the third deck of the boat),—all of this was so new, and so different from all to which I had been accustomed, that I felt myself quite rapidly developing into a sort of superior creature.

Having turned my sick over to the proper authorities in St. Louis, I returned to Cairo and reported to Dr. Simons.

# CHAPTER III

I did not stay in Cairo long. The number of sick in the district was rapidly increasing and it had become necessary that the hospital accommodations should become largely augmented. The town of Mound City, four years old and of speculative origin and growth, stood on the right bank of the Ohio river, about eight miles above Cairo. It was then a very little town, just on the river bank, a long row of three or four-story brick houses, or rather warehouses, built to accommodate the anticipated business of the future city. As a speculation they had up to this time been a failure, and the buildings stood finished as to their walls, but unfinished as to their interiors. They were just in that state, from which they could readily be converted into a general hospital, three hundred feet long in front, by one hundred feet deep, capable of accommodating from eight hundred to one thousand patients comfortably. This building, the medical director had selected for the great general hospital of the district, and I was sent by him with full instructions to accomplish the work, and to take charge of the hospital when completed.

Accordingly to Mound City I went at once, and put up at the hotel of the place, situated not far from the river bank. There was rather a stir in business at that time in the new little city, as four of the Mississippi ironclads, the "turtles," as they were afterwards christened, were being built here by Captain Eads, for the United States government. These were to be covered by iron slabs ten and a half inches thick, arranged like the roof of a house, and at such angle as would best turn or deflect any shot or shell striking them.

They proved to be a success, and afterward played a prominent part in the operations undertaken to open the Mississippi River. Many of the chief workmen or master mechanics employed on their vessels boarded at the hotel to which I went.

One of my first cares was to provide quarters for myself; and here I was so fortunate as to find the first floor of a little house or shop, which suited me exactly, two communicating rooms, capable of holding whatever I might choose to put in them. So with a little cot bed with bedding and mosquito netting from the hospital stores, with my big blue blanket for a carpet, a stove and a looking glass, a pitcher and a wash basin, I established myself at once in a most luxurious manner. My landlord was a little German apothecary from Hesse, who lived next door with his wife. They had not been very long in the country, and were very nice people. My breakfast and tea were furnished me by my hostess, and her omelets were unexceptionable, and the coffee well made. The whole establishment was quite cozy and economical. I paid four dollars a month for my room rent, and my provisioning was on an equally modest scale.

It would be hard to understand the difficulties I had to overcome before I could get my hospital into a condition to receive even one or two hundred sick. However, I stuck to my work, and eventually, before I was relieved from the charge of the hospital, I had succeeded in bringing it to a satisfactory state. A year or so later, after I had learned something about hospitals

(I mean military ones), I am sure I could have accomplished in a few hours the work that cost me so many weary days of labor and nights of thought at Mound City.

One of my chief troubles at this place was the difficulty,—and, I may almost say, the impossibility, of procuring the necessary men to do the work incident to the formation of a large hospital. In a city, or where the command was large, this difficulty would not have existed, and men could have been obtained. But the garrison at Mound City at this time was but a single regiment, and to this regiment many duties were assigned. The presence of the iron gunboats, in process of building, was a tempting bait to the enemy, who practically held the opposite bank of the river, and our men were constantly on the alert against surprise. At first we were very defenceless, but later, guns and a battery were sent up for our protection. Every day or two an alarm would be raised and we would be told that the enemy were in force on the opposite shore, and our scouting parties would be sent out to reconnoitre. During my stay, however, the excursions never resulted in any practical end. The "enemy" would usually turn out to be scouts of our own from camps below Cairo.

Had I rightly appreciated my position at this time, I should have known that I was really well off. I had every authority I could wish for, I was comfortably situated, and nobody to interfere with me, and, as far as I knew, enjoyed the confidence of the Medical director. But the fact was, I was lonely, dreadfully lonely; the men by whom I was surrounded were not to my liking; I did not understand their rough, western, good-hearted ways and I longed at that time to be among those whom I called "gentlemen." I am afraid I did not try to make myself popular and I am sure that I received more consideration than I deserved. I am sure, too, that I fretted a great deal more than was at all necessary, about my hospital, though it was hardly to be wondered at, considering I had only half-sick men, or the prisoners from the guard house, to do my work. Scrubbing, sweeping, putting up beds, and making beds, and that sort of thing, was, to use the western formula, "women's work," and these gawky western men insisted upon it that they did not come into the army to do anything else but fight. It was astonishing to me how slowly these fellows did work, even with a guard behind them. In fact, they seemed only to work when my eye was upon them. Just as soon as my back was turned all exertion ceased.

But if the men were bad, the women were worse. Just at this period the craze spread among our good people that the women of the country could make themselves very useful by acting as nurses for the sick and wounded. So out they came, these patriotic women of the North. The Secretary of War, the generals commanding departments, divisions or military posts, were besieged by them. By strained construction of certain paragraphs in the army regulations, and of acts of Congress, positions, paid positions, were devised for them. They besieged all officers and persons high in authority, and these, on the general military principle of sending a disagreeable person as far away as possible, sent the fair petitioners to as far away positions as they could. And the women went, and on the arrival of certain trains would stalk into the office of district commanders, and establish themselves solemnly against the walls, entrenched behind their bags and parcels. They defied all military law. There they were, and there they would stay, until some accommodation might be found for them. In self-defence the adjutant general would send them to the medical director, and he, gallantly or not, as might be his nature, would forward them to the surgeon in charge of hospitals. To him at last these wretched females would come. "They did not wish much," not they, "simply a room, a bed, a looking glass, someone to get their meals and do little things for them," and they would nurse the "sick boys of our gallant Union Army." "Simply a room." Can you fancy half a dozen or a dozen old hags, for *that* is what they were (our modern efficient trained nurses were unknown), surrounding a bewildered hospital surgeon, each one clamorous for her little wants? And rooms so scarce and looking glasses so few! And then, when you had done your best, and had often sacrificed the accommodations for the sick to their benefit, how little gratitude did one receive! Usually nothing but complaints, fault-finding as to yourself, and backbiting as to companions of their own sex. In short this female nurse business was a great trial to all the men concerned, and to me at Mound City soon became intolerable.

I determined, therefore, to try to get rid of them from the Mound City hospital. In answer to my request to the Catholic authorities of, I think, North and South Bend, Indiana, a number of sisters were sent down to act as nurses in the hospital. These sent were from a teaching and not from a nursing order, but in a short time they adapted themselves admirably to their new duties. I have forgotten the exact title of the order to which they belonged,—I think they were sisters of Notre Dame. I remember their black and white dresses, and I remember also, that when I asked the Mother, who accompanied them, what accommodation they required, the answer was, "One room, Doctor," and there were in all, I think, fourteen or fifteen of them. So I procured good nurses for my sick and the whole tribe of sanitary "Mrs. Brundages" passed away. The sick patients gained by the change, but for a few days I was the most abused man in that department, for the newspapers gave me no mercy.

A great deal has been written about the bountiful supplies sent by the North to the army. Undoubtedly, this was true in the later part of the war, and in the early part of the war, as far as the army of the Potomac and the eastern armies generally were concerned. But we in the west fared badly at first (notice that I use the pronoun "we" in the plural for I was fast becoming a military man in my military sympathies); not perhaps while I was at Mound City, but later when I had the honor of being a member of the military family of one who was to become the great "Captain" of this war. We, in the west, then, I say, were badly armed, and not well supplied with the medical equipment, necessary for the active preparations we were just entering upon. But I will say more of this hereafter.

I have spoken of the objection of the western man or soldier to doing certain kinds of work. Nevertheless, he possesses a certain degree of independence, and of marked individuality. An outcome of this is "lynch law," essential, perhaps, to the development of the western land, but from the influence of which it is hard for the western man entirely to free himself, even when the necessity for it has passed away. Should any necessity for it arise, he turns to it again naturally. In illustration I may state that the Eighteenth Illinois Regiment (infantry) was stationed here. It had the reputation of being a somewhat wild regiment. One evening a private in that regiment, in cold blood, shot a private of his own company, for some petty grudge. The regiment was on the point of moving, and was waiting for marching orders in a few hours. The man could not be tried by martial law, as Illinois was a loyal state. He could not be tried by a civil process, as the witnesses would move with their regiment. There was but one solution, and that was for his comrades to take the law into their own hands, in fact for the matter to be settled according to the stern and summary procedure of "lynch law."

This was accordingly done, a jury of twelve was chosen from his own company, a judge was selected, and a court established. There was a counsel for the defence and a counsel for the prosecution. In the interests of justice, witnesses were heard. I think I was asked if the victim died from the effects of a gun shot wound. I know, that at the time, I could hardly believe that this was all in real earnest. The prisoner was found guilty by the jury and was sentenced to be hanged on the following morning. As I was informed, a commission from the regiment waited on the Colonel, and requested him to go to Cairo early in the morning, to make purchases. He obligingly complied and left the camp betimes. As I was eating my breakfast on the morning following the so-called trial, the regiment in good order, and headed by the Lieutenant-Colonel, marched past to a strip of woods just beyond the borough limits. The prisoner was placed in a cart, a rope around his neck; the officiating executioner, who sat in the fork of the tree just above the doomed man's head, made all fast; the cart made off, the man was hanged and justice done. Someone suggested to the military officials in charge the advantages of a grave for the dead man. "A damned good idea," remarked the functionary, "Dig one under him as he hangs and drop him into it." This was done, the grave was dug, the body lowered and dropped into it. The hole was filled up, the executioner jumped down from his perch, the regiment formed in marching order, and then moved off to their daily duties. All parties felt that they had performed a virtuous act; and perhaps, as things go, they had.

After a while the Colonel came and pretended much surprise.

The matter was reported to General Halleck at St. Louis in a mild way, and there was some correspondence. It was rumored that it would go hard with the regiment, or at all events with the officers. But events were pressing, the regiment moved off, and no more was heard of the matter. After all, it was war-time, justice had been done, and the men themselves, the parties concerned, had acted. This was my only experience during the war with "lynch law," a rough code, it is true, but in this case it produced a most salutary effect. The regiment which had been a wild one, was sobered, and I doubt if anyone who witnessed that hanging ever forgot it.

During my short stay at Mound City hospital, I first learned what it really was to be in authority. The responsibility which to me, was always commensurate with the authority, weighed heavily upon me. I did my best to get for the patients in the hospitals all the comforts I could, not only from the government supplies but also with the aid societies, which at that time were springing up everywhere in the west and the east. For you must remember that this was a "people's war," and that those who remained at home worked hard to supply with comforts those who were in the fields. The men gave money, the women fitted up boxes containing every imaginable and unimaginable convenience and comfort for "our boys," which they were only too glad to send on request. A good many of these "soldiers' boxes" reached me, and most useful they proved. It was a great thing to have these extra stores which one could dispense at discretion, and for which no special return or account had to be given. I do not know how it was in the east at the early period of the war but in the west, few delicacies or extra stores of hospital clothing or linen could be procured from the department of the medical purveyor.

The supplies at this time sent to the western troops by the government were scanty, and it was not until after Dr. William A. Hammond became surgeon general, that much improvement took place in this respect. But I will speak of this hereafter, and shall now content myself by referring to the boxes which reached me from Philadelphia and from Newport, R. I. The former, furnished on my own request, contained all sorts of underclothes for patients in hospital; wrappers and slippers and shirts and drawers for the convalescents. Then too there was clothing for the dead, and I ought to state that I had at first no chaplain to perform religious services, or to bury the dead and more than once I was obliged to perform these gloomy services myself.

I referred just now to a box from Newport, R. I. This was sent by Mr. J. C. Van Renselaer. I remember that box particularly. It contained some "good" wine, and some "very good." This I was authorized by the donor to apply for my own personal benefit, and I can distinctly recall that "Old Constitution Madeira," figuring prominently on my New Year's dinner at Cairo on January 1st, 1862. I may say that at this time I took very good care of myself and I am afraid that I was in some respects a "featherbed soldier." I know that I swallowed my quinine regularly to prevent the occurrence of chills; and that I was very careful of my precious self in every way. I do not know after all that I should be blamed, for that region was a most malarious one, although let me say that while I have often been *near* a malarious country, or place, or town, I have never yet been anywhere, where the inhabitants would openly and honestly admit that unhealthiness prevailed *just* there. Thus at Cairo, below the level of the waters of the two rivers, and at the time of which I am speaking unhealthy to the last degree, I never could find any Cairo-ite who would frankly acknowledge the fact. If questioned, the answer would always be, "Unhealthy, no indeed: how can this place be unhealthy with a strong breeze blowing all the time from the Ohio to the Mississippi River. Now Mound City, seven miles above, is unhealthy, everyone knows that." Yet at Mound City, I would be told "There is no malaria here. If you want to find that, you must go to Cairo, where everyone has the chills. Here we are entirely protected by our belt of woods." Probably each one of these speakers carried quinine in bulk in his pocket, and took it daily, almost without regard to definite doses. And so I have gone through the world chilled to my back bone, and yet never have been able to find any locality, city or town, where any loyal inhabitant would admit the presence of the dreaded influence.

While at Mound City I felt an intolerable desire for home. I was homesick to the last degree. I had no society, no associates of my own rank, and although the contract assistant surgeons who reported to me, tried to help me, still I had not been long enough from home to have learned how to accustom myself to new companions, and how to be satisfied in the novel and changing circumstances in which I found myself. So chafed was I at all my discomforts at this time that I wrote to my cousin, Dr. John McClellan of Philadelphia, and afterwards to either Arthur or George, I forget which, begging that I might be ordered to the Army of the Potomac. Fortunately for myself, my request was unheeded by my cousin, General McClellan, who was at this time in command of the Army of the Potomac, and my letter remained unanswered, and I remained where I was. Had I only known it, I was very well off, and I should have felt very happy and comfortable. Mound City, barring its malaria, was really not a bad place to be in. It had even almost historic associations, for it had grown up close by the abandoned sites of the old villages or towns of Trinity and Unity, which date back to the earliest settlements of the French. These little villages were situated on a sort of stream, or canal, which connected, once upon a time, the Ohio and Mississippi rivers. This stream was once known as the "Cash" River, a contraction for "Cache," and was nine or ten miles long; the name indicated, I suppose, that at sometime or other provisions or supplies had been buried or hidden near its banks. The channels of the stream had been obstructed and the towns had disappeared, although vestiges of the stone foundations of the houses were still traceable, and one could see evidences of the clearings in the woods. Tradition, if the term be here admissible, referred the foundation of these deserted villages almost to the time of Father Hennepin and the Sieur de la Salle, who passed down from Canada to the mouth of the Mississippi.

Another curious feature of this place was the mound

from which the city took its name, "Mound City." This mound or tumulus was a circular pyramidal mound, about thirty feet in height, situated not very far from the right bank of the Ohio river. It was undoubtedly of Indian construction, but when built, or exactly by whom, no one knew. I never heard that it had been pierced, or that any search had ever been made as to its contents. I suppose that it had once been intended as an Indian burial place. At the time I knew it its sides were green, and the top was surmounted by two or three trees, under which I liked to sit and smoke my pipe— thinking of home.

One of the first things I learned at this station was how to answer a sentry's challenge, and how to give the countersign. The guard line ran between my hospital and my quarters, and it used to make me a little nervous at first to be stopped after work by the hoarse "Who goes there" of the sentry, and his imperious "Halt," and then my very prompt answer, "A friend with the countersign," and then again the "Advance, friend, and give the countersign." All this is simple enough on paper, but when the challenge was emphasized with the sharp click of the musket lock, there was a reality about it, which was unpleasantly startling. I can well remember how cautiously the "Friend" (that is I myself) used to advance, dodging that bayonet and that confounded muzzle, which seemed to glitter so brightly, no matter how dark the night, and which seemed to be pointing in every direction at the same moment, and how carefully, how distinctly I would whisper "Banks," and then hear the sentry's answer, "Correct, pass on." Such was the formula every time I went to my hospital at night: Banks, Halt, Anderson, Grant, Concord, Wool, and the like were the favorite words. The countersign was sent to me every night just before dark, written on a paper done up in a mysterious, three cornered cocked hat of a note; and I have more than once in my after military life forgotten the word, and had difficulty in recalling it.

Here, too, I learned to salute; and that, let me tell you, is no little accomplishment.

My days were thus busily occupied, and in the evening I used to look over my accounts and write my letters, and amuse myself in killing mosquitoes, or in touching their bites with a solution of ammonia. Very powerful and bloodthirsty were these pests, grey-backed, huge and insatiate. Then, too, in the evenings I spent a good deal of time in studying up my "Army Regulations," which is one of the best things an officer can do, especially if he happens to have many executive or administrative duties to discharge. At the same time I also paid some attention to riding. It is true that I had not yet a horse of my own, but I was lucky enough to procure for my ambulance a good pair of horses from the quartermaster, which went equally as well in the saddle and in harness.

By the 13th or 14th of October, I had some 250 or 300 men in hospital, and at this time I was instructed to lose no time in raising the hospital capacity to 800 or 1,000 beds. Besides the small regimental tent hospitals, the only other accommodation for the sick was the district hospital at Cairo, under the charge of Acting Assistant Surgeon Burke, a resident of the town, and the capacity of which was only eighty or a hundred.

At this time, Cairo had become a center for the concentration of troops for future contemplated operations; the forces in Cairo and its dependencies at Fort Holt on the Kentucky side of the Mississippi River, and Byrds Point on the Missouri side being about twenty regiments of infantry and one or two of cavalry, used for patrolling and scouting duty. All of the troops were much exposed. The camps were close to the river, the malarial influences were subtle and overwhelming, the hygienical conditions were bad, the men had not learned to take care of themselves, nor had their surgeons as yet had sufficient military experience to be able to cope with the difficulties of their new positions. The supply departments were inefficient, the medical stores in the hands of the medical purveyor at Cairo were meager and not altogether suited to the necessitous condition of the command. The quartermaster's supplies were also scanty, and even when plentiful in his hands, were grudgingly and unwillingly issued to the medical department. All complaints of the latter were met by the assurance that supplies could not be obtained from St. Louis, and it may be that a want of general military organization did at this time exist at this city, then the military headquarters of the department. At a later period, their deficiencies were remedied, probably owing to the examinations and reports made by careful inspectors from the regular service, but in the earlier period of which I am now speaking, disorganization, rather than organization, prevailed.

I suppose that all this medley of affairs was unavoidable, and was in great part due to the newness of the war, and to its gigantic proportions. It took time to learn how to carry on so great a struggle and to fully appreciate the idea that it was all in dead earnest. There was great friction at first in the movements of the vast military machine;—its elements and component parts were freshly made, and often badly put together, and the men who managed it were inexperienced. The troops were raw, filled with home ideas, and I know that we, the officers of medical corps, had much to learn. For those who passed from civil professional life, into what I may describe as purely professional military life, such as the treatment and charge of sick and wounded soldiers, it was not so very hard. Some paper work undoubtedly there was, but it was not excessively onerous. Far different, however, was it with those officers of the corps of brigade surgeons, who, standing high on the roll of their corps, found themselves, fresh from civil life, suddenly forced into positions demanding a high degree of executive and administrative ability. Not a few were early called upon to assume the responsible duties of medical directors of corps, armies and departments. In the old service, I mean the regular service, and in the natural order of events and by the force and operation of the law of seniority, the men who discharged these functions were men of advancing age, and who had had lifetime experience in the routine and *paper* duties of the department. In the exigencies of our national strife, from the magnitude and pressure of its demands, officers fresh from civil life were called upon at a moment's notice, and without previous training, to discharge these high duties; how to do so properly they had yet to learn, and that in the face of pressing events. In this position I soon found myself, and it happened more from the kindness and good will of my great commander, rather than from any merit of my own, that I was enabled to carry myself without discredit.

# CHAPTER IV

## CAIRO, 1861

Towards the end of October, 1861, Dr. Simons, Medical Director of Southeastern Missouri (that is Cairo and its dependencies), relieved me from duty at Mound City General Hospital and placed me on duty in the medical director's office. This, as I discovered in a few days, was merely preparatory to my temporary appointment as Medical Director of the District, during the proposed absence of Surgeon Simons, who had applied for leave to visit his home in Baltimore. On arriving at Cairo, I took up my quarters in the fourth or fifth story of Safford's Bank Building, at that time occupied as the headquarters of General Grant. The office of the medical director, was, if I remember rightly, in the third story front room. I fancy my presence was rather agreeable than otherwise to Dr. Simons for, as I have said before, he seemed to be dreadfully lonely and much in want of someone to talk with. He was a typical southerner, an old army officer of the Mexican War type. It seemed to me, however, that something must have happened in his previous life which had soured him,—but he was very kind to me, and I liked him.

On Wednesday, the 23rd of October, I made a very pleasant trip on board a flag of truce steamer down the Mississippi, to Columbus, far in the enemy's country. The description of this trip I quote in part from my letter to my Mother, dated October 24th.

"About noon on the 23rd of October, I started in a tiny steam tug under the command of Colonel N. Baford, who had been educated at West Point, but had been long in civil life. He was a fussy old gentleman, an old granny, but kind and amiable; he had with him two or three aides, and Dr. Simons and I went as inquisitive passengers in the expectation of bringing up some wounded men. We had on board a reporter for the New York *Herald,* a very busy man, who after a while got very drunk. The boat was the smallest steam boat I had ever seen, hardly large enough, in fact, to carry the party. We steamed down the river with a white sheet tied to our flagstaff, away down the river for twenty-six miles, until we came in sight of the high bluffs, on the left-hand side just above, and overtopping, the town of Columbus, Kentucky, the first town within the river limits of 'Secessia.' "

The noble bluffs were covered with tents and swarmed with men, and the big guns pointed their ugly noses up the river in a terribly menacing manner. We were all expectation, and I, for one, could not help wondering what would happen next. However, our saucy little boat floated quietly down, gradually approaching the hostile works, the ragamuffins on the bank running along the river edge, when, Bang! a blank cartridge was fired from a 64-pounder. We whistled three times and then steamed on (which we ought not to have done), until we came right under their works. "Bang!"—again went the heavy gun, and we came to, and just in time; for as we were afterwards told, a shotted gun was trained on us to check this abuse of a flag of truce. A shot from such a gun at a 500-yard range would have been indeed no joke, especially, aimed as this one was, by Captain Blake, a graduate of West Point. "Had you not finally laid to when you did," this person told me himself the next day, "I should have sunk you."

And so, tardily shutting off steam, we slowly drifted down until we reached a steamer, anchored by the sloping banks of the changing western river. Here our chief, Col. Baford, when challenged, asked for General Polk. "I am General Pillow" was the answer, "come on board," and so we did, and then ascending to the saloon of the steamer, we were all presented to the Warrior Priest, Bishop, and Major General, Polk. This gentleman had been educated at West Point, but subsequently took orders, and had become bishop, I think, of Louisiana. At the outbreak of the war, he laid aside his lawn, and again assumed the shoulder straps. He had formerly, in 1827, been commissioned in the U. S. Army, as second lieutenant of artillery. He was killed in 1864 during General Sherman's Atlanta march.

General Polk, who was in full major-general's uniform, received us kindly, and shook hands with us all. He was a rather tall, thin fellow, toothless, and bland to a degree. He talked a good deal, and his manner seemed to me to be somewhat flippant. He was not altogether priest *or* soldier, and the admixture of the manners of both was not happy. However, we were all received very cordially, and were invited into the cabin, where we took a drink of brandy and water all around, to the toast of "Washington and his principles," a sentiment in which we could all join, no matter what was the color of the uniform.

General Pillow was a very quiet, gentlemanly person, who said little. Our New York reporter was very busy; he kept close to the Secession generals, and picked up his items like a veritable newspaper bee. After a while, champagne was brought, and as there seemed to be some difficulty as to the ice, we offered some from the stores of our little tug, but they would not receive it. Laughingly, Dr. Simons and I promised to send it to them some day, when they sent us a flag of truce, a promise which we liberally kept a few days later. While the seniors were talking (of what I never had the faintest idea), the two staffs fraternized, and we had a very merry time, and here it was that the *Herald* man was overcome by the enemy, and became quite hilarious.

The Confederate surgeons were very polite to me. They took me on shore, and I passed with them through the streets to the hospitals. The latter were poorly appointed, but the inmates were apparently in good condition. The other members of our party were not allowed to land, that permission being accorded only to the medical officers. The people in the streets seemed squalid and unhealthy; they were ragged in appearance, and offensive in their manner and words. As we passed by they called us all manner of names, "Lincolnites," "Damned Yankees," "Abolitionists," and other such pet-names. Had we not been in the company of our Secession friends, we would indeed have fared badly.

The uniforms of the Confederate officers were generally of a shabby dirty gray, with a good deal of tinsel and cheap gold lace ornamentation, entirely too much. Their arms were poor. Several of the officers were West Pointers, and these talked freely on passing events. Of their ultimate success they seemed to be certain. They laughed at the idea of defeat or subjugation. From one of their officers, a Captain Blake, of Polk's staff, I learned a good many war items, of confederate coloring, interesting to me then, but now long forgotten.

Another of their officers was a Captain Polk, of the same staff. He had been educated at West Point, and was a nice talkative, rather boastful young gentleman. We had a good deal of chat among ourselves, during which he said if he was hurt, he would rather be treated by Northern than by Southern surgeons, and he laughingly added, "Should I ever be wounded, and let you know, will you bring me into your lines, and take care of me?" This I afterwards did. He was wounded at the Battle of Shiloh, and lay outside of our lines, in a little Confederate house where he was attended by his wife and friends. He wrote to me, as I was on General Grant's staff at the time, and reminded me of my promise. I went out under a flag of truce and brought the wounded man (as also two or three pats of fresh butter which had been set aside by Mrs. Polk), to our hospital transport, as I shall relate hereafter.

After two or three hours' pleasant chat, we prepared to start for Cairo, taking with us a few of our wounded men. Where they had been hurt I do not know,—I suppose in the various skirmishes which were constantly occurring between the pickets and the observation parties of the two armies.

I saw at this time quite an affecting sight, the parting of one of our wounded men from a wounded Confederate soldier. They had been wounded in the same encounter ten days or two weeks before, had lain side by side in the same hospital, and had mutually cared for each other. They seemed loath to part, and their leave-taking was strange to see.

All of the Secession wounded, who were able, came down to the wharf to see our wounded placed on the boat, and the good-byes were cordial and prolonged. We then steamed away to Cairo, not in our little tug, but in a boat of theirs, which carried us to our own lines, when their steamer returned to Columbus. And this was "Civil War," and this my first observation of it. The Confederate officers, whom I met, spoke freely of their commanders. General Joe Johnston, they ranked first; then a General Smith,* and Beauregard. General George B. McClellan on our side, they had a high opinion of; but they considered that he was not supported by good generals, and they felt confident of beating him badly.

On my return to Cairo I remained on duty in the office of the Medical Director for two or three days, and on October 28th, the following order was issued.

"Headquarters Dist. S. E. Mo.,
Cairo, Oct. 28, 1861.

[SPECIAL ORDER]

Surgeon James Simons, U. S. A. Medical Director, having received leave of absence, Surgeon John H. Brinton is appointed to act in his place. He will be obeyed and respected accordingly.

BY ORDER OF BRIG. GEN'L. GRANT.
(Signed) John A. Rawlins, A. A. G.

To DR. JOHN H. BRINTON,
Brigade Surgeon, U. S. A."

And so, at Cairo, after two months' actual service, I found myself the Medical Director of a geographical military district of considerable extent, and occupied by many thousand troops. To superintend medically the welfare of so large a command, was no easy work, espe-

* Probably Maj. Gen. Gustavus W. Smith who took command, for a day or so, of the Confederate Army before Richmond after the wounding of Maj. Gen. Jos. E. Johnston and before Robert E. Lee arrived to assume command.—E. T. S.

cially when it is borne in mind that most of these men were fresh levies, all from civil life and many from agricultural districts. In fact, as far as their health was concerned, they might almost have been looked upon as children. The men from the country had often not passed through the ordinary diseases of child life, and no sooner were they brought together in camps, than measles and other children's diseases showed themselves, and spread rapidly. The malarial influences of the rivers too, produced a most depressing effect upon men brought from higher regions, and more healthy surroundings. Violent remittent, intermittent and low typhoid fevers invaded the camps, and many died. The general hygiene was bad, the company and regimental officers did not know how to care for their men, and the men themselves seemed to be perfectly helpless. This inability to take care of themselves seemed to me to be one of the strangest peculiarities of the volunteers at the beginning of the war. And here it must be remembered that this time, the summer and early autumn of 1861, was the patriotic era of the national volunteers. "Conscription" with which we were afterwards so familiar, had not yet been thought of, and bounties, tempting fat bounties, were unknown. Men volunteered willingly for the war and in a patriotic spirit; young men of good families were in the ranks, men of education and attainments. In many instances, farmers eagerly became soldiers, and left their families, their farms, and their business without hesitation. These men, numbers of them, had been accustomed to think and act for themselves, and to take care of others; and yet just as soon as they entered the ranks and became soldiers, it seemed as if all individualism was lost; they ceased to think for themselves, and became incapable of self-protection. They had to be thought for, and cared for as children,—they were no longer the self-relying men they had been in civil life. And there was difficulty, too, in regard to their caretakers, for the men who suddenly found themselves officers and who were the natural guardians, as it were, of the rank and file, were utterly inexperienced, and in every way unaccustomed to take charge of others. The commissary of subsistence, whose duty it was to feed the troops, was, if he were a volunteer, ignorant of the details of his office. So also was the quartermaster, and yet on the efficiency of these officers much of the comfort of the private soldier depended.

The medical officers, the regimental surgeon, and the assistant surgeon were in a somewhat different relation, for they brought to their new positions the professional attainments of civil life, and they had only to apply their every-day knowledge to the military surroundings. Some fresh details, it is true, they had to acquire, but with a little experience, and by careful study of the army regulations, supplemented by a reasonable share of common sense, they became fitted for their duties.

The brigade surgeon had more to learn, for his higher grade placed him in a broader field. He most frequently found himself in charge of general hospitals in the larger cities, or of great divisions and corps hospitals with armies in the field. In many instances, however, he advanced at once to the grade of "medical director" it may be of a division or corps, or even of an army itself. In these instances he was on the staff of the general, who depended upon him in no slight degree for information as to the health of the command, and as to its general availability for active operations. His suggestions were usually listened to kindly and respectfully, and orders touching the hygiene of troops and camps were often issued at his instance. From my own observation, I would say that the greater the general and the more liberal his views, the more was he disposed to listen to the words of his medical director. From all this you will understand how difficult of discharge were the duties of a medical director of a district or department or army, and how delicate, too, at times they were. It was his province to see to the health, as it were, of every man in the command; to so provide that a bed should be ready for every sick or wounded soldier whenever and wherever it might be called for; to see that medicines and medical supplies should be on hand at every depot, or with every column; and to anticipate all future demands by bringing fresh supplies from the central stores. Then too the medical director had to think of the medical officers over whom he was placed. He was a sort of bishop to his military flock; his duty was to help on the diffident, overworked, or lagging; to encourage by advice or instructions those who might be perplexed or weary; to restrain and hold in check the overzealous.

It was oftentimes no easy thing to answer the pointed questions of perplexed regimental surgeons, who in the early days of the war in their ignorance of the "army regulations" regarded all rules as fetters and denounced all system as "red tape." These officers, yet civilians at heart, felt deeply for the sick and injured of their individual commands; they naturally wished to procure instantly for them those things of which they stood in need and they disliked the formality of requisitions, which they deemed unnecessary. They were impatient of delay, and yet they did not know how to make haste; they hurried to the office of the medical director for information, and he alas! (I speak for myself) often knew little if any more than his questioners. To anticipate a little the story of my own doings in my new office, I can only say, that "Men learn by teaching," and I learned the regulations, and how to do things by studying these same regulations and by trying to teach others. And then, too, a little later than this, I was taught a good lesson by Captain, now General, Hawkins, U. S. A., then in the subsistence department. "Doctor," he said to me one day, when I consulted him on some puzzling paragraph of the regulations, "Do this; when your servants come to you in ignorance and want to know what to do, tell them kindly if you do know. If you do not know, open the book of regulations for them, at the proper chapter, tell them to read it carefully for fifteen minutes in your office, and then they will understand it. Should they not do so, you will then explain it to them. And then run down to my office or General Grant's, state your trouble, and I am sure you will be helped out. You will not have to do so often." This advice I followed literally, and never did I in my ignorance apply in vain either to my good friend Hawkins, or to the great general, who seemed to me to be amused by my troubles, and at the same time to take pleasure in helping me out of them. I shall have much to say of him as I write, and I will not now anticipate, as I prefer to take up events in order, so that you can judge for yourselves how my opinions were formed, and my judgment crystallized.

On the departure of Dr. Simons for the east, I found myself with a load on my shoulders; yet although the responsibility was great, at times almost crushingly so, I did not dislike it, but tried as well as I was able to be efficient, and somehow or other got along.

For a few days, I was busy enough, inspecting the regimental camps, examining their hospitals and assisting the regimental surgeons in obtaining their requisitions, by which I mean their supplies medical and otherwise. Everyone supposed that we would pass the winter in more or less quietude, in the neighborhood of Cairo; and of active operations we had little anticipation or knowledge. I see from my letters that late in October the staff whispered some rumor of a move in thirty or forty days, but whither we did not know. Flags of truce were occasionally passing to and fro on various pretences. Southern union men would be coming north, or men from the north with southern friends would be passing southwards, or women of all sorts of political proclivities would be sent over the lines, sometimes I daresay freighted with letters full of treason, or with percussion caps, or morphia and quinine, which were already becoming scarce in "Dixie's Land." These flags of truce were often much abused, and I fancy at times did a good deal of harm. It was hard to vouch for the loyalty of those who availed themselves of them. I have a memorandum of a pretended union man, who sprang from a truce boat into the stream and swam for the southern shore, which he failed to reach, being drowned in the attempt.

One of the earliest difficulties, and one of the most pressing with which I had to contend, was a scarcity of medical men, especially of young medical men, who possessed the slightest pretensions to decent medical attainments. The regimental officers were good enough of their kind, but more than these were wanted to supply the depot hospitals, which were being established at various points. The men who supplied most of these subordinate medical positions were known as "contract physicians" or "doctors," to use the common phrase;— in the true military parlance of the Surgeon General's office "acting assistant surgeons." These gentlemen held no commissions, but signed a contract with the medical director for the time and place being, which contract would be approved by the Surgeon General in Washington. The pay was usually from eighty to one hundred dollars per month, and was charged to the medical appropriation, expended under the orders of the Surgeon General.

The regular paymaster of the United States Army had nothing to do with the contract physicians. The grade of medical men who at this time, early in the war, held these positions, was often low. Many ignorant physicians, or those who had been long out of practice, if indeed they ever had any, obtained contracts. Not infrequently it happened that charlatans and impostors succeeded in forcing themselves into these appointments, and the soldier, as would naturally be supposed, suffered in consequence. This condition of affairs obtained probably to a greater extent in the western armies than elsewhere. One of my first efforts was to reform this abuse, as far as I could, by obtaining a better class of young doctors from the east, and from some of the larger cities, but the scarcity of good surgeons to do the every-day work in the more remote hospitals of this region was undoubtedly a great evil, which existed for some time after the war began in this portion of our country.

I have already referred to General Grant's friendly treatment. I find in a letter to Dr. DaCosta, dated Nov. 20th, 1861, this allusion:

"General Grant (an old regular) is very kind to me and helps me out of many a tight place, so also does

Captain Hawkins (regular). We are quite intimate. Grant is a plain, straightforward, peremptory and prompt man. If I ask for anything it is done at once, the great secret in all military matters."

By the early part of the month of November, my new duties had become very pleasant to me, and I had become more than reconciled to my position. I felt that I was making headway, and I could see daylight ahead. My chief trouble at this time was the malarial influence of the country. Cairo enjoys, and I think most deservedly, the reputation of being thoroughly unhealthy, and this bad reputation had, up to this time of which I am speaking, always acted as hindrance to its development. One would suppose that the location of the town, on the tongue of land at the very confluence of the Ohio and Mississippi Rivers, would have been in itself sufficient to insure its rapid progress. But the place had lagged in its growth, despite the attempts of speculators to force it. It was here, I think, that many years ago, a sort of colony had been established, in which the Rev. Dr. Ely, a man of wealth, and the father-in-law of the late Dr. Samuel McClellan, the uncle of General McClellan, was largely interested. Money, a great deal of money, was spent here, but the immediate outcome was a disappointment to all concerned. The place could only grow by commerce, and this took time. Topographically considered, as a stopping place of exchange, or inland port for the steamers of the two great rivers and their tributaries, Cairo was exceptionally favored. On the other hand, as a pestilential hole fraught with all malarial poisonous influences, the town unquestionably is preëminent. The levée, a high stone bank on the Ohio River side was a good one, and at the time I went to Cairo, a good many steamers were coming and going.

On the top of the levée was the railroad track, which ran down to the St. Charles Hotel, near the end of the tongue of land. The levée, of course, was made of land, and nearly all of the houses and warehouses on it were of wood. Safford's Bank, then used as the headquarters building, was, I think, almost the only stone or brick structure. The levée and its bordering buildings, were infested with rats, many of them of a very large size, and at night they swarmed out of their holes. I have often known them to be crushed by the wheels of the railroad cars.

Cairo at this time was not altogether a pleasant place, but yet I learned to like it, and I soon came to care very little about the rats, although I never could quite bring myself to think kindly of the swarms of merchants, peddlers, produce dealers, and the like, who infested the levee, and its neighborhood. Yet I must make an exception, there was one fellow, hook-nosed and black-bearded, who sold everything and anything, and especially apples of such size, color and tartness, as I have never met since. These apples were my delight, for the craving for acid fruit was upon me. The truth was I was beginning to feel the influence of the climate and was becoming malarious and jaundiced. This was a wretched condition to fall into; I did my best to fight it off, but to no use. I stuck to my office and did my routine work, but was scarcely able to go downstairs to my meals, or to see anything of General Grant's staff, of which I was a temporary member, although I had an idea that something was in the wind, but what, I knew not.

At last, horribly nauseated, I was compelled to take to my bed. One of the ladies in the house, a Mrs. Turner, an Englishwoman, and the wife of a sort of an English

doctor under contract, kindly saw to having some food
sent to me, but which I could not eat. I felt wretched,
and finally on the morning of November 6th, after having been in bed nearly two days, my nausea was so
excessive that I put a large mustard plaster on the pit
of my stomach, hoping for some relief. The plaster
had just begun to burn comfortably and pleasantly, and
I was trying to force down a few mouthfuls of soup,
when Mrs. Turner knocked at the door, and then came
hurriedly in to tell me that the General, with a good
force, was on the eve of starting to attack the enemy,
somewhere or other. "And you won't be able to go,"
she added. The importance and suddenness of her information started me, and begging her to go out of the
room, away went my mustard plaster, and I was out of
bed in a minute, poultice on the floor, hunting for my
clothes, with my head swimming, and myself in a generally disordered condition. I managed to get into my
uniform, and hurried downstairs to the General's office.
He welcomed me warmly, saying that thinking I was
too sick to go, he had ordered that I should not be disturbed, and at once directed that I should be provided
with the best horse available.

The charger with which I was supplied deserves a
fuller mention. He was loaned to me by the quartermaster, and was a roan stallion, possessed of few virtues,
and many vices, like Byron's corsair. Chief among the
latter were his proneness to kick, and the delight he
experienced in bending his neck around and biting the
rein. He gave me much trouble early in the day, but
later proved himself a faithful creature. Having procured him, I made the best arrangements I could for
the medical department, and then provided for myself;

that is to say, I had my india-rubbers and blankets strapped to my saddle, and confided my instruments to the care of my clerk, who was to act as my orderly. Equipped and prepared for whatever event of war might happen, I waited our departure.

# CHAPTER V

In the meantime, the troops were being embarked, chiefly infantry, of which there were five regiments, two companies of cavalry, and two guns, in all, a little over three thousand men. It took a good deal of time to get all the troops safely on board and the expedition did not start until afternoon. Under the convoy of a couple of gunboats, the "Tyler," and the "Lexington," commanded by Captains Walker and Stemble, U. S. N., it steamed down the Mississippi and anchored on the Kentucky shore about six miles above Columbus. I am sorry to say, however, that of what took place during this afternon and evening and night, I knew very little. I was quite ill, in fact, scarcely able to stand, and with the General's permission, I lay down in a berth until my services were necessary. Here I slept pretty well until it was morning, when all were aroused, as the expedition steamed across the river, and prepared to disembark the troops on the Missouri shore, just about three miles above Belmont. I should say here that I accompanied General Grant in the "headquarters' boat," and that as Medical Director of the District, I was the ranking surgeon of the command, and the Medical Director in the field.

Shortly after sunrise the disembarkation of the troops was completed, and the men were drawn up in lines at right angles to the river, extending in front of a cornfield and out into the woods. Pickets were immediately thrown out and the whole force prepared to advance. It was while the disembarkation was being effected, that for the first time I saw a shot fired in earnest. It happened thus: The bluffs above Columbus are very high on the Kentucky side, I cannot really say how high, but the batteries appeared to be high up in the air, and the guns were very large, some of them I afterwards learned being rifled columbiads of ten or eleven inches bore. They were distant from our transports about three miles, perhaps a little less. As I stood on the front of our boat, a transport, I saw a puff of smoke afar off, and in a few seconds a huge projectile flew past us, and far above our heads. It was not exactly in line, and was rather high, and so passed harmlessly by, falling far to our right. But the man who fired this shot soon improved his aim, for when the next puff showed itself, it seemed to give birth to a black line, at first well up above the Mississippi, but gradually sinking as it came nearer. It seemed to me to be making a bee-line for my eye, but fortunately changed its mind, and passing above our heads, and apparently between our smoke pipes, buried itself in the dirt of the Missouri bank of the river. I was immediately seized with a covetous desire to possess that shot, and thereupon offered two darkies on the boat half a dollar apiece if they would dig it out for me. They at once set to work, and as I went up the bank, I left them digging away industriously. The next day they presented me the shot, which was a round conical shell about eighteen inches long, which had been filled with lead, and fired as a solid shot. I paid the money and secured the prize, but found, when I had it, that it was an elephant on my hands. When I left Cairo

I left it, and what became of it I never knew. I daresay it is a household ornament somewhere at this moment.

The shots of the enemy were replied to by our gun-boats, and I could see the shells from their big sixty-four-pounders bursting over the buttresses on the bluffs. On reaching the level, a sort of clearing in front of a cornfield, with wood roads, one leading towards Belmont, and one off to the right, I found our army, for I must so dignify the expeditionary force, forming in line of battle, ready to move onwards. It was a grand and new sight to me to see how real war was to be carried on. I am afraid that at first I thought more of that than of my own particular department, so I could not help riding up and down the line to take it all in. The early autumnal morning was delightful; the air fresh and invigorating, without being cold; and while I was still nauseated, it seemed to do me good. As I have already told you, I had been provided by the quartermaster with a vicious roan horse. I had not at first very much confidence in him, he had such an ugly look. Nor do I think that he had any great trust in me, since he showed a marked unwillingness to suffer me to mount him. Then too I was heavily encumbered with a surgeon's paraphernalia, but finally with the assistance of several soldiers, to wit, one to hold the beast by the head, one to keep him from turning around side-ways to bite, and one or two to boost me up, I succeeded in reaching the saddle, and when at last ensconced, felt confident of my position and certain that nothing short of an earthquake would unseat me.

So I trotted fearlessly along the line of soldiers, when suddenly my horse gave an extraordinary sort of jump, forward one time, backward one time, then a sensation of vibratory unrest, and then *da capo,* one, two, three;

and the more I said "Whoa, boy, be quiet," and tried to stroke the horse's neck, the more he essayed this confounded buck jump. Then, too, the more I tried to look unconcerned, the more the men laughed. I felt quite sure I should not be thrown, I was too deeply entrenched in my saddle for that; but why couldn't, or why shouldn't that wretched horse stand still! Soon the mystery was solved. A kindly looking soldier stepped up to my side, and raising the scabbard of my sword, showed me that the end of it had dropped off, and the sharp point of the blade was pricking the rear hind leg of the animal at every step, which was more than horse flesh could stand. So I saw at once that I could not wear the sword that day, and took it off, and left it for the time, at a little one-story house on the edge of the woods, which I had occupied as a field hospital, and had placed in charge of my friend, Dr. Amos Witter, of an Iowa regiment,—the same who had spent a night with me at Mound City.

The good doctor kindly took charge of my sword, but this was the last I saw of it, for later in the day, as our forces were returning to their boats, the enemy followed rapidly, and occupied this building before our wounded were fairly out of it. As I afterwards learned, my sword passed into the possession of a southern surgeon, and I hope he had a new end put on the scabbard.

One of my first cares was to make the best arrangements I could to take care of the wounded (should there be any), when brought to the rear. The little hospital I have referred to was organized, and I then rode on in search of headquarters, which I knew would be well to the front. The command had plunged into the woods, advancing rapidly, and my only guide was the firing, which was becoming every moment more and more heavy, showing that the fight had begun in earnest. I was alone, but anxious to rejoin my General, so I spurred on my horse, sometimes keeping to a wood path, and at other times striking through a primitive forest, as the firing led me. The first wounded man I saw was an Irishman, who had been grazed in the abdomen by a bullet. He was lying on the ground, alone, and yelling with pain. The injury was insignificant, but his mental perturbation was great. When I told him the truth, he became calm, and gathering himself up, marched off for the transports. The next day I saw a fearful case; a shell had exploded behind, but close to, the back of a soldier. He was dying when I saw him and evidently in a dreadful condition, so I dismounted to render him what help I could. I have never seen a worse wound, before or since. The whole of the skin and muscles of the back from the nape of the neck to the thighs and on both sides of the spine had been torn away, as if the tissues had been scooped out by a clean-cutting curved instrument. The surfaces were raw and bleeding, and the sight was a horrible one, and one which I have never forgotten. In a moment or two he expired, and I remounted and rode on.

In looking over my letters, I find one to Dr. DaCosta, dated November 10th, 1861, from which I think it worth while to quote a few sentences:

"At 6.30 on Thursday morning, we disembarked four miles above Columbus on the Missouri shore. Our force consisted of 2,800 men in four steamboats and two gunboats, with one hundred men each, and six sixty-four-pounders, in all 3,000 men with a number of brass guns, and about 250 cavalry."

"I was mounted on a fast horse I had got from the Quartermaster, a kicking beast. We immediately threw out scouting parties, and as we commenced to do so, the first shot was fired from the bluff batteries at Columbus. This was replied to by our gunboat 64's, and I could see the shell bursting right over the enemy's pieces. Their shots passed over our gunboats, which now ran down below our point of disembarkation and threw their shell quite lively. I now pressed forward with the staff, a half mile. Here we found, in order of battle, ten pieces of artillery in the rear, two in the advance, and the infantry thrown out on the wings. As Chief Medical Officer, I then directed the surgeons to take position on the margin of a wood, and at that moment, with heavy volleys of musketry, our whole line advanced, driving in skirmishes of the enemy. As I considered our rear unprotected, I ordered our hospital up nearer the main body, stationing them in a little log hut, our main hospital. I then seized all the water, placed it under guard, stationed my surgeons, ordered the assistant surgeons to their regiments, and advanced myself to the front. I shortly met men being carried to the rear; the first man had his hand shot off, the second his arm blown away, and his whole back torn by a shell. As I advanced slowly to the front, with my orderly carrying my instruments, I arrested temporarily the hemorrhage of the wounded I met, and ordered the ambulance wagons to hurry to the hospitals, and then to return to the front; all I am now speaking of took only ten minutes or thereabouts, and shortly the heavy dull roar of artillery burst through the woods, and the fire of musketry was continuous and rolling, as much so on both sides as at a review. We now reached a cornfield, and came in range of the batteries, and here a good many were killed, but our boys cheered and dashed on, driving the enemy before them, storming their guns and taking them. Most of the mounted officers lost their horses from the rifle fire. Passing the cornfield I again pushed into the woods for a mile or more, dressing the wounded as I went, and kept moving slowly on. After a long time, we having by this time gone forward some two and a half or three miles, we came to an open plateau, immediately behind Belmont, and exactly opposite Columbus. Here I had a fine view of the artillery practice. The gunners changed the position of their guns several times, and finally opened on the camp of the enemy at two or three hundred yards.

"The enemy retreated under the bank of the river, and sought refuge under the fire of their guns from Columbus. We then burned all their tents, while a brisk fire of shell was kept up on us from the opposite bluff. Fortunately their range was too high, the shell passing through the tops of the trees, and making a terrific racket. Here I attended a number of wounded officers. In a little while our men formed into an irregular column, and as they were doing so, I saw the pipes of two steamers going up the river. I thought to myself, 'These cannot be our gunboats,' and so rode up to General Grant and pointed them out to him. He would not at first credit these as the enemy's transports until I drew his attention to their course, as shown by the direction of the motion of their pipes; he then expressed surprise, but immediately ordered our men into line. Very shortly after this, a force of the enemy appeared on our right, in the direction of the river, and somewhat later a considerable body, in regular order, advanced from the woods, into the opening on our left. Whether these troops were the runaways whom we had driven under the bank of the river, or the fresh reinforcements, or both, I never knew.

"Our men quickly went into line of battle, but still in considerable confusion; some were tired out, and some did not care much about further fighting. Here the volunteer spirit showed itself; they had done their day's work, and wanted to go home."

"I now mounted some wounded men on wagons, put an officer or two on an artillery caisson, and threw out a judicious suggestion, as I thought, to some officers, relative to hurrying their men into line, and then stopped to look on. The two lines stood bravely up, exchanged a few volleys, and our men pushed on towards our original landing place, Generals Grant and McClernand leading. We had a number of wounded whom we did not bring off. I should have told you that we had already taken some 160 prisoners, four guns, and about thirty horses. We brought off the horses and two guns, spiked two others, and left one caisson behind. Our whole command now pushed vigorously on, and I started with it, but was stopped by Major Butler."

From what I have written, you will have learned that I followed our army as fast as I could, merely stopping to give the necessary directions on my way. On my arrival at the open Belmont plateau, the fighting was still going on, the enemy were retreating, and in a very short time their tents were in flames. I busied myself in gathering up our wounded, and in sending them to the rear hospital, directing the slightly injured to walk, and putting those who were more seriously injured into such wagons as we possessed. It was at this time that I joined General Grant, when the fire was pretty hot, and the big guns on the bluffs on the opposite side of the river were beginning to open. He was good enough to tell me that a doctor had no business there, and to get away. However, I had business there in caring for our wounded, and I did what I could. Then when our exodus or retreat was ordered, I watched our people rallying in line, and I thought that even if they had scattered a little to pillage the enemy's camp, they were still a brave set of men. Some of them, however, were as I thought, foolish, notably one officer, evidently a German, who had two pieces of artillery in charge, which he held upon low ground, while the enemy were hurrying up in good force. I was standing on a little hill and saw the possible catastrophe, "Come up here," I called to him, "bring your guns up here." He did so in a twinkling, when I ordered him to open on the approaching gray mass. This he did right manfully, and after a couple of rounds, the gray column passed to the right and out of sight. My major's shoulder straps seemed to inspire him with confidence, and he did what I told him, even to trotting off with his guns, when the rest of our men moved backward.

About this time, I learned for the first time the sound of a bullet. A good many big trees were on the ground, buttonwood trees they were, which had either fallen or had been cut down, when the camp was formed. Their leaves, dried and withered, were yet on the boughs, and I could hear all around me the whiz of the bullets, and the dry pat as they cut through the dead leaves. At first I could not think what the noise was, but soon one fellow came unpleasantly near my ear, and as I saw and heard the dry leaves rip and fly, and saw the holes which were left, I then knew what it all meant. Then, too, men were hit near me and I began to feel uncomfortable; I felt as if I would like to ride away, but I knew it would never do to show fear, even if I was afraid, so I walked my horse over to where General Grant was, which drew upon me the kind of rebuke I have told you of. In my heart, I do not think I deserved it, for I am afraid I *was* afraid.

Yet all the same I had my wits about me for I noted a good many curious events passing around me. I particularly remember a Confederate soldier, who had been shot in the left arm, for he was supporting his elbow with his right hand. He was a tall fellow, in butternut brown trousers, and without a coat or hat. He was evidently suffering great pain, and the pain had produced a peculiar excited delirium. He noticed nothing which was transpiring around him, nor did he even seem to see our soldiers, but he kept steadily running up and down, forwards and backwards, by the side of a huge fallen tree, always turning exactly at the same point and retracing his steps to and fro, jumping over some bush at each tour. I watched him for some minutes with curiosity and was about to ride up to him, when my attention was diverted by the stream of our passing men, and I saw the necessity of following them, if I wished to avoid being taken prisoner, so I turned my horse's head and moved off with our men.

The enemy were in front of us as we were then marching, facing towards our boats, and the firing was rather brisk, but we were pushing them, and they were giving way, allowing our men to force their passage. As I rode with them, a Southern officer dressed in a gray uniform, and lying on the ground in a fence angle of a clearing, called to me, asking me to dismount and help him, "if you are a gentleman." Urgent as the position of affairs was, I could not resist his appeal. I dismounted, knelt down by him, examined him, and found that he had been shot through the liver, and was rapidly sinking. He told me that his name was Butler, "Major Butler of Louisiana," that he had formerly been Secretary of Legation at Berlin, and that he was a grandson of Mrs. Lewis Washington, or Washington Lewis, of Clarke County, Virginia. He said, too, that his mother had been a school friend of Mrs. George McClellan. He asked me how long he could live. I answered "but a very short time." He then said to me: "Please send a message to my father,—by the first flag of truce,—tell him how you found me,—and tell him, too, that I died as behooved me, at the head of my men." I did all I could for him, stimulating him from my flask. He was very grateful and said, "Oh, Doctor, I wish I had met you before this." He begged me to remain with him, and when I told him that our troops were on their way to their boats, he offered to protect me while he lived, if I would only stay. I assured him that his own people would find him, and that I must go. So I mounted and reluctantly left him on the ground. I afterwards learned that he was carried alive to Belmont, but died shortly after reaching the town. I was also informed from home that his mother had been one of the bridesmaids of my Aunt McClellan. In the course of a few weeks, I also received a letter from Ex-Governor Vroom of New Jersey, formerly our United States Minister to Prussia, at Berlin, stating that Major Butler had been his Secretary of Legation, and that he had been a very clever fellow.

On leaving poor Butler, I rode after our retreating army, but no sooner had I reached the verge of the woods than I found myself confronted with quite a number of our gray-clad enemies. I came upon them suddenly, and they instantly covered me with their rifles. Fortunately for myself, I wore a civilian's overcoat of black cloth, and my uniform was, therefore, not very conspicuous. I immediately raised my hand in a deprecatory, and at the same time in an authoritative sort of a way, and they lowered their guns. In a moment, and almost instinctively, I wheeled my horse to the left, struck him hard with my spurs, and dashed through a dogwood thicket, and was out of their sight in half the time I have taken to write the last line. My horse carried me splendidly, and seemed to understand the exigencies of the situation. The men tried hard to follow me, but I was well mounted, and they were on foot, and the bushes thick, and so I escaped.

I have spoken of my spurs; let me say here that those I wore in this action were the silver ones marked "George Brinton, September 11th, 1779," and which descended direct to me from my great-grandfather, having been made from silver dollars. I wore them this day, so that I could say they had been used in battle, and I feel sure that they will be honorably worn hereafter by my descendants.

Leaving my enemies behind me, I rode at random, not knowing my true course, and after a long circuit, I again struck one corner of the battle field, over which I rode alone. It was desolate enough now; there were no active combatants upon it, only the dead and wounded. I left it as soon as I could, and again sought for our men, or our gunboats, but somehow or other I rode in exactly the opposite or wrong direction, and emerged from the wood upon the river bank, along which ran a road between an open field and the river. Here, on the fence, I found two old darkies, one of whom was blind and the other lame. At first they seemed afraid of me, but when they saw I was a Union officer—in their own lingo, "one of Massa Linkum's sojers," their confidence returned. I told them how I came there and that I wanted to reach the gunboats above. I could scarcely believe my ears when they told me that I was far below Columbus, and I even doubted my eyes when, looking up the river, I could see the whereabouts of the town. I took some five-dollar gold pieces out of my pocket, and offered one to each of them, if they would pilot me to the boats. This they were afraid to do, but they tried to do the next best thing, namely, to show me how to find my own way. The blind man seemed to be the intellectual partner, and he told his lame colleague to draw with his stick in the dust of the road a chart of the course I should follow. This he did, and then, thanking him heartily, I left. I must add here that they absolutely refused to accept the money from me, their reiterated reason for not doing so being "that I was Linkum's sojer."

So again I struck into the woods, determined, if I could not reach our boats, to make the best of my way to Bird's Point opposite Cairo, twenty-five miles higher up. As I had neither guide nor compass, I must have steered in an uncertain course. I remember wondering at the time how Robinson Crusoe felt when he discovered his own footmarks. After a while I fell in with another wanderer, and we two went quietly together for a little way, when we differed as to our course and parted, he going his way and I mine. And here let me add as sequel this curious coincidence. More than a year and a half afterwards, when I was stationed at Washington, I was travelling in the train from Baltimore to Washington. In front of me sat a most dilapidated and gaunt man, without decent clothing. He mentioned to his neighbor that he was just from Andersonville (the dreaded Confederate prison camp in Georgia) where he had been taken after his capture. "And when were you captured?" he was asked. "On the seventh of

November, 1861," he replied. Hearing that, I leaned forward and asked him if he had been captured at Belmont, Missouri. He took a long look at me, and then said, "Major, your way was right, after all—mine was wrong, for it led me to Andersonville, which I have just left." He was on his way to Washington to report his case. I was always sorry that I did not learn his name and follow him up. The second meeting was odd indeed, odder still that he was able to recognize me.

To return to my ride, after parting company with the unbeliever, as before described, I wandered aimlessly around, trying to keep a general direction parallel to the Mississippi River. Suddenly, in the midst of a dense forest of primeval trees, I was startled by the loud report of a heavy gun, directly in front of me, and by the whiz and bursting of a shell in the tops of the trees above my head. It instantly flashed on my mind that there must be a force of the enemy just ahead of me, and that our gunboats were firing into them, with possibly too great elevation of their guns. I checked my horse at once, and stopped to think what I had best do. If I advanced, I should inevitably fall into the hands of the enemy, if they were where I supposed them to be. If I rode backwards, I would run the risk of being killed by our own shells, which were falling behind me. I felt very uncomfortable, not so much at the idea of being hurt, as at the idea of being away from all assistance in case of injury. My horse, too, became demoralized; he stopped and shook all over and there seemed to be none of the spirit of the morning in him. Then, to add to it all, a great shell struck the top of the tree under which we were standing, and cut all of the upper part of it squarely off, and down it fell, point foremost; I remember it all most distinctly how that stem of the tree looked as it struck the ground perpendicularly. Just then the direction of the fire seemed to shift, and the missiles seemed to strike more in front and to my left. So I rode away, and after a while struck the bed of an unfinished railroad. Along this I rode for some time, and then, hearing voices, I reined in my horse, and waited to see who might be coming. Soon I saw through the trees (here of small size) a body of horse, in our uniform. I joined them, and found that I had fallen in with Dollin's cavalry, an independent company of cavalry attached to our command. They seemed to be in rather a bewildered condition, and their leader, noticing the major's gold leaf on my shoulder straps, consulted with me, and indeed asked me to tell him what to do. I do not pretend to be much of a soldier, but I have a dread of being surprised or taken at a disadvantage, and I observed that just at that moment we were in a most dangerous position, and that if attacked in any force, we might all be destroyed or captured. We were riding, all huddled together, with an impassable slough of mud and water close on our right. I suggested that we should move more to the left, throw our scouts out on the left side and in advance, and march rapidly and quietly. This was done, and after advancing in this order for some distance, we were able to cross the swamp, and bearing to the right, we came on a sort of road, and soon reached a poor log house. The occupants pretended to know nothing as to the position of the river, or the whereabouts of our boats and troops. We were about to take a guide by force, under the persuasion of a cocked pistol, when one of the women recognized me. She was the mistress of the little cabin or farm house I had occupied as a hospital early in the morning. In doing so, I had given particular orders that her property should be respected, and these had been obeyed. Bitter rebel as she was, she was grateful for what I had done for her, and seeing me, she volunteered to send her young son along to show me the way to a road, whence I could reach the point of the morning's disembarkation. The boy, after having been warned as to the probable results of treachery, trotted along quietly enough by my side until we reached the turn of the road near the river, where I left my cavalry friends, and riding on, soon saw one of our gunboats looking for stragglers. I hailed the boat, and was told to ride on further, where I could find a transport moored to the shore. This I did and reached the boat about half a mile higher up the river, and after some little trouble, succeeded in leading my horse down the steep bank and crossing the gangplank, thus placing both him and myself in safety. By the time I embarked, it was dark, and I was quite worn out. I had been in the saddle almost since daybreak, without food, and what was worse, without water, save one or two horrid mouthfuls I was forced to take from the half stagnant water of the slough or swamp, or back water, whatever it might have been called.

# CHAPTER VI

### INCIDENTS OF THE FIGHT

During this day's long ride, several little matters fell under my observation, which may perhaps be of interest. In the first place, I might have been shot by a cowardly hound of our command. As I was riding forward in the morning toward Belmont, I came across a fellow, unhurt and fully armed, who had evidently skulked away from his company, and was on his way to the rear, or to some place of safety. I came on him suddenly, saw what he was after, and demanded his name, company, regiment. Taken unawares and off his guard, he answered me, and I have no doubt, truly. I added, "you are a coward and are skulking, and I will report you," and then I rode on. In a second or two I had an instinctive feeling that the fellow might shoot me. Looking back over my shoulder, I saw him deliberately aiming at me, at a distance of scarcely ten yards. I turned my horse to one side and drew my pistol. My movements disconcerted the man, and he slipped away behind a fallen tree. I was too busy to think of him, and rode on, but I always felt that my escape was a narrow one.

I was much struck this day with the behavior of animals when terrified. Thus, my horse, when he and I were exposed to the terrific shell fire of the gunboats, was thoroughly, may I say, "unhorsed." He was no longer the kicking, fractious beast of the morning. He was entirely subdued, and trembled and shook, and seemed scarcely able to stand. Then, too, he appeared to recognize *me* as his master, and when I dismounted to see the wounded he showed no disposition to wander or leave me, but stood with his nose close to me. It was scarcely necessary to hold his bridle, he was so quiet and companionable.

Again, when I rode over the field alone, several mules followed me closely,—they could not get too close to me. One fellow in particular, without a bridle, a big white creature, with extraordinary ears, stuck to my side, as if we had been friends all our lives. I suppose he was what was then called a "secesh mule" captured or set free at the destruction of the enemy's camp. I mounted more than one wounded man on him, and he did not fall behind. It was upon him that a poor lad, not more than sixteen or seventeen, who had been shot through the lung, died. I reported his case in my paper on "The Instantaneous Rigor of Sudden or Violent Death," in the *American Journal of the Medical Sciences*. In this lad's case, the rigor was so quick and marked that I had much difficulty in removing his body from the animal, so tightly were the legs clasped around the sides of the mule. This string of mules accompanied me until I reached the river bank.

One other incident relative to the behavior, not of animals, but of men, remains in my mind. While the lower deck of one of our transports was filled with men, a flock of duck or geese settled in the river, not very far from the boat. At the same time a small output of the enemy appeared on the bank, and a desultory fire was opened on our men in the boat. This was returned from one side of the boat, while the men on the opposite side practiced at long range on the birds. This, I think, occurred at or before the disembarkation in the morning.

The shelling of the woods, which occurred as I approached the river, took place, as I learned afterwards, through a force of the enemy in the cornfield and woods incautiously exposing themselves to the fire of our gunboats. The latter was very effective and caused great loss to the enemy. Some of these shells flying high passed over my head, and caused me to infer the presence of an enemy in front of me.

After reaching the transport, and getting my horse safely on board, I went up to the Captain's office, in the "Texas," to see the Captain. He was just uncorking a bottle of "champagne." I have tasted many a glass of wine since, but never one which tasted better than did the fictitious champagne of that evening.

In the cabin of the steamer, I found about sixty or seventy wounded men, and one or two surgeons. I joined them and had plenty to do as we steamed up the river. On our arrival at Cairo, the wounded were immediately sent to the post hospital, under the care of Dr. Burke, and to the regimental hospitals, which had been organized in the town.

We reached Cairo about nine or ten o'clock in the evening, and I immediately hurried to the telegraph office to telegraph my safety to my mother. The operator expressed much surprise at seeing me, and said, "Doctor, you have just come in time, I was just about to send this paragraph east," and he read me this slip: "Surgeon Brinton, the Medical Director, was killed; he was seen to drop from his horse under the enemy's fire." This looked very odd to me, and while I felt sure it could not be true, yet to prevent mistakes, I did telegraph my safety, and this I learned afterwards was one of the early intimations in Philadelphia that a battle had been fought. The night following the battle was for me a busy one, but there was plenty of help, and the wounded were soon comfortably housed in the hospitals I have referred to.

On summing up my experience in my first battle, I see from my letters home that at that time I felt I had gotten well through the day's incidents. I had done my professional duty as well as a new man could, and then, having kept close to headquarters, I had acquired some little credit as a valiant doctor, which, by the way, I do not think was particularly deserved, for after all, in a battle with long-range weapons, the rear is almost as dangerous as the front. I certainly was very fortunate in escaping capture, wandering as I did at random, and with no sense of the points of the compass, or of the direction of our forces. I know that I determined to procure for myself at once a compass, and that I wrote home asking that a good serviceable instrument be sent me.

For the few days following the battle, I was kept very busy, not only by the administrative duties of the medical director's office, but also by the professional work I did. The surgeons under me were willing, but as surgeons, they were inexperienced, and I had to do many operations, and also teach them how to do them.

Here let me relate a little anecdote of one of my surgeons, a member of one of the Illinois regiments. He was a very earnest man, but at that time rather deficient in professional, or at all events, surgical training. In his hospital lay a patient whose leg, seriously injured, demanded amputation. The surgeon came to my office one afternoon, confessing that he had never done, and had never seen an amputation, and moreover had no idea how one should be done, and begged me, at the appointed time, to perform the operation for him. I explained to him that this would never do; his position in the regiment demanded that he himself should remove the limb. And then I explained to him how the amputation should be done, and made him go through the motions, promising him that I would help him through when the time came. On the following morning I did so, and he operated very well, and to the satisfaction of the lookers on. Somehow or other this amputation established his reputation. He at once took rank as an experienced surgeon; nor, better still, did his newborn confidence desert him, for at the battle before Fort Donelson, some months afterwards, I was informed by one of the hospital stewards that a great surgeon was busy operating in one of the field hospitals in the rear of our lines. I at once rode over to see who this person was, and found the operator busy in the second story of a little country house, to which many wounded men were being carried.

I found bloodstained footmarks on the crooked stairs, and in the second-story room stood my friend of Cairo memory; amputated arms and legs seemed almost to litter the floor; beneath the operating table was a pool of blood, the operator was smeared with it and the surroundings were ghastly beyond all limits of surgical propriety. "Ah, Doctor," said the new-fledged surgeon, "I am getting on, just look at these," pointing to his trophies on the floor with a right royal gesture. And after all he seemed to have done good work, and from that time he was a recognized surgical authority among his confrères.

At this point I must record the sad loss of my cherished surgical instruments. On entering the service, I had not drawn from the Medical Purveyor any of the surgical instruments issued by the Government. They were, in fact, good enough, and a fair selection, but I preferred to use my own, and I, therefore, carried with me a select assortment. Many of these I had brought with me from Paris; others which had formerly belonged to the late Professor Mütter, my old preceptor, had been given to me after his death, by Dr. S. Weir Mitchell, who had either inherited them, or received them as a gift from Dr. Mütter's widow. All of my stock of surgical tools had been wrapped together, and in the hurry of leaving, not having time to select, I took with me the package containing all, onto the field at Belmont. I unstrapped the package from my saddle, and gave it to my orderly, a lad of eighteen or twenty, to carry for me. But alas! under the artillery fire from the bluffs, he became greatly demoralized, and in utter fright ran away, and I remember distinctly seeing him "scudding" off holding the heavy package on his head with his two hands. It was a ludicrous sight, to watch him disappear from the open into the woods, and with him my precious instruments, none of which I ever saw again. Both were captured and the instruments fell into the possession of a Mississippi surgeon, who, as I learned, shortly went to his home, taking my instruments with him. I made a touching complaint to General Grant, who on a flag of truce later attempted to get my possessions back, but obtained nothing but the above history of their whereabouts. However, the General was good enough to offer to barter in my behalf,—thus: It seems we had captured a cream-colored pony, which had been given by a lady to a Confederate officer. He was a beauty, with long silver tail and mane, and his former possessor was as anxious to recover him as I was to obtain my instruments.  An exchange was proposed, but it never was consummated.  My instruments are, I suppose, still in the South, and the pony, too conspicuously dangerous to be ridden in action, was sold for a trifle and sent to Chicago.  As to this charger, I remember that we were told, that his former "secesh" owner and his friends had threatened that they would shoot, if they could, any Northerner who might ride him.  He was said to be of Arabian stock.

I append here the reports which I made of the Battle of Belmont, to General Grant:

"Medical Director's Office,
Cairo, Missouri, Nov. 20, 1861.

General:—

I have the honor to submit the following list of soldiers, wounded in the recent fight at Belmont, Mo. The total number of injured as reported to this office amounts to 274.  Of these as will be seen by reference to the subjoined statement, 10 have already died.

It should, however, be stated that from one Regiment, viz., the 7th Iowa, no report has as yet been received. The number of casualties to this corps have been more in number than in any other regiment, and when the report of the Surgeon, Dr. Witter, shall have been received, the list, as already submitted, will probably be augmented by some 30 or 35 names.  The reason for the delay in regard to the report of the 7th Iowa arises from the fact that immediately after the 7th inst. the regiment was ordered to Benton Barracks, one portion of the wounded being left behind at this place, and in Mound City, whilst another portion were taken northward with the Regiment.

Many of the wounded at present in our Department and General Hospital present cases of unfavorable nature, owing to the fact that they fell into the hands of the enemy, and were left exposed on the field of battle for at least eighteen or twenty-four hours. Had the Medical Department of your command been provided with the proper ambulance train, this disastrous and mortifying result might have been readily avoided. The only means of transportation for the wounded which I had were two or three army wagons, which I obtained from the Quartermaster's Department, and these being destitute of springs, and the country over which they passed being woody and rough, the wounded suffered much unnecessary pain.

I would state that Surgeon Gordon of the —30th Ill. and Asst. Wm. Whitnell of the 31st Ill. fell into the hands of the enemy and are still prisoners. It affords me pleasure to testify to the efficiency of Brigade Surgeon Stearns and the corps of surgeons generally, and I would especially instance the conduct of the Asst. Surgeon Kendall, of the Cavalry, who freely exposed himself under fire in his efforts to rescue and aid our wounded.

Very respy. yr. Obt. Servt.

J. H. BRINTON,<br>Brigade Surgeon and Act. Medical Director.

Brigadier General Grant,
Commanding."

# CHAPTER VII.

On the 14th of November, 1861, I received the following order in the handwriting of General Grant:

> "Head. Qts. S. E. Mo.
>
> Cairo, Nov. 14, 1861.
>
> SPECIAL ORDER
> NO. ———
>
> Surgeon J. Brinton, Medical Director, will proceed as soon as possible to Cape Girardeau, Mo. to inspect the hospitals, and to make such changes and orders as he may deem necessary for the benefit of the sick.
>
> (Signed)  U. S. GRANT,
>
> To                    Brig. Gen. Com.
> Surgeon J. Brinton,
>    Medical Director,
>       Cairo, Ill."

Accordingly, on the 15th of November, I came up to the town of Cape Girardeau, sixty miles above Cairo, on the right bank of the Mississippi River, and in Missouri. My business was to inspect the hospital, for there was a regiment or so stationed there. Of this, I remember little, but the town itself made a strong impression on my mind. It was not an American town, but a French one, a remainder from the French occupation of this region, and consisted almost wholly of one long narrow street leading upwards from the river, with high flag stones for crossings, and deep ruts for wagons, almost as in the days of Pompeii. The houses were low, mean looking, and with projecting roofs or eaves. French was the language of the town; and the air of quietness and repose, which prevailed, almost banished the idea of civil contest. I stayed at an inn, which strongly reminded me of a little *auberge* at a miniature town some twenty miles distant from Marseilles, where I was once landed, and where the whole population came out to assist the customs officers in the inspection of my very modest valise.

On the 17th of November, I found myself at Cairo, and on the 18th or 19th, started with General Grant and his staff, and a good force of men, on an expedition after General "Jeff" Thompson, who was raiding somewhere or other on the Missouri side of the Mississippi River. Our expedition was well planned, two commands having been directed to converge to meet our own at a given point, where and when it was supposed that "Jeff" would be cut off and caught. But he was too wary a swamp fox to be thus trapped. At the appointed spot, we found only a few released Union prisoners with a note from Thompson, addressed to General Grant, stating that as he had released more Union prisoners than his opponent, the latter, meaning General Grant, was "still so many men in his debt." I remember that General Grant was greatly amused at this incident, and showed the note to his staff, with full appreciation of the joke. So we returned to Cairo without our prisoner, and "Jeff" went off through the swamps.

At this time, at Cairo, we were much annoyed by newspaper correspondents, who were ever on the lookout for news, and who did not hesitate to thrust themselves forward on any pretext. A flag of truce was for them a great opportunity, and as "flags" not infrequently passed between Cairo and the enemy, every effort was made by these gentry to accompany them. On one occasion, three of them smuggled themselves on a truce boat. They got entrance by carrying on their heads cots,—as the boat was about to bring up wounded. Once on board, they stowed themselves away, but were soon detected by the Colonel in command. He immediately locked them up in the wheelhouse and gave them no food for twelve hours, and one of them by accident, or possibly by intention, was sent to the guardhouse on the return of the "flag" to Cairo. Here he stayed for a week and only obtained his liberty by writing to General Grant. The victims in this matter kept very quiet, but the joke was too good to be kept, and the effect upon obtrusive correspondents was useful and lasting.

During these months I suffered a good deal from boils, in fact, physically, I was wretched and could scarcely move. At one time, I had eleven of these wretched sores in full blast. I was then living in a suite of rooms in a little shanty near the St. Charles Hotel, but below the levée. The building was a sort of annex to a restaurant, and I had the floor to myself. The restaurant was kept I think, by a German, who furnished a fare much above the western diet. My Thanksgiving dinner was a great success, turkey, dressed celery and mince pie. The latter I think was made of dried apples, and the meaty part had a peculiar flavor, suggestive of levée rats and Chinese ideas.

By the end of November, a good many troops had been collected at Cairo, and of course, with them, came a number of surgeons; almost all were western men, from Illinois, Iowa, Michigan and Missouri chiefly.

Many of these were rough, but I think that at first I underrated them. Their hearts were good, and they were professionally zealous. In order to bring them together and for our mutual improvement, we organized the "Army Medical and Surgical Society of Cairo," which met once a week at the Medical Purveyor's business quarters. A good deal of interest was shown by the members, and our discussions were prolonged, and I now think that they must have been useful. The society flourished and continued its existence long after I left Cairo.

The town of Cairo was essentially a frontier town on the very borders of "Secessia." The proximity of the enemy, and the sending of occasional flags of truce, thus afforded good opportunities for the transmission of private letters to friends within the lines of the rebellion. In this way loyal families could communicate with their relatives in the south. All such letters passed through the military headquarters, and baskets full of such letters would accumulate, awaiting transmission. When the privilege of sending a letter was granted, it was understood that it would not be abused, and that the communication should not contain any military information or treasonable news. Letters were sent open, and were liable to inspection at headquarters. This duty General Grant occasionally imposed on the different members of the staff, and very tiresome and disagreeable it was to read other people's letters.

A prominent Southern physician was at that time living in Philadelphia. He was anxious to write to his family, and a mutual personal friend wrote me, begging that I would have his letter passed through without the usual examination of contents; assuring me on the writer's word of honor that nothing improper would be conveyed. On my mentioning the request to General Grant, he at once assented, but added that for form's sake, he would ask me to open the letter and assume all responsibility in the matter, and he would consider the enclosure as examined, and order it passed on. I did so, and at once saw that the sheet was full of treasonable military information as to the Northern forces, their disposition, strength and commanders. Without a word, I cast the dishonorable note into the fire on the hearth. The General smiled, and simply said, "I expected as much; I am not surprised."

I mention this to show how little honor prevailed at this time in places where one had a right to expect good faith.

On the 29th of November, Dr. John K. Kane arrived from Philadelphia. I had previously written, telling him that if he wished to see something of military surgery, I would make a contract with him. This I did immediately on his arrival, and assigned him to duty as a "resident surgeon" at the depot hospital, which was then under the charge of an Irishman named Dr. Burke, an eccentric, jealous, assuming man. He soon, I think, took to Dr. Kane, and they got along very nicely, although Kane's daily ablutions in an india-rubber bath tub were at first regarded as a very undignified proceeding; but as he was the brother of the distinguished arctic explorer, his new comrades concluded to look upon his daily wash as a purely individual peculiarity, which in a stranger should be leniently considered.

All of which reminds me of another vanity, this time my own. I was the happy possessor of a gray dressing gown, lined and trimmed with scarlet flannel, and which I had made for me in Vienna in 1852. When I was stationed at Cairo I had it expressed to me, and during the time I was living at Safford's Bank, our head-quarters, General Grant saw the gorgeous garment and determined to have one like it. So it was borrowed by Mrs. Grant, taken to Chicago and served as a model for a similar gown for the General.

In the early part of December Dr. Simons returned to Cairo, and resumed his duties as Medical Director of the District. I was not, however, sent away, but was kept on duty in the office and in fact I was treated by him with the greatest consideration and kindness. I was very glad indeed, to be left quietly in the office, for my boils were growing worse, and some days I could scarcely move. During the days preceding Christmas, I received some boxes from home, full of nice comfortable things, and the letter which came to me at that time, you may be sure, made me feel homesick. On Christmas night, I left for St. Louis as my teeth were troubling me, and greatly in need of the services of a dentist. I was fortunate in finding a good one, and in a day or two the necessary repairs were made.

On the 30th of December I returned to Cairo, reaching there in the night, and strange to say, feeling also as if the dirty old town was sort of home to me. New Year's Eve I spent at General Grant's at a sort of small party, after which I wrote home my New Year's letters. I remember it all so well, and chiefly I remember the famous batch of home letters which had accumulated at Cairo during my absence, and the wondrous pleasures I had in going through them, one by one.

On New Year's evening, January 1, 1862, which fell on a Wednesday, I gave a little New Year's dinner of my own. I was not at that time, physically speaking, in very good shape, for in my New Year's letter to my mother, I tell her that there are certain positions which

I cannot well occupy in consequence of my aforementioned boils, and that these positions were "sitting, standing, lying down, walking, riding and running." So you see at once how disconsolate I must have been. Nevertheless I determined to have my New Year's dinner in the little frame shanty in which I then had my quarters, the conspicuous feature of which was an iron stove, in which I burned large quantities of wood. My guests of the day were Medical Director James Simons, Dr. Aigner, a very clever German, who represented the Sanitary Commission, and Dr. John Kane, who was then one of the resident assistant surgeons at Burke's post hospital. Our dinner, a very good one, and rich in game, was washed down by some excellent wine, chiefly that sent by Mr. John C. Van Renselaer of Newport, R. I., for the Christmas dinner which I did not eat in Cairo. I remember especially some burgundy, and some famous old "Constitution madeira," which its donor said had made the voyage round the world in that old warship; at all events it was sound wine, and served its purpose, and elicited profound wine stories from two at least of the diners around my modest table. So it all went off merrily, and I remember that good dinner more clearly than many a far better one since.

In the early part of January, 1862, rumors began to creep around the staff of an expedition somewhere, but the information was most vague. Soon, however, these took shape and on the 9th, I received an order from General Grant to accompany him on an expedition.

My guess as to the object of this expedition was correctly stated in my letter to my Mother, dated on the steamer "Esmeralda," at an encampment on the Kentucky shore, six miles from Cairo, as follows:

"I imagine the object of the expedition is merely to

prevent the enemy at Columbus (Ky.) from ordering troops away from Columbus to Bowling Green (Ky.). I think Buell is about to make an attack, and that we are put forward on the principle of 'Brag to support him.' " And in the same letter I add: "I just missed being Chief Surgeon to this expedition. Dr. Simons was sick, but he is well enough to come to-morrow, so I go with McClernand instead of Grant. Grant wanted me and paid me the compliment of ordering me peremptorily to come with him, but General McClernand claimed me, so I had of course to go. A little piece of vanity all this, but you need not tell."

So as will be seen, I went with Gen. McClernand, who was in direct command of the expedition, about 5,000 or 6,000 men. Gen. Grant accompanied, having his own body guard. Dr. John K. Kane volunteered, and asked permission of General Grant to go with him. The General was delighted, "I accept you, my boy," he said, and made him surgeon of his body guard. In this position Kane behaved admirably, and I may say here that he stuck very close to the General in a very hard, and at that time, much talked of reconnoisance which the General made around Columbus. The ride was from 40 to 50 miles, the day dreadful with snow and sleet, and cold. The General returned to his camp late at night with only Rawlins, Kane and an orderly or so. The rest of his escort was left on the way and struggled in as best they could afterwards. It was, I fancy, the recollection of this ride and its attendant weather, which lingered in his memory so long, and which prompted his description of "splashing through the mud, snow and rain," as given at page 286 of the first volume of his personal memoirs. The General never forgot either the ride or Kane. Only two or three years before his death, he recalled the circumstance to me, and asked, "How is little Kane?"

I ought to say something right here of General Mc-Clernand, for I was now serving on his staff. He was a fine, or rather let me say a good, specimen of an active, bustling western politician, and one possessed of a certain amount of influence. Doubtless he was a clever lawyer and shrewd politician, but he aspired to be something else,—a general. I do not think that he ever exactly comprehended what a real general was, or should be; nor do I believe he ever eliminated the idea of politician in his estimate of the soldier. The latter was by his standard not only a fighting, but also, a talkative personage. Placed by circumstances near Grant, he was even at this early day jealous of him; at least, it seemed so to me then. He was, however, kind to me, and bore me no grudge, as many a man would have done, under the following circumstances.

Shortly before this I had been stationed in charge of the general hospitals of the District of Cairo; General Grant was away from Cairo (at St. Louis I think), and General McClernand commanded in his absence. One of the latter's orders was to this effect: "That all able-bodied men in the hospitals in the District should be returned to their command, irrespective of the hospital duties they were performing, or the sources of their detail." The execution of this order, the superintendence of serving it and carrying it out, he entrusted to a chaplain. By the regulations of the army, a chaplain's functions were limited to his own department, and he was incapable of executing command. The order was clearly illegal, but apart from this, its execution would have instantly paralyzed the whole hospital department of the entire district of Cairo, at a time too, when its efficiency was most called for. I accordingly instructed my surgeon to disobey it, and by my own endorsement disputed its validity. General Grant on his return sent for me, showed me my rebellious order, and added, "Doctor, this is a very serious business." My answer to him was, "General, when you entrusted to me, as your Medical Director the care of the invalid of your command, you said to me, 'Doctor, take care of my sick and wounded to the best of your ability, don't bother over regulations.' Now, General," I added, "I have done this to the best of my ability. If I have done right, you will support me; if I have done wrong, you know what to do with me." The general looked at me a moment, took the paper, and put on it the endorsement which lives in my memory: "The object of having a Medical Director is that he shall be supreme in his own Department. The decision of Surgeon Brinton is sustained." I have always regarded this action of General Grant, the position of an old soldier, toward me, who was trying, perhaps ignorantly, to do my duty under novel and difficult surroundings, as very noble. I think that my veneration for his character, and my strong personal affection for him, dated from that interview. I doubt if another officer of his rank in the army would have so supported a medical officer under like circumstances.

At the time General McClernand was slightly annoyed, but he behaved well to me, especially on this expedition. He requested that I should go on his staff, and General Grant verbally instructed me to do so, and I was taken very good care of. I remember very well that in the afternoon, the boat, the Esmeralda, tied up at the shore, and General McClernand and his staff landed. I was in bad plight with my boils, and was very grateful to my commander, when he came to me, and said: "Doctor, you are so ill at ease, stay on board till morning, and land at your leisure." I thanked him, and went to my stateroom. He landed, but came back to the gangplank, and called the captain of the boat to him, when to my intense surprise, I heard him say, "Captain, take good care of my doctor, for he is a gentleman," I think he added, "A real gentleman." I was very much touched by his consideration, for it was unexpected. I never forgot it, and in one way or another, I did him good turns afterward, which he never knew of.

In the morning, I landed and mounted. I must tell you about this mounting, if I can supply such a term to the arrangement of my saddlery. I had one stirrup, the left one, very long, so that I could stand in it as it were with my right thigh supported at an angle over the saddle. The right stirrup was very short, so that I could, when resting my foot in it, be uplifted over the saddle. This latter was well padded with a blue blanket, —and so I rode in the saddle, but not of it, or touching it. I could not have looked like a warrior on a career of invasion; I know I did not feel like one. However, I had not at this time far to ride, only a mile or so up a wood road to our "Camp Jefferson." McClernand's headquarters were at a farmhouse, with a big chimney place and bright fire blazing in the kitchen. On the 11th of January, three Confederate gunboats came up the Mississippi; our gunboats saw them, and started down to give battle. A good deal of heavy firing ensued, but a fog suddenly sprang up, the firing ceased abruptly, and we all felt some anxiety as to the result. It was determined to send one of our transport steamers down the river to learn the result. I begged permission to go on her, and we started. Our crew consisted of the engineer, fireman, a hand or two, an engineer officer to observe, and myself. We steamed steadily along, watching the Kentucky shore, for fear of field batteries; at one time, we made out hostile tents, so we turned the boat around, and dropped slowly downward stern foremost, so as to be ready for a quick start homewards, in case of danger. As we neared the suspicious canvas, the tent walls vanished, and we found only some linen of an old woman's wash, hung out to dry on the bushes. Soon the fog cleared away, and we saw our own and the enemy's boats a little below us, and some distance apart. Firing began at once, and in a moment a shell from one of our ship's guns burst directly at one of the enemy's ports; the rebel boat immediately turned and steamed away with her consorts. We, that is, the engineer and myself, ran to our little fleet and boarded the flag ship. We were very kindly received (by, I think, Commodore Porter) and had a good luncheon. The ship or gunboat was one of the Mississippi ironclad fleet, designed by Captain Eads, and known as "Turtles," broad-bottomed boats, suitable for shallow waters, with sloping sides, or rather tops, plated with two inch iron, on which projectiles would glance. I was greatly interested by all that I saw here, for everything was in fighting trim, ship and men, and the smell of the powder was over all.

Having been furnished with the account of the naval skirmish, the engineer and I returned to our transport and went back to headquarters with our budget of news. I ought to add that the boats of the enemy had been industriously planting torpedoes in the river channel until stopped at their innocent work by our fleet, which pulled up these dangerous machines.

# CHAPTER VIII

On the 13th of January, 1862, I received an order from General Grant, informing me that I had been detailed as a member of the board of their medical officers to convene at St. Louis, January 16th, for the examination of officers, and directing me to proceed at once to that city. The object of this board, of which I was president by seniority, was the examination of regimental surgeons and assistant surgeons and contract physicians, who had appeared to be deficient in medical qualifications; and in other words, to find out the medical "black sheep" of the Department of Missouri, and very black some of them were.

Accordingly, I left the expedition, and I must confess, with regret, as I had by this time come to like the men with whom I was serving, especially General Grant, and had formed a conviction, I can scarcely say how arrived at, that he was the man destined to close the war. I was still physically most uncomfortable from my many boils, and horseback exercise was really torture. In one sense, therefore, I was relieved at being sent to St. Louis, though looking forward with pleasure to a speedy return as soon as I should be in better health. Passing through Cairo on the 14th, I arrived at St. Louis on the same night, or rather early in the morning of the 15th, and took up my headquarters at the Planters' House, the best hotel in the city, and crowded with officers and persons on military business.

In a letter to Dr. DaCosta of about this date, I wrote as follows about George McClellan, my cousin: "If he, (General McClellan) does not move, he will topple over. If Grant takes Columbus, or Bowling Green, George may find a rival. The people here are losing confidence in him. What does he mean? Is the fighting after all to be done here in the west?"

In this letter, too, I speak of a friend, whose acquaintance I here made,—Captain I. P. Hawkins, Commissary of Subsistence, U. S. A. He was a very honest and good hearted fellow, and a good friend to me who gave me a great deal of sound advice, which I tried to follow, and which I am sure was to my advantage in the service. One of his favorite teachings was, "Always be satisfied with your present detail of duty; do not pull wires, or try for something else, or seek to supplant any other officer; be content with what you have; do your duty as well as you can, and it will most probably turn out well. Services which are sought for, especially unfairly sought for almost always bring trouble and regret after them." All this was very good advice for me.

My time in St. Louis passed pleasantly. The duty was not hard, and the other members of the board were very congenial. I had a good deal of time to myself; office, or rather, board hours, were only in the morning, so I made friends and paid visits. Among the military men I knew at the time in St. Louis were Col. Woods, Col. Totten, Col. Thorn, of the Topographical Engineers, Generals Sturgis, Schofield, Sweeny, and Van Renselaer, and many others. The presence of the headquarters kept the city gay. The General in command of this Department, or rather I think of the entire west, was

General Halleck. I afterwards became a member of his staff.

The southern or secession feeling in St. Louis was strong and bitter. As I have already written, I had a good many friends, and soon found myself in St. Louis society, largely through the kindness of Mr. James E. Yeatman,* who was then the President of the Western Sanitary Commission, a very powerful organization. Mr. Yeatman was perhaps the most prominent Union citizen in St. Louis, and I believe was connected in some way with John Bell of Tennessee, a former defeated candidate for the Vice-Presidency of the U. S. Some of my friends in the army had spoken to Mr. Yeatman about me, and when I arrived in St. Louis as President of the Board of Examination, Mr. Yeatman called on me. He asked me if I was married, and when I said I was not, he asked me if I would like to see something of St. Louis society. I replied affirmatively, and very shortly (I mean an hour or so) I received a card to a Philharmonic Society, with an invitation to call at Mr. Yeatman's house, and accompany some of the young ladies of his family to the Concert Hall. This, I gladly did. I spent a pleasant evening, and the next day invitation after invitation reached me, and I was thus soon launched among a pleasant set of social acquaintances. I must also say here that although many of the men I met with in this society were, or pretended to be, loyal, the women were undoubtedly southern sympathizers. I found it best in public entertainment to wear my uniform as a sort of protection and thus show my colors.

In a letter of January 26th, 1862, when writing home,

*This gentleman was the original of the character of Mr. Brinsmade in Mr. Churchill's novel, "The Crisis." E. T. S.

I find I have thus spoken of the "secesh settlement of St. Louis":

"But General Halleck is fixing all that now. It is becoming a dangerous game to be too 'sassy.' The Missouri refugees are being quartered in the houses of prominent secessionists. 'I will tell you when I want them carpets took up,' said one of these half savage union refugee women to one of the secession ladies of St. Louis, her unwilling hostess, and who was on the point of removing her parlor furniture with a view to rendering the house as little comfortable as possible. The carpets were not 'took up,' as it was understood that General Halleck might possibly order them down again, and he was a prompt man, using little ceremony."

This was a time when everybody was having new experiences and learning new things. Even I was gaining my experiences, as appears by a plaintive appeal home: "Can you tell me any secret by which short buttons can be permanently retained on their respective sites? I haven't a button to my name."

About this time General Grant came up to St. Louis to consult with Halleck. I saw something of Grant then. He treated me kindly, and as an old friend. One evening I was seated at rather a low theatre, smoking and listening to the music and the wretched jabber on the stage, when I felt a hand placed on each shoulder, and looking up, I faced the General, puffing away at his cigar. "Oh Doctor, Doctor," he said, "if you only knew how it grieves me to find you in such a low place, and in such company," and he sat down, chuckling greatly. Before he returned to Cairo, which he did on the 27th of January, he told me that he intended to have me back at Cairo with him before long.

In St. Louis, I made the most of my time, doing my board work and going much into society, and then too, I repaired my wardrobe and bought new linen. I had a present, by the way, just at this time of a fine green silk scarf. It was given me by a little French Jewess, a Parisienne, whose husband was, if I remember rightly, post baker at Cairo, and whom I attended when sick. I charged him nothing, but she used to make me a nice French omelette at every visit, and give me a glass of delicious French light wine. I am afraid that the baker's bread was short of weight; he made a great deal too much money, and got into evil repute. I did what I could for them in one way or another, and so she gave me this green medical sash. I wanted it then, for the one I had was poor and mean and sashes were expensive. M. and Mme. Lazare prospered during the war, and long after the peace she became a very fine lady at Narragansett and her daughter was a piquante belle, and they forgot to remember the flour and the bakery.

As I did not always wear uniform, I had for St. Louis use, civilian's suits. I can never forget on one occasion going to a large ready-made clothing establishment in that city to buy a pair of citizen's trousers, urgently needed. They had none to fit me. "None?" said I, "None?" and I turned to go despondently through the street door. "Stop a minute, stop, my dear sir," said the master salesman. "I have a thought," and he went to the open hatchway, leading to the upper stories, and putting his hand to his mouth trumpet fashion, he shouted "Isaac, I-sa-aa-c, send down at once a pair of the 'short-fats!'"

On the fifth of February, I wrote to my Mother that I would probably start for Cairo soon; on the 6th. I add "That I am leaving in a great hurry this afternoon

for Cairo at my own request." On the 7th I sent her a
line to say that I had just arrived at Cairo and that Fort
Henry on the Tennessee River had been captured, and
that I would join General Grant at once. I remember
distinctly the arrival of the gunboat, which one I have
forgotten, confirming the news of the capture of Fort
Henry. She arrived at Cairo on the 7th, flying the rebel
or I suppose I ought now to say, the Confederate flag,
upside down, I think, and below the flag of the United
States. Her arrival created a great excitement at Cairo,
which spread rapidly over the whole country as fast as
the telegraph could convey the news.

# CHAPTER IX

I immediately started for Fort Henry to report to General Grant, in obedience to orders. I found him with his staff on board one of the steamers. I believe it was the "Tigress." I was now the medical director of the forces in the field, Dr. Simons, the medical director of the district, being sick at Cairo. I had at this time plenty to do and was busy all the time visiting the regimental hospitals (tent hospitals, of course,) of the forces which were hurrying up from every direction, and which were encamped around the captured fort on the higher and partially dry ground.

And here I ought to say something about Fort Henry, the first fort of any note which had been captured from the enemy. It was an earthen-work of some size, thrown up on the right bank of the Tennessee River, intended (in conjunction with another work, Fort Heiman on the left bank) to command the Tennessee River entirely and to prevent the passage of our gunboats along this river, and thus into Alabama, threatening Mississippi. Both of these forts when erected were some thirty-five or forty feet above the bed of the river and completely commanded it. Heavy rains, however, occurred and the river was greatly swollen; it had risen and was still rising rapidly, and the fort was now upon a level almost with the river; in fact the water had surrounded it, and so high was the stream that our gunboats fought at a great advantage, and were indeed almost able to throw a plunging fire into the work. Provided, as it was, with heavy guns (seized at our navy yard at the beginning of the war) the fort nevertheless offered but a feeble resistance to the effective fire of our gunboats. The enemy's guns were soon dismounted, the fort became untenable, and during the night of the 6th was abandoned by its garrison. When I visited it, shortly after reporting to the General, it was a dreadful sight. Great heavy columbiads* were overthrown, some with their muzzles pointing in the air, their carriages were broken and stained with blood. Here and there too, were masses of human flesh and hair adhering to the broken timbers. The interior of the fort was a mass of mud, the back water from the stream having flowed in from the rear.

It had been intended that the capture of Fort Henry, Tennessee, should be attempted by a co-operative effort of the naval and military forces of the Government, and for that purpose a considerable force, several thousand in fact, had been landed on the right bank of the river, with instructions to march up and occupy positions behind Fort Henry and between it and Fort Donelson, investing Fort Henry by land, while the fleet should operate from the river. The march of the troops had, however, been retarded by the inundation of the wooded banks of the river, and they did not reach their destination until after the fort had surrendered to the naval forces.

General Grant and his staff, of which I was a member, remained at Fort Henry until about the 12th of

*A columbiad was an enormously heavy iron muzzle loading cannon, throwing round shells of eight, ten or eleven inches in diameter. They were constructed for naval use and for sea coast defence and were smooth bored and not rifled. E. T. S.

February. Our quarters were on the steamer "Tigress." About the 12th the General and his staff started for Fort Donelson, some eight or nine miles distant from Fort Henry. Fort Donelson, afterwards so well known, was a strong earth-work on the slope of a hill, near the little town of Dover. It commanded the Cumberland River and the approach to Nashville. It was a strong fort, with heavy guns mounted high up on the hill, and a battery of very heavy guns low down almost on the level of the river, at all events, on its level, in the then swollen condition of the stream. Two roads led from Fort Henry to Fort Donelson; the army moved along both, the cavalry watching the space between, so as not to allow any of the enemy to escape us. The Staff moved by the left-hand or low road. I rode near the General on my black horse, a strong powerful beast, which I had bought at Cairo. He was possessed of a fast walk, and moreover he would push in front of the other horses on the Staff. I could hardly keep him back; he particularly and persistently would pass the General who rode his old favorite stallion "Jack." Finally, he very good-naturedly said to me, "Doctor, I believe I command this army, and I think I'll go first."

When we reached Fort Donelson, our troops were extended and kept well in line, so as to be ready for any outburst of the enemy. Wandering off from the Staff to give some professional directions, I somehow or other got in front of this line, and it seemed to afford the men great pleasure to close up so as to keep me from getting through. I, and a solitary scared dog, were in front. After a while, when the men had had their joke at my expense, I passed through.

We met with no opposition on this march and finally arrived near Fort Donelson. Our line of investment was soon formed. We marched in battle order, ready for action. The actual luggage of the staff was represented by a few collars, a comb and brush and such toilet articles, contained in a small satchel belonging to me. General Grant had only a tooth brush in his waistcoat pocket, and I supplied him with a clean white collar. Of whiskey or liquor, of which so much has been said, there was not one drop in the possession of any member of the staff, except that in my pocket, an eight-ounce flask, which I was especially requested by the General to keep only for medical purposes, and I was further instructed by him not to furnish a drink under any pretext to any member of the Staff, except when necessary in my professional judgment. But of this, I shall speak again.

We occupied the headquarters house on the afternoon of the 12th of February and here we remained until after the capture of Fort Donelson, and of the little town of Dover, which was included within the enemy's lines of defence. The kitchen had in it a double feather-bed and this was occupied by the General,—some small rooms in the other parts of the house were crowded by other members of the staff. I think for one night the General slept somewhere else than the kitchen, but came down because of the bed and the warmer temperature. The big open fireplace was attractive. On the 13th, I was busy fixing my hospitals and doing the best I could. The whole of this day was employed in establishing the positions of our forces, and in strengthening their lines. We threw up no breastworks, but depended upon the natural strength of the ground, and its "lay" for our protection, should the enemy attempt any sortie. But the idea of a sortie never entered General Grant's head, or if it did, it found no lodgment there. His ideas were fixed, that the enemy would stay inside their works and not readily venture out.

One of my hospitals, that nearest to the Southern lines, was in a ravine, within sight of the hostile troops. It happened that some heavy skirmishing took place on the 13th, chiefly along General McClernand's front, our right. Indeed it was more than skirmishing; for a time in fact a very lively fight. During this, a good many wounded found their way to this particular hospital, and not only wounded, but many, a great many faint-hearted ones, who disgracefully sought the hospital precinct as a shelter. This congregation hourly increased, and I began after a time to feel anxious, lest the enemy, noticing so many stragglers, might sweep down, and make capture of both hurt and unhurt. The hospital had only its sacred character to defend it, and this was being debased by the gathering crowd. Then too, most of our hospital stores, I mean the reserve supplies, were here, and I did not wish them to fall into the enemy's hands. So I accordingly went to General Grant and explained to him the exposed position of the hospital. His answer was, "Yes, Doctor, I see, but they will *not* come and capture you." And back I went to the hospital. Yet things went from bad to worse, the stragglers increased in numbers. The hospital supplies became more and more important, in view of a probable approaching battle, and my anxiety was greater every minute. The loss of this depot and its supplies would have been almost paralyzing to the Medical Department. Again I saw the General. Again I told him my fears, and again heard his answer, as before: "They will not come."

As the peril increased still more, I sought him a third time, and after saying all I could, I asked him "Am I exaggerating the risk, or the consequences of the loss of the medical stores of your army, removed as we now are from fresh sources of supply?" The General heard me as he always did, most patiently, and replied, "No Doctor, you are right, I know the exposure as well as you, and fully realize what a disaster would be the loss of our medical supplies; but yet Doctor, it will not happen; the enemy might capture you all if they chose; they could do it with a small force of cavalry, but, Doctor, they won't do it, so you need not worry, they are not thinking of anything, except holding their position, so make yourself easy. The enemy are thinking more of staying in than getting out, I know him." And this was all my satisfaction, and it all turned out just as he General said, but nevertheless, I felt that my fears had been well founded.

I do not intend here to give any military account of the attack on Fort Donelson. I am only telling about myself, but this is the schedule of the several days' operations. With about 15,000 men on February 12th, 1862, Wednesday, we left Fort Henry and arrived before Fort Donelson. February 13th, 1862 (Thursday), was occupied in extending siege, positions, etc., and skirmishing and fighting on right in front of General McClernand. February 14th (Friday), there was little fighting, with an attack by a gunboat fleet under Commander Foote,* which failed. February 15th (Saturday), the enemy made a fierce sortie and are repulsed, and retire into the fort. General Grant visits the fleet. February

---

*Andrew Hull Foote, the venerable Admiral and Christian gentleman worn out with hard service, died during the war while on his way to rejoin his fleet. Notwithstanding he had grog abolished in the Navy he was very much beloved by the sailors who often sung of him: "He increased our pay ten cents a day, And stopped our rum forever." E. T. S.

16th (Sunday), surrender of Fort Donelson to the Union forces under General Grant.*

My exact professional position at this battle was a peculiar one. The Medical Director of the District of Cairo, General Grant's command, was Surgeon James Simons, U. S. A. He, however, did not accompany this expedition, but sent me as his representative with General Grant.

Surgeon Henry S. Hewitt, U. S. Vols. (Brigade Surgeon) next in rank above me on the army list was the surgeon and medical director of the command of General Chas. F. Smith, who was under the order of General Grant, and who commanded the division originally stationed at, and around, Paducah, Ky.

Dr. Hewitt was, therefore, during the Fort Donelson campaign the acting Medical Director in the field of General Grant's forces, although himself attached to the staff of General Smith, outranked by General Grant. Dr. Hewitt and I arranged matters between ourselves. He would remain with General Smith to whom he was strongly attached, while I was to look after the hospitals, to see to their organization, the transportation of the wounded, and to the general surgery of the field, and this I did thoroughly, to the best of my ability. A great many operations I performed myself, and many others I assisted and directed in performing.

On the 15th, in the early morning, General Grant went

*For my official report of the "Account of the campaign of the Army of the Tennessee from February to June, 1862, including the capture of Forts Henry and Donelson, and the battles of Shiloh and Corinth, by Surgeon John H. Brinton, U. S. V., Medical Director of the Army of the Tennessee." See Medical and Surgical History of the Rebellion, Part I, Medical Vol. and appendix, Part I, Page 24, Paper 28.

down to the fleet on the Cumberland River to consult with Commodore Foote, who had been wounded on the previous day, and who had failed with his gunboats to pass or force the strong batteries commanding the ascent of the river. Several of his vessels had been badly hit, and it was necessary for him to return to Cairo, or rather to Mound City to refit. It was during this absence of the General from camp, about which so much was unkindly said, and has since been written, that the enemy made its famous sortie, attacking our right under General McClernand, and driving it back in confusion. Information of this was carried to General Grant, who hurried rapidly forward, to assume personal command and to resume the fight. What he did and how he did it, and how nobly he retrieved the day, and turned defeat into victory, and how the fort fell, are all now matters of history. On his arrival, he found our right in confusion, and driven back, although at a halt. The left of our line under General C. F. Smith was in excellent condition, and as yet unengaged. The center, in part, had gone to the help of our right, and its presence had been sufficient to check the onslaught of the enemy, and cause them to draw back within their lines. They had thus failed to cut their way out, but they still held their fort, strongly defended by earthworks, batteries, and with most formidable abattis. It was through an obstruction of this kind that our men had to pass to enter the fort. General C. F. Smith, who commanded our left, was ordered by Grant to lead his command through the abattis, and to pierce, if possible, the enemy's lines. This he did at once, and about 3 o'clock in the afternoon led his men forward. The move was one of difficulty, the abattis was dense and the enemy fought at great advantage. At one time, at the outset, our troops wavered in pushing through the obstructions. General Smith rallied them with curses. In a letter to Dr. DaCosta from Fort Donelson, dated March 2nd, 1862, I remark: "You ought to have heard old C. F. Smith cursing as he led on his storming regiments. 'Damn you gentlemen, I see skulkers, I'll have none here. Come on, you volunteers, come on,' he shouted. 'This is your chance. You volunteered to be killed for love of country, and now you can be. You are only damned volunteers. I'm only a soldier, and don't want to be killed, but you came to be killed and now you can be.' And so the old cock led them with a mixture of oaths and entreaties over the breastwork. The loss was heavy, but he never flinched, but sat straight on his horse, his long white moustache, his stature and his commanding presence, making him a conspicuous mark. He was every inch a soldier, and a true disciplinarian. Without Grant and Smith there would have been no such result, so no more sneers about the regulars. They are the men; without them volunteers are but a rabble. I believe that with the splendid material for the ranks, all we want are good officers to have the most magnificent army in the world."

Seeing his front line shrinking and wavering, the General turned to my friend Surgeon H. S. Hewitt, U. S. V., who was by his side, saying, "Hewitt, my God, my friend, if you love me, go back, and bring up another regiment of these d—— volunteers. You will find them behind the bushes." And this Hewitt did, leading the men forward, himself mounted, and the yellow staff trappings on his black horse, making him a most conspicuous object, as he headed the regiment until the abattis was reached. With the regiment he passed through by the side of his General, until a lodgment was effected inside the hostile lines. This gallant assault of General Smith, and his success, ensured the surrender of Fort Donelson on the following morning.

I ought to say something here of these two men, so typical of their kind. General C. F. Smith was the very *beau-ideal* of a soldier, I mean the real soldier; at the time of which I am writing, he had been thirty-seven years in the service, having been appointed a brevet second lieutenant in the Second Artillery in 1825 (eighteen years before General Grant entered the service). General Smith had, I think, been commandant of the Military Academy of West Point when General Grant was a cadet, or if not, he was on duty there at that time. He was tall, six feet three, I should think, slender, well proportioned, upright, with a remarkably fine face, and a long twisted white moustache. He was a strict disciplinarian, fearless, determined, grim. Altogether, he was a typical military man in his appearance, air and manner. He had served in the Mexican War with distinction, and was respected in the old army. He had some of the faults of his kind, but a braver, bolder, more determined soldier, never lived. Dr. Hewitt was a surgeon in my own corps, one of the Brigade Surgeons, afterwards known as Surgeons of Volunteers, U. S. A. He had originally been an assistant surgeon in the regular army before the war, but resigned, and on the outbreak of the rebellion, entered as a Brigade Surgeon, standing third on the list. His name was next above my own. He was a very brave man, impulsive, easily irritated, but kind and generous. He had a somewhat poetic temperament, and I have copied here his "Song of the Shell"; written under fire, I think, he told me, on the field of Shiloh, where he greatly distinguished himself for his professional efficiency and personal gallantry.

## SONG OF THE SHELL.

There's a music aloft in the air,
As if devils were singing a song,
There's a shriek, like a shriek of Despair,
There's a crash which the echoes prolong.

There's a voice like the voice of the gale,
When it strikes a tall ship on the sea.
There's a rift like the rent of her sail,
As she helplessly drifts to the Sea.

There's a rush, like the rushing of fiends,
Compelled by some horrible spell,
There's a flame, like the flaming of brands,
Plucked in rage from the fires of Hell.

There's a wreath, like the foam on the wave,
There's a silence unbroke by a breath,
There's a thud, like the clod in a grave,
There is writhing, and moaning, and Death.

# CHAPTER X

Before speaking of the capture of Fort Donelson, I must call attention to some events of the investment of the place. The weather was terrible during almost the entire time, alternating between sleet and snow, especially at night. It was very cold, and the sufferings and deprivations of the men were excessive. As our lines extended close around the works, it was necessary to conceal the exact position of the soldiers as much as possible. Fires, therefore, on the front lines were not permitted, and I wondered at the time how our poor fellows could endure the long cold nights without fires and with insufficient coverings. This latter statement may seem strange, but the fact is that in the march across the country, many of the men had found their blankets and overcoats cumbersome, and had left them by the roadside, or placed them in wagons, which had failed to make a redistribution. As it was, very many of the troops laid on the ground at night, tentless, fireless, and with scanty covering. In spite of all this exposure, no cases of tetanus occurred among the wounded at Fort Donelson.

Another matter which caused the Medical Department much anxiety was the removal of the wounded to the rear.

This was a sort of double matter, a removal by two stages, as it were. The first one was to transport the wounded man from the place where he fell to the advanced point where the ambulance could reach him. The second stage was his conveyance to the hospitals in the rear. The latter part of the trip was comparatively easy. All the regimental ambulances and extra wagons had formed themselves into a sort of ambulance train, which ran steadily and systematically to and from the hospital centers. The train was under the charge of a commissioned officer, who proved himself efficient and intelligent. The first part of the trip, however, was a matter of much more difficulty, for it was no easy undertaking to carry the wounded, those helplessly wounded, from under the guns of the enemy. Yet this was accomplished, and shortly after dark on each day's fight, all of the injured were brought in and sent to the rear hospital.

To accomplish this required much cool courage, and one of the most remarkable cases of heroism I witnessed on the last day's battle. A Methodist clergyman (a chaplain, attached to one of the regiments, I believe), devoted himself to the removal of the wounded. He was a man of about thirty years of age, tall, strong and well built, of quiet, yet resolute manner. He had his horse and spent his time riding to the extreme front, absolutely under the enemy's fire. Here he dismounted and selecting the worst of our wounded men, he would lift him into his saddle, hold him there with one hand, while with the other he would lead his horse back through the lines to the rear hospital. Sometimes, he would bring off two wounded men at one trip. I watched him do this, and I must confess, felt a high appreciation of his courage, moral and physical, and the sincerity of his religion. I was glad to know on the next day that he had escaped unhurt. I cannot but think that his chivalric

126 *Personal Memoirs of John H. Brinton*

bravery was appreciated even by the enemy, who seemed to have spared him while on his self-imposed, self-sacrificing task.

The behavior of the medical officers at this battle was admirable. General Grant thus speaks in his "Personal Memoirs," Volume I, page 300, "Up to this time," (the 13th) "the surgeons with the army had no difficulty in finding room in the houses near the line for all the sick and wounded; but now hospitals were overcrowded. Owing, however, to the energy and skill of the surgeons, the suffering was not so great as it might have been. The hospital arrangements at Fort Donelson were as complete as it was possible to make them, considering the inclemency of the weather, and the lack of tents, in a sparsely settled country, where the homes were generally of but one or two rooms."

During the continuance of the Fort Donelson campaign, I had ample opportunities of witnessing the military operations, and of seeing what was going on. I had not only to supervise the surgery of the rear hospitals, and in a general way to see that the wounded were being attended to, but I had also to superintend their transportation. Moreover, I had a certain responsibility with regard to General Grant and his Staff. I was thus kept moving from one point to another, and very many strange, sad, and sometimes amusing things passed under my eyes.

I have spoken of the odd character of many of the western doctors, who were now regimental surgeons. One of these, a Doctor, or let me say, Surgeon Henry Winter Davis (I think of the 18th Illinois Infantry), was a most impulsive, efficient, outspoken man. On the last day's fight. I found him with a gun in his hand, firing away with great spirit. I rode up to him, and said,

"Doctor, this is hardly the work for you to be doing, you ought to confine yourself to strictly professional work." He was kneeling on the ground at the time. He stopped his shooting, looked up at me with a queer expression, and said, "I'm all right, Doctor, I have done all the surgery of this Regiment, and have fired forty-five shots, by G-d." Then he added, "I am glad to see you here. I am glad you're not a feather-bed doctor," and he went on with his belligerent pastime.

This same surgeon, I think, had a curious case. A soldier was brought to him, with a dreadfully crushed leg, apparently greatly swollen and distorted. He promptly amputated just above the knee, when out rolled a 12-pound shot or shell, from the tissues behind the knee joint, and the upper part of the leg where it had been concealed. I learned of this case verbally, and on inquiry, found that this actually occurred, though I was not able to procure the projectile, for the Army Medical Museum at Washington.

I remember well one funny incident which happened at this time. General Grant had a body servant named Frank, French Frank we called him from his nationality. He was a great talker, and boastful, and often expressed a wish to see real fighting, and as he expressed it, cannon-shooting. It happened on the 15th, that he wandered away from headquarters and several of us, riding on a wood road near the front, met him. "Why, where are you going, Frank," we said, "do you want to be shot?" Just at that time, there happened to be a lull in the enemy's battery in front. "I have curiosity," said Frank, "much curiosity, and I must go see the enemy's fight." He was told "Go on, that road will surely bring you to them." Our party rode on, but Frank took us at our word, and in reality did march on in the half open space towards the enemy. Suddenly, we heard a terrible noise of musketry and artillery behind us. When next we saw Frank, he greeted us thus: "I have now no more curiosity; it is satisfied, it is all gone; the enemy did allow me to come near them, then all at once, they did begin to shoot at me, but I escaped them, and behold me!"

I have already referred to our headquarter's accommodations at Mrs. Crip's. In this little house, I was a witness to one or two strange incidents, which as far as I know have not as yet found their way into print.

The enemy made their last sortie on the 15th, which was unsuccessful. As I happened to be in our kitchen bedroom in the after part of the day, I heard General Grant give orders to Captain Hiller, an aide-de-camp, to get ready to go down the Cumberland River at once by boat to Smithland, a little station at or near the junction of the Cumberland and Ohio Rivers, and the nearest point of telegraph. When he should reach there, he was directed by General Grant to send a dispatch to General Halleck, the Commandant of the Department, informing him that "Fort Donelson would surrender on the following morning." I am not quite certain whether General Grant sent a written telegraphic message, or whether he simply verbally directed Hillyer to do so on his arrival at Smithland, but of the tenor of the message, and I think even the very words used, I am positive. When I was alone with the General, I said to him, "General, was it not a little dangerous to send so positive a message as to what the enemy will do tomorrow? Suppose he don't do it?" "Doctor," said the General to me, "he *will* do it. I rode over the field this afternoon and examined some of the dead bodies of his men; their knapsacks, as well as their haversacks, were full of food; they were fighting to get away, and now that they have failed, they will surrender. I knew their Generals (Buckner and Pillow) in Mexico, and they will do as I have said." I felt at that moment that I was talking to an extraordinary man.

The night was inclement. Our troops slept on their arms, General C. F. Smith's division being absolutely within the lines of defense around Fort Donelson. All apparently passed quietly enough, no sorties were made by the enemy and no attack by us. General Grant slept at his headquarters in a feather bed in the kitchen, and I remember that I was curled up on the floor near the fire with my head resting in the seat of my saddle. Early, very early, an orderly entered, ushering in General C. F. Smith, who seemed very cold, indeed half frozen. He walked at once to the open fire on the hearth, for a moment warmed his feet, then turned his back to the fire, facing General Grant who had slipped out of bed, and who was quickly drawing on his outer clothes. "There's something for you to read, General Grant," said Smith, handing him a letter, and while he was doing so, Smith asked us for something to drink. My flask, the only liquor on the Staff, was handed to him, and he helped himself in a soldier-like manner. I can almost see him now, erect, manly, every inch a soldier, standing in front of the fire, twisting his long white moustache and wiping his lips. "What answer shall I send to this, General Smith," asked Grant. "No terms to the damned rebels," replied Smith. Those were his actual words. General Grant gave a short laugh, and drawing a piece of paper, letter size, and of rather poor quality, began to write. In a short time, certainly, not many minutes, he finished and read aloud as if to General Smith, but really so that we understrappers could all hear, his famous "Unconditional surrender" letter, ending with, "I propose to move immediately upon your works." General Smith gave a short emphatic "Hm!" and remarking, "It's the same thing in smoother words," stalked out of the room to deliver the letter, which was shortly followed by the return answer of surrender. I recollect distinctly every feature of this visit of General Smith, his magnificent appearance, soldier-like bearing, and his abrupt mode of speech. The exposure of these nights must have told on him severely; he felt the cold and thrust out his feet and said, "See how the soles of my boots burned; I slept last night with my head in the saddle, and with my feet too near the fire; I've scorched my boots."

I shortly went about my professional duties, and later in the morning, about eleven o'clock, I learned that the surrender had been consummated, and that General Grant and his staff were on a boat. Here I joined them, and found that the stateroom adjoining the General's, had been assigned to me.

About this time Lieutenant-Colonel McPherson,* soon to become so famous, and to die so gallantly, visited our headquarters. We were then all living in a small frame house known as Mrs. Crip's. While he was there I came to know him well. In the first place, I took to him greatly; he was so winning and yet so manly. He suffered with a cystic tumor of the neck, low down, which pressed apparently backwards, and interfered with tracheal respiration. For this, he consulted me. I must add that he was a good friend of my old friend, Major,

*James Birdseye McPherson, killed at Atlanta while commanding the Army of the Tennessee, temporarily succeeded for a few days by John A. Logan, and then to the close of the war succeeded by Maj. Gen. Oliver Otis Howard.—E. T. S.

afterwards General Hawkins. So from one cause or another, in a few hours, we became very good friends, and one evening he told me, "Doctor, my breathing is bad, and I will sleep awhile in the cold, out on the porch; come, lie down with me, I want to ask you some questions." I did so, and rolled up in my buffalo robe close to him. Then he told me, "I have been ordered here, and instructed to obtain special information. All sorts of reports are prevalent at St. Louis (the headquarters of General Halleck, Grant's superior officer), as to General Grant's habits. It is said that he is drinking terribly, and in every way is inefficient. I am fond of him, and want to do him justice." I told him as earnestly as I could the truth,—that the reports were unfounded, that I knew they were false, and assured him that to my knowledge there was no liquor on the Staff, that the contents of my pocket flask was the whole supply, and that I had been cautioned by General Grant as to its disposal, being positively forbidden to give any to any of the staff, except in medical urgency. I explained to McPherson that there were men near the General who disliked him and were jealous of him; yet, knowing this, and their attempts at detraction, he still moved on, undisturbed. I think, indeed I am quite sure, that Col. McPherson believed me, and said that he would so report to General Halleck on his return, and was glad to be able to do so. He did do so, as he afterwards assured me when I saw him at St. Louis.

Shortly after the surrender, I went down to the headquarters' boat on which General Grant was. On my way, I noticed that the Confederate soldiers were doing a brisk business, by selling their bowie knives and small arms to our men who were buying them eagerly as trophies. I myself, had bought a very beautiful knife with a brass lion head, for which I had paid one dollar, and handed it to my servant to bring on board. I casually mentioned this traffic (but not my purchase), to the General. As all captured arms were the property of the Government, he issued an immediate order to the guards to confiscate all such arms, wherever found. As they went to the shore to carry out the order, it happened that the first person met was my contraband (negro) servant, carrying my luggage and prominently displaying my recently purchased lion-headed bowie knife. My servant reported the loss to me, and I begged hard for my knife from the General, but he would not accede to my request. However, a day or two afterwards, he picked out a handsome Confederate sword from a pile of captured arms, and gave it to me, as he said "to make up for my loss." The sword, a Solingen blade, has C. S. A. on the blade, and the same letters on the brass hilt, which I was told was cast in Mobile, and is roughly finished. This sword I still have. At the same time General Grant gave me a wooden handled bowie knife, which had been made from a Southern cornstalk chopper.

About an hour or so after the actual, but informal, surrender I entered the fort, passing through the abattis and I at once hunted our headquarters. General Grant's table was placed behind the dingy curtains, which separated what I suppose had been the ladies' cabin from the general cabin. When I went in, the General was writing his official report of the surrender. A number of officers were present. I quite vividly remember that at the time I was offering my congratulations to the General, that I said very kindly to him, "General, you are going to be the President of the United States. If I ask you then for a not improper office, will you give it to me?" He laughed, and said, "Doctor, I will; what do you think you will want?" "I should like to be Secretary of Legation to Paris," said I. "You shall have it," he replied, "when I am President of the United States."

I often thought of this afterwards. My imaginary choice was based upon the fact that Dr. DaCota and I had often thought what a nice position that must be for a young unmarried man. We remembered a Secretary of Legation who always received his visitors in the last of seven or eight salons, "en suite." It *was* impressive.

The capture of Fort Donelson, and what it carried with it was immense, not less than 15,000 men and many guns. The force under General Grant's command was less than 30,000 men. A great many of the enemy escaped in the night preceding the surrender, and with them, Generals Floyd, Pillow and Forrest with his cavalry force. At this time I had frequent opportunities of talking quietly with the General, and I was much impressed with his magnanimity. Once, probably on the day of the surrender, I asked him how soon, or when, the enemy would be paraded and the formalities of surrender gone through with, such as the lowering of the standard and the stacking of the guns, and the delivery of the Confederate commander's sword. "There will be nothing of the kind," said General Grant to me. "The surrender is now a fact; we have the fort, the men, the guns. Why should we go through vain forms, and mortify and injure the spirit of brave men, who, after all are our own countrymen and brothers." All this seemed very strange to me whose mind was filled with the pageantry of European warfare, as I had lately been reading Jomini, Thiers, and other books on warfare and war history. But it showed the kind of man Grant was.

Grant was a ready writer; he wrote tersely, rapidly and very rarely struck out or altered; occasionally I have seen him interline a word or two. If any one was present whom he trusted, he would read a line or two aloud. I remember once, while on the boat at Donelson, he was writing some report; he had arrived near the bottom of the page of the first half sheet, and was about to sign. Looking up, he saw me, read what he had written, and asked me what I thought of it. I remarked that its termination seemed a little abrupt. He read it, and said, "So it is," and then adding two or three lines, he carried over to the next page, and signed, saying, "It does look better now."

My chief occupation at this time was looking after the wounded and having them transported to the boat, fitted up for their reception and transfer, as fast as possible. They were put on board, carefully attended to and dressed, and then moved in the hospital boats to the great hospitals at Mound City, Cairo, St. Louis, Louisville and Cincinnati. Among our prisoners, I found several of my old students, who were serving in the medical corps of the enemy. I was glad to see them, but the pleasure was somewhat inconvenient, as I had to share my underclothes among them, as they were all destitute of linen. One or two of the southern surgeons (I do not refer to any of my old friends) served us a shabby trick. It was reported at headquarters that some distance, seven or eight miles, up the river, and on the opposite shore, a rebel colonel was lying, grievously wounded. Two of the rebel doctors were sent under parole to see to him, and bring him in. They went, did not visit him, and then vanished to their homes or elsewhere. The poor fellow, thus abandoned, again sent to headquarters, complaining piteously of his condition and his neglect. I was ordered to go and look after him. I did so, gave the necessary directions, and succeeded with much difficulty in boarding a down-going steamer, returning to Donelson.

I ought to tell you that the river at this time was very high, forty feet above its ordinary mark. This flooded a great extent of country and swept away large trees, frame and log houses, and created a terrible current. At one time, when we were occupying Fort Donelson, and the adjoining town of Dover, the water was rising an inch an hour. Our boats were moored to the bank, and the rise and subsequent fall of the water kept the captains of our boats constantly on the watch. Our horses were stabled on the boiler deck, and it was strange to see how soon they became accustomed to these quarters, and how thoroughly they associated the idea of home with a boat, in no way disturbed by the peculiar and noisy machinery of a Mississippi steamer. I was riding at that time a fine black horse, who swam very high out of water. He was not a pleasant-tempered horse, but he had sort of a good feeling toward me. He liked his boat, and on one occasion when the river was falling, and the descent of the river bank to the boat was somewhat difficult, having occasion to go on board of our headquarters boat for a few minutes, I left my black steed standing on the bank above. Whilst on board, it became necessary to change the mooring of the boat, and to do this, the Captain unmoored and began to back off from the shore, intending to come in again to a satisfactory spot. When he had gone several feet from the shore, I happened to come down to the boiler deck. As I was on the stair,

I was startled by a shuffling, sliding sound, a rush, and in a second my horse landed quite satisfactorily on the boat, having made the leap from the shore, across open water. He did not intend to be left behind.

The arrangement of the great wastern steamers was well suited for the accommodation of animals. They were packed in tightly, and in the main got along in a friendly spirit. On one occasion, I was walking on the lower deck, when I met General Grant limping terribly, and rubbing his leg. "Why, what is the matter, General," said I. "Nothing. Oh nothing, Doctor," he replied. "I have just been to see Jack" (his big favorite stallion), "and he seems a little playful this morning," and off he limped, and all day continued bragging of Jack's playfulness and general Christian disposition.

About this time among the horses tethered, Major (afterward General) Rawlins, Grant's Chief of Staff, had a very fine bay, with a splendid tail, which he was always admiring, saying to everyone, "Just see that splendid tail. It almost touches the ground." But, alas! the animal was tethered in front of a mule, and one morning the tail was changed, the hair had disappeared, and the bones stuck out bare and ragged, not very much longer than your hand and wrist. The fact was reported to Rawlins, and we went with him to examine the catastrophe. The report was true. At that time, Rawlins was very profane, even under ordinary circumstances, but this incident was overwhelming to him. At first, supposing this mutilation to have been the deliberate work of some malevolent person, his indignation knew no bounds, he could scarcely find anathemas sufficiently strong to do justice to the occasion. When at last, it was discerned that the ornamental tail was *eaten* off for the salt in it, by the rear mule, Rawlins was dumb with wrath.

And now that I have written Rawlin's name, I want to say something about him, for he was a most extraordinary man, and by his faithfulness toward the General, his good judgment, his fearless and outspoken expression of his convictions, and his quick sense of right and wrong, greatly assisted his chief in arriving at just conclusions, and in withstanding the temptations by which he was surrounded.

You will scarcely believe or comprehend the dangers which encircled the General at this time. Bad men were ever approaching him, seeking to further their own plans and interests; some wanted promotion; some, place; and others, contracts, or the equivalent, recommendations, by which they could covertly grasp money. So specious were their propositions, and so cunningly were their tricks devised and concealed, that even the most wary could be deceived. And just here it was that Rawlins's cleverness and good sense were evinced. He was a young lawyer from Galena; he had known Grant in civil life; he understood him and knew the amiability of his disposition and his attachment to those whom he regarded as his friends, and it seemed to me even at that early date, that he deliberately took it upon himself to guard his chief, and to assume the part of the watchdog at the gate, a duty which he discharged to the great good of the General and to the advantage of the country.

Rawlins had set his mind upon one thing, that there should be no liquor used on the Staff, save for medicinal purpose. I well remember that on one occasion, a distinguished officer of the regular army was assigned to duty on the Staff. In due time, he arrived; his baggage was a very small portmanteau, and a quite large keg of whiskey. The fact was reported to Rawlins, who was the Adjutant-General of General Grant's Staff. His direction to the orderly was this: "Start the bung of the keg, then throw it into the river, and then carry the valise upstairs." And it was so done, to the chagrin of the officer, who thundered as loudly as one of his own guns. But it was too late, the keg floating away on the stream.

Grant, as the world knows, was a man of gentle disposition, yet he could be stern, where the discipline of his profession was involved. While we were at Donelson, it was reported to him that some wanton burning and destruction of property had been permitted by one of his favorite colonels, who had a command up the river. This officer had paid a visit to our headquarters, and had left the General only a moment or so before the report came in. It was apparently truthful. Grant's action was prompt. Turning to one of his aides, he said, "Captain, follow Colonel ——, arrest him, take his sword, and order him to report to me at once." The unfortunate Colonel was arrested, to his intense surprise, before he had reached the top of the river bank, but I believe he made his peace, as the charge was exaggerated.

About the 24th of February, as nearly as I can fix the time, General Grant, with his Staff, went up to Clarksville by boat. This place had been evacuated by the enemy, and then occupied by General C. F. Smith, and his division, acting under General Grant's order. The town had some comfortable houses, but yet it seemed lonely and desolate. On the following morning I think, we returned to Donelson; on our way down, while making a bend in the river, we came in sight of a number of transports, crowded with troops coming up. The General, who was sitting at a table in his headquarters on the cabin deck, talking to Rawlins, when informed of arriving troops, brought his hand down sharply on the table, and exclaimed: "Rawlins, I have it; this is probably Nelson and his command. I will order him to report to Buell at Nashville."

The interview between Grant and Nelson was a short one. In a few moments the latter was back on his own boat, and the dense cloud of black smoke, which rolled from her smoke stacks, told plainly enough that no time would be lost by "Bully Nelson," strange mixture and compound of sailor and soldier that he was.

So Nelson passed up to occupy Nashville, and Grant in high good humor sailed down to his old position beneath Fort Donelson. On the 27th or 28th of February, Grant with all his staff started up the Cumberland River to Nashville. The town looked sullen enough; there had been but little real Union feeling there, although everyone pretended to hold Northern sentiments. Nearly all whom I saw were traders, anxious to establish themselves, and to replenish old stocks now exhausted. As we passed, we noticed Buell's troops at Edgefield, on the opposite side of the river from Nashville. He had not yet been able to cross, lacking transportation, and Nelson was still in command of the town. Before we left, General Buell, with a full staff, came over to Grant's boat. Buell's staff seemed large and formal, and far better appointed than ours. All the same, I imagined that there was a great difference in favor of our General, between the two commanders. The interview was formal, but I thought not particularly cordial. I fancy that Buell was disposed to fault-finding. Some of his words could be heard, and such was the impression conveyed to me, and to others. However, the interview was soon over, and we turned homewards,—that is, Donelsonward.

While at Nashville, we all narrowly escaped a bad accident. The bridge at Edgefield had been burned, but the stone piers still stood. Our boat was above the piers; the river level was twenty-five or thirty feet above ordinary, with a furious current. The navigation between the piers was very difficult, and to strike the piers would have been the destruction of our boat. Our steamer in coming down, swerved, lost her headway, and was in great danger of striking the pier sideways. A catastrophe seemed inevitable, but somehow or other, the pilot brought her head around a little, and we passed through, with scarcely an inch to spare. I never could understand how we escaped; for a moment it seemed as if we had not a ghost of a chance.

I have frequently spoken of Grant's humor. Here is an illustration apropos of a little question of mine. A great deal had been said about the water battery at Fort Donelson and I had asked the General what a water battery really was. His answer had been "I will tell you some day, Doctor." On this trip, as we were ascending the river, an orderly came for me in great haste, saying the General wanted me immediately, that I was to report to him without delay. I obeyed instantly. He took me by the arm, led me to the "Texas," and then pointing to the muzzle of a single gun, he said with great glee, "There is a water battery, study it well, and you will learn more than the engineers know."

We reached Nashville on the evening of the 28th, and my business at this time required me to be a good deal among the troops stationed there. On one occasion just after the capture, I rode through Dover, a little town, and seeing a number of soldiers gathered in the court house, I went in. I found a number of men in the record room. A fire was burning in the corner, into which they were busily piling the written leaves of the registers of deeds and wills. This I stopped, and then looking a little carefully, I found one man, sitting on a pile of large rebel ammunition with a lighted pipe in his mouth, and pleasantly occupied in tearing or picking out the cartridge ends. I had him and the rest of his friends out of that dangerous corner in very short time, and notified the Provost Marshal of that perilous unknown arsenal. Soldiers are often more silly than children. At times, they seem absolutely unable to take care of themselves.

At this time, I was riding a dear little "secesh" sorrel pony with a dark-brown tail. She was as tame as could be and would follow me anywhere. I did not tie her but used to leave her at the door when I went into a hospital, and she would wait. On one occasion, I went into a house to see a sick soldier, leaving her as usual. When I came down, I found her in the entry, patiently waiting for me. To reach there, she had ascended one or two porch steps, had then crossed the porch and entered the open house door. She was a charming sociable little nag, and I parted from her with regret when the time came. She had been loaned to me by the Quartermaster.

The question of courage, personal courage, is a strange one. At the storming of Fort Donelson was a young regimental lieutenant, who distinguished himself by his lack of personal bravery. When his regiment advanced, he became demoralized, in fact to use the western phrase "stampeded." Instead of leading his men on, he dropped back, and lay down behind a fallen tree. For a while he was safe, but while endeavouring to stalk still further to the rear, he was wounded from behind, a stray ball injuring his knee joint. He refused all operation, and died a few days later from septic poisoning. He did not appear to greatly fear death, but although he knew he was disgraced in the eyes of his comrades, he still had an idea that he was, after all, a martyr. I saw him not very long before his death, and as I parted from him, his last words to me were, "Doctor, the tree of liberty is watered with my blood." His poor old father, quite a prominent officer of a neighboring state, felt deeply the stain on his name. He said to me that under the circumstances he would rather his son should die than live. He was a brave old Spartan; his great desire was to enlist as a private soldier in the regiment in which his son had been and thus try and obliterate the disgrace of his name. This attempt on his part was absolutely forbidden; but I can never forget the grim set of the old man's jaw.

The interior of the fort was a sorry sight, I mean that portion near the bank of the river; a great amount of crude pork had been piled under the bluff by the Confederates before we took the place, and was insufficiently salted. Salt in the Confederacy was scarce then, and under the influence of the rain and the rising water, it had been decomposed and formed a horrid mess; it was good for nothing and had become a nuisance. The salt had indeed lost its savor. Yet, in the end, it served to make much trouble, and almost caused the loss of a commander to the Army of the Tennessee, and possibly to the country, and thus. Busybodies had spread the report that after the capture of the fort, General Grant had allowed the destruction of much valuable property (which, as Rawlins once told me, meant "that pork"). Then, too, it was asserted that his living was irregular, that he had disobeyed orders, and in fact, that he had lost his head, and wandered up and down the river, in an aimless manner, thus permitting his army to become a mere mob, disorganized and unmanageable. The truth was that Fort Donelson once taken, Grant saw with a true soldier's eye that the next moves on the checkerboard of war would be the occupation of Clarkesville and Nashville, and the penetration of the southern land by columns moving from Nashville. But his superiors at St. Louis and Washington thought otherwise; Nashville was to be taken by Buell, who was heading thither at a snail's pace. Grant at this time, having captured Fort Donelson, was anxious to occupy Nashville, but his orders forbade him. It was only when Nelson's division on transports met Grant upon the river above Fort Donelson (having been ordered to report to him while the siege of Fort Donelson was in progress), and reached the fort, now ours, when their services were not needed, that the idea struck Grant that he could order Nelson to report to Buell at Nashville, Buell, not having reached there, and Nashville not having been captured by Union troops. So Grant captured Nashville with Buell's men, Buell himself being an unwilling spectator from the opposite, or wrong side, of the river. These facts were perfectly well known upon Grant's staff, and caused not a little unkind feeling on the parts of Generals Buell and Halleck. Buell was an angry man. He had but a poor opinion of Grant, and in one of his dispatches either to Halleck or McClellan, he used the expression, "My troops are being filched from me." This I have seen in official form.

And here I wish to add a note explanatory of the

circumstances under which I saw these dispatches for a second time, and at my leisure. At a later period in the war, I was stationed at Washington, and detailed on duty in the office of the Surgeon-General to prepare the Surgical History of the War. Grant was at that time in the neighborhood of Washington with his headquarters at the War Department. Wishing to refresh my memory on the events of the period on which I am now writing, I asked and obtained permission through Rawlins, to look over the old record and dispatch books on file in the office. This permission was readily granted, and as I knew so many of the old staff well, I had every opportunity for study, and was thus enabled to read what I pleased. Not a little rough manuscript which I then compiled was afterwards printed in the Medical and Surgical History of the Rebellion.

I find in a letter to Dr. DaCosta, some opinions of what was taking place around me. My letter is dated:

"Headquarters, Fort Donelson, March 2, 1862," and reads in part as follows:

"I have not had time to write you since the battle with its stupendous results. *We* took Nashville, not Buell, for it fell in consequence of Donelson. I am afraid Buell, who has now 125,000 men, is too cautious. He sent down yesterday, or the day before, for Smith's command of 2,500 men, to Nashville, when he had 40,000 or 50,000 there. He should push on, and not allow the enemy time to fortify at Murfreesboro. Grant would do it. By the way, our General is a good soldier and prompt. He means what he says, and says what he means. He is not afraid of responsibility. On the Friday before Donelson, he told me, 'Doctor, if I was a little more assured of my men, I would storm with every man at twelve tonight, but I am not sure of them in a night melée.' The place must fall to a moral certainty. On Saturday night, he was certain of it, and told us in the morning that we would be in, and so wrote to Halleck. He and I have the biggest kind of military talks, and it would do you good to hear me expressing my views as to the next steps. Grant told me the other day, 'Doctor, wherever I go, I want you to come,' and he would not allow me to be moved from his staff when Dr. Hewitt joined. He was on Smith's staff, but very generously applied to be relieved, as he saw Grant wanted me. He did not wish to interfere with me, so now I rank everybody, unless some old regular surgeon should be sent here."

On March 4th, General Grant and his staff left Fort Donelson and rode over to Fort Henry, taking up our quarters on a steamer. At this time an expedition was fitted out to ascend the Tennessee River. It went under the command of General C. F. Smith. Grant remained on the boat at Fort Henry, and I stayed with him. The country around the fort was thoroughly inundated, and as a consequence, the health of the troops who had encamped there, had suffered greatly, especially from camp dysentery and fevers.

On March 6th, I rode over to Fort Donelson, to look after the sick and wounded, and this done, on the following afternoon started by boat to go round Fort Henry again. We steamed pleasantly down the river, the night was brightly moonlight, and I was sitting on the upper deck by the side of the big smoke pipes or stacks. Of a sudden, without warning, we were enveloped, that is, I was, in dense smoke. We were steering very close to the shore, and had run into an immense sycamore tree which grew on the bank. Our huge pipes were instantly broken off and lay prostrate on the deck, volumes of thick, choking smoke rolling from their stumps. Fortunately, I at that moment was sitting close to the ladder, which led to the lower deck, and although in utter darkness, I was able to creep down and find refuge below. By moderating the fires, the dense smoke was in some way eliminated, and we crept slowly along, reaching Paducah the next morning. Here I found thirty-eight transports loaded with men, waiting to ascend the Tennessee River. In a short note to my sister, mailed from here, I find that I refer to a photograph sent her of General Grant, which probably was the first I had of him. I told her "I will send you an autograph of Grant's to put under the photograph. By the way, his name properly is U. Grant; this, he told me himself;—the cadets nicknamed him · U. S. Grant, (Uncle Sam). It crept into the army register as U. S. Grant, and so he has always written it since."

At Paducah, I found many newspaper reporters and was surrounded, and pumped for battle-field anecdotes. My imagination was then vivid and I gave it scope. The same day "Nigger" and I went up the river and reported at headquarters. "Nigger" was my jet-black horse, so named by my servant. I called him "Nig" for short, and he soon learned his name. On reaching the old headquarters, I passed several very pleasant days. One thing I particularly remember. We had a washerwoman on board, who not only could wash, but could also darn, so I had an opportunity of overhauling an important part of my wardrobe, and was for the present relieved from the unpleasant necessity of tying up my stocking toes to get rid of the holes.

It was at this time, that a remarkable occurrence took place which might have influenced not only the after career of the General, but indeed possibly that of the nation also. I have already referred to the dissatisfaction felt by General Halleck, and by the War Department authorities at Washington with the events which followed the surrender of Fort Donelson, and how blame was heaped upon the head of General Grant, a victorious general, and so far, the only successful general of the war. Matters soon culminated. On March 2nd, General Grant was ordered back to Fort Henry, and on the 4th was ordered to place General C. F. Smith in command of the expedition up the Tennessee River. On the 6th of March, General Halleck severely reprimanded Grant for neglect of duty after capture of Fort Donelson.

On the 7th, and subsequently on the 11th, Grant asked to be relieved from duty in the Department. After the 7th, the day on which, at Fort Henry, he received Halleck's letter of the 6th, he was practically in arrest, and so continued until the receipt of a letter from Halleck, dated St. Louis, March 13th, 1862, refusing to relieve him from duty, as he had requested, and closing thus: "Instead of relieving you, I wish you, as soon as your new army is in the field to assume the immediate command and lead it on to new victories."* The communications of Halleck to Grant, I saw when they were received, and of the virtual arrest of Grant on the 7th of March I was cognizant, Rawlins having told me of it at the time, and General Grant having spoken of it to his staff.

It would seem as if these discourtesies, and the practical arrest of the General were the result of communications passing between Halleck at St. Louis and General McClellan at Washington, and somehow or other, I also formed the opinion at the time that General

* Official records, War of the Rebellion, Series 1, Vol. X, Part 11, p. 32.

Buell's complaints had not a little to do in leading to the misunderstandings.

The treatment received by General Grant from his superior officers at this time cut him bitterly. In a letter written by me to Dr. DaCosta from Fort Henry, dated March 11th, 1862, I alluded thus to passing events: "Grant has been demanded to be relieved from this department. Halleck did not arrest Grant, but ordered him to remain here, as bad, if not worse. Out here, we are destitute of good artillery men, and cavalry officers, and were it not for the innate pluck of the troops and officers, we should be in a bad way. I have seen the telegrams and dispatches and was never more surprised in my life, than when I read the one putting the General on the shelf. It was infamous, and the blame rests with his superior officers, and that confounded ——, a Chief of Staff, a Miss Nancy of the worse kind. I traveled with him, and he is the only man I ever saw who watched a checked piece of baggage. When this thing comes out, defend Grant. He obeyed his orders to the letter, and had he not been stopped, would have been at Chattanooga at this time. His fault was in being too strong and active."

His headquarters at Fort Henry were on a steamer, I think still the "Tigress." During this interval between the 6th and 13th of March, 1862, when he was under a cloud, I passed on one occasion, into the back part of the cabin deck, that part curtained off as the ladies' saloon, used at the time as the private office of headquarters. My own stateroom was near to Grant's, and opened into the office of Generals Logan, Ogelsby, Cook, Lawler, who, with others of the staff, recently created brigadiers, at Grant's recommendation, were there. Several of them who had been at the Battle of

Belmont were known as the Belmont Colonels. They had just presented a sword of honor to General Grant, and it lay upon its open case upon the table. The General had received it when presented, but unable to answer and overcome by his emotions, he turned and went back through the cabin door on to the open deck. I was at first ignorant of what had happened, but was told. In a little while most of the officers, indeed, I think, all, had left the headquarters office, and shortly afterwards I went out on the guards, and there stumbled across the General. The tears were on his face, unmistakably. He took me by the arm, without a word, led me back to the round table on which the sword lay, in its open case, pushed it as it were, toward me, saying, "Doctor, send it to my wife, I will never wear a sword again." The incident made a deep impression on me at the time, and has never since passed from my mind.

While here, Grant actively and regularly pushed forward the regulations for the expedition up the river under General Smith. Anxious to give me every chance, he ordered me to report to Sherman, who had a command with General C. F. Smith on this expedition, but as I saw that Sherman did not want me, but did want Surgeon Hewitt, and as there was a difficulty as to my rank, I ventured to suggest that I should remain behind with Grant, and so I was relieved of my order to him, and returned to Grant's headquarters. When I told him, he took me by both hands, saying, "My boy, I knew you would not leave me; stay with me." Kind as he had always been, and always was afterwards to me, this was, I believe, the only time at which he was familiar to me.

I might mention here the manner and deportment of

Grant and Smith. Smith had been commandant at West Point when Grant had been in the academy as a cadet. The latter in one sense still looked up to him in the memory of his old office; and yet I could not help feeling, and noticing, that there was an unconscious deference on the part of Smith to Grant as a soldier. It was apart from rank; it seemed indescribable; but it was there, it was the recognition of the master. On the evening before the expedition sailed, as the two walked up and down the guards of the boat, the last walk they ever took together, this relationship seemed to me stronger than ever.

The week I spent on the boat at this time, and after Smith had sailed away, and left our headquarters deserted and lonely with the troops all away, seemed sad enough. The General was depressed, Rawlins was out of spirits, and everyone, down to the very orderlies, was feeling below par.

# CHAPTER XI

About the 13th or 14th of March, Grant was restored to his command, "let loose" as it were, to start on that career of destruction of the Confederacy, which ended at Appomattox, Va., April 9, 1865. Once in command of the new levies and reinforcements which were pouring up the Tennessee, he made arrangement to go up with his staff immediately. The water in the river at this time was very high, fully fifty feet above the low water, or ordinary level of the river. The forts and the fences, erected by the enemy at various points, were, therefore, untenable in most instances. Our vessels and gunboats commanded them. Then, too, the width of the river had been enormously increased, and dry banks were so far removed, that the enemy could find no vantage ground from which to annoy our transports. The flood of water swept down with irresistible force, carrying away small houses, mills, sheds, lumber, trees and everything which could float. Navigation for our heavily laden boats was therefore somewhat difficult. Sometimes, at nights, our boats would be carried by the waters into the roads, stick there until daylight, and then have to be cut out with axes, so that they could find their way back into open stream. However, by great care and watchfulness, all of the transports, from eighty to a hundred in number, were successfully conducted to Savannah, Tennessee, and to Pittsburgh Landing, a few miles above on the opposite shore, soon to receive such bloody notoriety. Nearly all of the enemy's gunboats had been captured or destroyed. The one or two which had escaped and gone up small creeks, were neutralized by our own war vessels.

About the middle of March, our headquarters moved up the Tennessee River. We were received with great joy by many of the inhabitants, and it seemed very strange once more to see the old flag hoisted on impromptu flag poles, and to hear the loud cheers of the poor, upon the banks. The people had been hardly treated. The men had been dragged off, often marched at the tail of the cart, to the southern armies, and their homes had been ransacked for supplies. Whatever might have been the case in other portions of the South, it was unquestionably true that a strong and genuine Union feeling existed along the banks of the river in Hardin and McNairy Counties.

At Savannah, our boat rested. Here we found that General C. F. Smith had established his headquarters in a small house, not very far from the landing. While we lay at the landing, I spent a good deal of time on shore, and saw something of the inhabitants. I remember one family which was 'secesh' to the back-bone. It consisted of five daughters and two sons, the latter away in the rebel army. I soon became quite intimate with the young ladies, and after a while they would sing to me their Secession songs.

One was:

> "Wait for the wagon, the dissolution wagon,
> And we'll all take a ride."

Another:

> "To arms, to arms in Dixie land."

Another, and this was the most favorite one with them:

"And, *one, two, three,* we'll crush them!"

I remained here until the 22nd of March, 1862. A great amount of sickness existed at this time among the troops, malaria, dysentery, typhoid; and in fact all the diseases partook more or less of the typhoid type. I was fighting all the time to obtain proper food, medicines, and medical supplies. Fresh meat was in great demand, and although I knew well the commissary of subsistence, Major Leland, one of the famous Leland brothers, hotel proprietors of New York City, it was only by positive threats of preferment of charges, that I could succeed in procuring the necessary fresh food for our sick. So pressing was the demand for all of these necessities, that General Grant determined to send me to St. Louis to procure what I could by personal interview and request from General Halleck. The following was General Grant's order in his own handwriting:

"Headquarters, District of Tennessee,
Savanna, March 22, 1862.

SPECIAL ORDER
No. 32.

Surgeon J. H. Brinton will proceed to St. Louis, Mo. without delay, and procure through the Medical Director and Purveyor of the Department, the necessary medical stores and supplies for the growing wants of this District and return.

By order,

U. S. GRANT,
Maj. Gen. Comg."

In obedience to this order, not a very agreeable one, I started by boat for St. Louis, down the Tennessee and Ohio and up the Mississippi Rivers. I had a rather strange meeting on the boat. As we were nearing St. Louis, a long-haired, shabby, lank individual, looking wonderfully like a Southerner came up to me, and said, "How d'ye do, Dr. Brinton?" I thanked him, and said, "Who are you?" The answer was, "A spy." I started, and asked him if there was not a certain risk in openly avowing such a dangerous calling. "Not at all," he said, "You won't betray me." I asked him how he knew me. He said, "Do you remember many years ago in company with Camac, Heyward and others, dissecting a long negro subject at the Jefferson College? I was one of the others," he said. He asked me if a young man named DaCosta was not a friend of mine. Then he said, "I am from West Chester (or Chester) County; I came out to Memphis, Tenn., to settle, and practice my profession. When the war broke out I was getting along nicely, and had married. I was called an abolitionist and driven away. My poor wife was turned out of the town without shelter. Her baby was born by the roadside. Mother and child both died. Then I swore vengeance on the Southern cause. I let my hair grow and turned spy. I have done them a world of harm, and will go on doing it. I do not care for my own life, if I can only hurt the enemy." I asked him where he had been last. "With Pillow's command," said he. "I had the clothes of a young Virginian officer, who was killed in the east, and I have passed myself off for him, and have been some days in camp down the river. But they became suspicious, and I have come up to report to Halleck." When I saw Halleck afterwards, I told him of this man, and I afterwards learned from some headquarters source that his story was a true one.

On my arrival at headquarters, I reported to the Medical Director and General Halleck on March 28th. The latter listened to all I had to say, and told me he would do the best he could for me. On my way to St. Louis, I had stopped at Cairo, and had obtained from the Medical Director, Surgeon Simons, additional facts as to the deficiencies, and also as to the hospital resources of the District of Cairo. Returning from St. Louis, I stopped at Cairo, and was there on the 31st of March, detailed on a board to examine into certain alleged abuses at Mound City Hospital.

The battle of Pittsburg Landing or Shiloh Chapel occurred on April 6th and 7th, 1862. At that time, I was on board duty from which I was immediately relieved, and ascended the river to Pittsburg Landing to report. On my way up the river, we passed one or two hospital steamers coming down. They were crowded with wounded, additional accommodations having been established by the pitching of the hospital tents upon their upper decks. On arriving at Pittsburg Landing, I found a busy scene. On Sunday, the 6th, the great battle of Shiloh, or Shiloh Chapel had been fought, the enemy having attacked our army in their camp, and driven them well back. Late in the afternoon, General Buell with the Army of Ohio had arrived. The army bivouacked in the rain during the night. Early in the morning, on Monday the 7th, Grant ordered a general advance along the whole line. The enemy fell back, at first slowly, afterwards rapidly, and retreated to his works at Corinth. His dead and many of his wounded were abandoned. About this time, Surgeon Simons, U. S. A., came up from Cairo, and for a short time discharged the duties of Medical Director of General Grant's army of the Tennessee. Before long, on April 24th, he was relieved and ordered to report for duty at Cairo. At the same time, I received the following order:

"Headquarters Department of the Mississippi,
Pittsburg Landing, Tenn., April 24, 1862.

SPECIAL FIELD ORDERS
No. 26.

Brigade Surgeon Brinton will perform the duties of Medical Director of General Grant's Army until Surgeon Simon's return.

By order of Major Genl. Halleck,
And
C. Kemper,
Asst. Adj. Genl."

Surgeon Brinton.

I acted as Medical Director for a little time until the coming of old Dr. McDougal, U. S. A., who had arrived toward the end of April, and who acted as the Medical Director of the Armies of the Tennessee. His office was on the headquarters' boat at the landing. I remained with Dr. McDougal until the 2nd of May, when he sent me to General Halleck's headquarters in the field, to represent him. My title was "Medical Director in the field"; my duty to report to him and keep him informed. General Halleck came from St. Louis about April 11th or 12th, and assumed chief command of the Armies of the Tennessee, of the Ohio (under Buell), and of the Mississippi (under Pope). This large joint consolidated army was sometimes spoken of as "The Army of the Tennessee," or "The Armies of the Tennessee."

General Halleck's headquarters were not very far removed from the "Landing" on a high bluff. During the time I was at the "Landing," I lived on General Grant's headquarters boat. At first, as can be seen from my orders, I was with Medical Director Simons, and afterwards with Medical Director McDougal. By each one of these I was treated with the greatest kindness. During my stay with these gentlemen, I was very busy. I occupied a sort of inspection position. My duties were to ride from camp to camp, to visit the hospitals, to inform myself of their wants. If anything was wrong, I would look into and report it to my chief. I had a great deal to do in the matter of transportation, and in getting the sick and wounded to the hospital boats, and in seeing that they were started in as good condition as possible.

In all this apparent turmoil, many incidents of interest occurred. In the pages on the fight of Belmont, Mo., I have spoken of a Captain Polk, of the Southern service. He was a nephew of Bishop General Polk, who had formerly been educated at West Point, and then, having entered the Episcopal Church, had later been consecrated Bishop. Captain Polk, I met on a flag of truce, sent from Cairo to Columbus. He and I quite fraternized, and he asked me to promise that in case he should be hit at any time, and would let me know, that I would come to him, bring him in our lines, and take care of him. And so it happened. About the 14th or 15th of April, he did send me word that he had been hit in the leg, was completely disabled, and was lying at a Confederate hospital, some seven or eight miles away from Shiloh within the southern lines. He asked me to come with an ambulance, and bring him into our lines, where he could be well cared for. I placed the matter before

General Grant, told him of my former promise, and asked his permission to go with a truce flag and bring Polk in. This he declined, but finally consented that I should take an ambulance, stretcher, and one or two hospital attendants, and go absolutely unarmed, at my own risk, as it were, but with the express stipulation that if I should bring in the wounded man, he would be regarded as a prisoner of war.

So on the 16th of April I went after him, riding by the side of the empty ambulance, without any white flag. I soon passed our picket lines, and entered into the lonely neutral country beyond. It was very lonely, and so quiet, that even the birds seemed to be afraid to sing. After a while, I caught sight of the enemy's pickets and someone advanced and inquired if we were the "Doctor's party." On my affirmative, he said that he had been sent to meet us, and to take us to the little hospital where Polk, I think they called him Major, was. I went there and found him. He was most glad to see us, welcomed us to the hospital, gave us an excellent dinner, with some delicious fresh butter, which had been sent to him by his wife. I explained to him that I would take him to our hospital boats, and do the best that I could for him, but although he would come voluntarily, he still would be a prisoner. "All right," he said, and sticking his hand into his pocket, and pulling out a roll of notes, he added, "See here are a lot of Lincoln's pictures; I'll get along." So as it was time to return, his friends lifted him carefully into the ambulance, put in some vegetables and fresh butter, and I started off. The Confederates passed us through their pickets, and took leave of us, with many expressions of good will. Then I took him to the hospital boat under Dr. Turner's care, and here I left him, with instructions that he should be kept on the boat for the present. He remained for a trip or two, when finally the fact was discovered by the patriotic citizens of Evansville (or some town on the river), who, on hearing that a wounded rebel major was being accommodated on board a hospital boat, forcibly carried him to a U. S. hospital. I heard that his leg was afterwards amputated, but that he had recovered. I have never seen or heard of or from him since.

This ride afforded me an admirable chance of seeing the extreme limits of a battle field, and the track of the enemy's retreat. The roads were all in a bad condition, the rain had been heavy after the battle, and the artillery and baggage trains had cut deep ruts.

During my stay at the "Landing," I was constantly dispatched on detached duty. On the 25th of April, 1862, I was sent by General Grant on a tugboat to Savannah, Tennessee, twenty miles below, to see General C. F. Smith, who had been very sick, and who was reported to be sinking. I found him unconscious and moribund, and during the night he died. He was said to have been perhaps the handsomest man in the army, erect, six feet four in stature. He was fond of the army, was universally esteemed, and left the reputation of a good and faithful soldier. In the execution of duty, he knew no friend, but duty over, he was a most genial commander.

My old friend Dr. Henry S. Hewitt, used to tell the following of him. On one occasion late at night, Hewitt and he were engaged in a fierce discussion on theological points, and notably, on Purgatory. The utility of such a state was stoutly challenged by the General. "Why, Doctor," he said, "do you mean to say that I shall ever go to Purgatory?" "General," was the answer, "the time will come when you will die, will go up to Heaven's gate, and claim admittance." 'Who comes?' St. Peter will demand. 'I, Charles F. Smith, Major General of the United States Army.' 'Have you passed a proper stage?' 'No, I come direct, and plead my mortal life and claims.' 'General,' will be St. Peter's answer, 'I know you well; I know your life; you have been a spotless citizen, an obedient son, a kind and loving father, an affectionate and tender husband; you have been a brave soldier, a true patriot, a gallant and distinguished general; but General, you, of all others, should know that discipline must be preserved, and that you must spend a few days in Purgatory.' " As this climax was reached, the General in surprise and admiration drew himself up against the door of the stateroom, which yielded to his weight, and he stumbled backwards, landing in his berth, muttering strangely, "So discipline must be preserved, and I must spend a few days in Purgatory; St. Peter thinks so."

I remember, too, another amusing incident about General Smith in which Sheridan (of whom I will have more to say in the next chapter), and I, and some amazing mint juleps, all played a part. It happened that as Sheridan and I were riding together one afternoon, he checked his horse and began sniffing. "I smell mint," said he, "we must find it," and he did and returned to camp with a generous supply. That night, we, or rather he, made mighty juleps, greatly appreciated by those who participated. Someone said, "How old Smith would enjoy one." Now, General C. F. Smith was asleep in his tent at the time, and it was not well to disturb him, but I volunteered and the julep was made. I went to his tent, separated the hangings, and reached in my arm, holding the tumbler at full length. Smith had been reading, and was half asleep, the candle flickering on the campstool at the head of his cot. The noise roused him, he raised himself on his elbows, anathematized his disturber, and then catching sight of the glass, crowned with green, he stared and stared. Finally the great truth burst upon him. "By G— this is kind," he said, and sliding from beneath the coverings, he crept slowly forward, grasped the glass, and muttering, "Kind indeed!" hurried back to his bed. But he never found out who did it.

# CHAPTER XII

About the 2nd of May, 1862, General Halleck determined to move out in command of the army, to the front, wherever that might be found, in the direction of Corinth, the intersection of the two great railroads. Dr. McDougal being almost too old to go into the field, and there being much for him to do at Pittsburg Landing, he determined to send me with General Halleck's headquarters as a medical director in the field, with instructions to keep him informed of all matters of medical interest which might take place. Accordingly I started to report at headquarters, and was ordered to come with them. On making my few preparations, and returning, I found that the headquarters had already moved. The tents had nearly all been struck, the ground was littered with empty boxes, cans and bottles. The only officer I could see was a little man with black hair, and rather scant beard and mustache, who was flitting about vigorously doing something or nothing, I could scarcely tell which. I entered into conversation with him. He said his name was Sheridan, Captain Sheridan, and that he was a sort of headquarters quartermaster, to look after the staff comforts. He did not seem to have a very exalted opinion of his duties, rather regarding himself as a fifth wheel. He inquired as to my name, rank and duties, and I think remarked that my own position and duties were as vague and shadowy as his own, as neither of us had distinctive position or abiding place on the staff. "Who are you going to mess with, and how will you live when you get there?" he asked me. "I am sure, I don't know," I said. "Then, let's live together," said he. "We'll join our mess kits. I'll find the transportation, and we will do the best we can. Do you think you could get a bit of ice from your medical resources?" he asked me. I said yes, that we had more than we could use. "Good, get a wagon load, and I'll find four animals to pull it, so we'll start housekeeping with an ice house." And so began my acquaintance with Sheridan, Philip H. Sheridan, who figured so largely in the after conduct of the war. And here I might say that either on this day or the next, he broke his wrist as he was mounting, his horse jumping forward when Sheridan's left foot only was in the stirrup. He was jerked off and forward and in falling fractured his wrist, I think the left, an oblique fracture of the radius just above the wrist joint. The top of a cigar box, a little triangular block, a chip left by the axe, where a tree had been cut down, and a bandage served to dress it. It made an excellent cure. Sheridan was anxious that no one should know what the injury was, or that it had occurred while he was mounting his horse. And so no one ever knew how Captain Sheridan *sprained* his arm.

And so we arranged that Sheridan and I should mess together. I rode out after the headquarters with my negro servant; the rain poured in torrents, and the road was in dreadful condition. Just before reaching the plateau at Monterey, where the headquarters camp was to be pitched, I came to a little frame building used as a small hospital. Here I found General Halleck and his chief of staff. The latter was evidently uncomfortable. He was always called "Miss Nancy," and disliked any exposure. His ride in the rain, the mud and the general discomfort of all surroundings had been too much for him; he was completely upset, and was nosing around for creature comforts, when I found him under pretence of finding something for General Halleck. Confidentially, he spoke to me on the subject, and I said that I would see what might be the resources of the medical department. The doctor in charge of the hospital was an excellent quick-brained fellow. In a few moments he had a fine steak broiled, with plenty of gravy, potatoes and mustard. This I sent to the famished Generals, who were good enough to devour it in silent majesty, and afterwards expressed to me their admiration, and wonder as to how such a dish was improvised.

After a while we settled down in camp, and I found myself ensconced in an excellent wall or officer's tent, side by side with Sheridan. And strange as it seems now, I was the ranking officer, and so my bunk was the highest up.

General Halleck treated me very kindly while I was on his staff. He seemed to regard me as sort of a literary character, an opinion based upon the fact that I received every week, by the headquarters mail, my number of the London *Punch,* which the General enjoyed as much as I did, and read regularly. I had for years been accustomed to read *Punch* every Sunday afternoon at the office of my dear old friend, Dr. Charles S. Boker. When I went off to the war, he thoughtfully and most kindly remembered it, and for a long time *Punch* followed me to the "Headquarters in the Field," and indeed until I reached the east again.

General Halleck's headquarters remained at Monterey,

an imaginary cross-road's blacksmith shop, until May 15th, when they were moved forward four or five miles to a point at the Corinth road, just where it crosses the Mississippi line, and close to Corinth, Mississippi, in and around which the enemy were said to be strongly posted. General Grant's headquarters were close to those of Halleck's. Grant, nominally second in command, had at this time no real duties, and no immediate command. His position was an anomalous one, and under which he greatly chafed.

I remained on General Halleck's staff until the twenty-fourth or twenty-fifth of May, when I left for Washington. During those days, my life was a very pleasant one. I was in general medical superintendence of the army in the field and it was my duty to keep my chief, Dr. McDougal, the Medical Director of the Army, advised of all that was going on in our department. Then, too, I had to see in a general way to the care of the wounded and sick. For this purpose, I directed the establishment of a large field hospital at Monterey with a capacity of from one to two thousand beds.

As I have said, Sheridan and I messed together, and saw a good deal of each other. I frequently rode with him, and he was forever proposing that we should take a little ride to see the land, as he would say, "It is always a good thing to get the lay of the country." Many a little thing we picked up in this way.

I was very kindly treated on this staff, and have a pleasant recollection of Col. Kelton, the Adjutant General, and Colonel Thorn, the Engineer. General Halleck, too, interested me greatly. I had formed, I hardly know how, a very high idea of his military abilities. I thought he was a really great man. I suppose I had been more or less influenced by his military nickname "Old Brains."

He had a large head and a thoughtful expression. He seemed quick intellectually, with acute perceptive faculties. In speaking, he went at once to the heart of the topic under discussion, and his questions were direct, to the point, and rapidly put. He wore a big conical hat, and he talked like an able man. Physically, he was somewhat inert; he was fond of good living, and of good wine,—notably of hock. After dining, he was often sleepy. From my after knowledge of him, I think that at first I overestimated him. I saw a good deal of and attended him in one or two slight attacks of illness.

About the 3rd of May, I received an order to report at Washington for special duty, but on the 16th, I was released from duty on this order, by a counter order bearing the private endorsement of Dr. McDougal as follows: "The Medical Director tenders his congratulations to Brigade Surgeon Brinton. Will be glad to hear from him."

Imminence of battle was responsible for this change of detail. Military affairs, however, dragged along slowly without much change. Our lines were slowly advanced and daily contracted more and more around Corinth, a rifle pit and embankment being thrown up at evening on each day's forward move. A battle, a great one, I mean, was daily expected, but which with great regularity did not take place. About the 22nd or 23rd of May, I heard from Washington that I was expected there, and on the 23rd I received a telegram, directing me "to obey the order of May 3rd, directing me to proceed to Washington."

So I had my wish at last to get away from the west, and to go east. I had been dazzled by the idea of getting one of the recently created medical inspectorships, and of leaving the western armies. Had I only known it, I was best off where I was. The western life, the western men, really suited me. I was among the men who were day by day making the nation's history, and who were destined to become the heroes of the war. In part, I felt this, but yet I did not realize it sufficiently. On one occasion, General Grant asked me how I would like to leave the Medical Department, and become one of his aides. I suppose I ought to have taken advantage of this offer, but my professional love was too strong, and I lost the chance of my life. Glad as I was to leave, I still felt a sort of grief at parting with those who in eight months' intercourse had become very much endeared to me, and with some of whom I had formed a friendship which lasted for years.

I took with me from the army headquarters, or rather from Cairo, where I had been collecting them during my service in the west, to Philadelphia, a box of fragments of shot and shell and bullets, intending to illustrate any course of lectures on military surgery which I might give. They passed by this order:

"Headquarters, Department Mississippi,
Camp Corinth Road, May 24th, 1862.
Authority is hereby given to Brigade Surgeon Brinton, U. S. V., to ship a box containing shot and shell, etc., from Cairo to Philadelphia, Penna. The contents of said box have been collected by authority and for professional purposes.
By order of Major Genl. Halleck,

J. C. Kelton, Asst. Adjt. Genl."

Under a like order from headquarters of the Department of the Cumberland, Nashville, a further quantity of shot, shell and projectiles, broken and mutilated weapons, and preparations of gunshot wounds were sent to Philadelphia, and now form part of my collection.

And so I turned my back on the old staff, rode back to Pittsburg Landing, and to the steamer "Polar Star," the boat on which the Medical Director had his headquarters. Here I remained a few hours finishing up my business affairs, chief of which was the sale of my big black horse. Strange to say, I did not lose on him, but absolutely realized his cost. He was a fine animal, and I had become quite used to him, and he to me. So I parted with poor old "Nig," and started down the river on the boat.

I do not remember much of my journey east, except this, that my travel led through Philadelphia. How glad I was to see my Mother and sisters. Although I had been away from home only nine months, yet it seemed as many years. But there I was at last, thinking that my service in the west was over, but in military matters, one can never foretell the future. I looked quite a soldier, and traveled with sword, saddle box, trunk and valise, just as if I were a man of importance. I was very warmly welcomed in Philadelphia; men from the western regions were rare birds then in the east. We had been doing heavy fighting, and winning battles, but in the east the armies had not as yet got fairly into motion.

# CHAPTER XIII

## SURGICAL HISTORY OF THE REBELLION

### TO WASHINGTON. THE ARMY OF THE POTOMAC

In a very few days, I hastened to Washington in obedience to my orders from the War Department, and having reported to the Surgeon General, Dr. William A. Hammond, received from the Adjutant General's office of the War Department, an order to serve on a board for the examination of candidates for the position of Brigade Surgeon.

On the 4th of June, the Surgeon General handed me also the sub-order, telling me that a room would be assigned me in the Surgeon General's office.

"Surgeon General's Office,
Washington City, June 4, 1862.
Sir:—

In accordance with special orders No. 98, Adjt. General's Office of May 3, 1862, directing you to report to the Surgeon General for special duty, you are assigned to duty in this office to prepare the Surgical History of the Rebellion.

I am Sir, very respectfully, yr. obt. Servt.

(Sgd) WM. A. HAMMOND,
Surgeon General U. S. Army.

Brig. Surg. J. H. Brinton,
U. S. Vols.
Washington, D. C."

On reaching Washington, I had gone at once to Willards Hotel, then the largest and best hotel in the city. It was crowded with officers and politicians, and was a busy center. At my first dinner, the cards of my colleagues on the examining board, Drs. Clymer and Warren Webster, were brought to me. The former, a Brigade Surgeon of Volunteers, was considerably older than myself, a Pennsylvanian by birth, who had practiced formerly in Philadelphia. He was a contemporary of Goddard, Gerhard and men of that age, and had been a Professor in the Franklin College, and Physician to the Blockley Almshouse. He was a man of the world, of considerable ability, and I subsequently came to know him quite well, and to like him.

The appearance of Washington City contrasted strongly with that presented in July, 1861, when I saw it last. *Then* all was absolute confusion, chaos; *now* a certain sort of order or system was being inaugurated; the military elements were being brought into shape; the departments were being extended and developed in accordance with the work they had to do. The Army of the Potomac, as organized by McClellan, had moved down to the peninsula, and was about entering on its long bloody career. Government, the departments, generals, soldiers, and civilians, were awakening to the magnitude of the task; politicians were alive to the chance of the future, and army contractors dreamed golden dreams.

The Medical Department of the Army, which for the first few months of the war had shown almost imbecility, and which had been conducted on the basis of the army establishment of the Mexican War, had undergone a change. An active man, Dr. Wm. A. Hammond, impulsive, it is true, but of far-reaching view, and sanguine temperament, had been raised to the office of Surgeon-General, and had infused fresh life and energy throughout the whole Department.  Much has been said against him, heavy charges have been pressed, but from an intimate knowledge of the man, and his surroundings, I am convinced that much injustice has been done, and much undeserved obloquy has been cast upon him.  He was not always wise or prudent; his ways of doing things were not always judicious; but he sought to make the Medical Department of our army efficient, and to render it capable of caring for the sick and wounded, and that, too, in no niggardly or tardy spirit.

When he was first appointed as Surgeon-General, I was on the Tennessee River at Pittsburg Landing.  Shiloh had been fought.  Thousands of wounded and sick were lying on the ground, and unprotected.  Of bedding and covering there was great scarcity, and transportation was insufficient.  The Medical Department was at its wit's end, and almost frantic.  On one afternoon, I sent (I think by Dr. McDougal's order), a pitiful telegram to the new Surgeon-General, begging for God's sake aid for our wounded.  Early the next morning a telegram arrived from him, stating that on that afternoon ten thousand mattresses would start by Adams Express to Shiloh; and they came with wonderful quickness.  In a letter to me at Pittsburg Landing, May 23, 1862, while I was in camp, near Corinth, on Halleck's staff, Medical Director McDougal wrote me:  "Hammond is sustaining me nobly, for which I am thankful; I have not liked him heretofore, but I will never say a word against him again."

Up to June, 1862, the Brigade Surgeons, of which I was one, formed a separate corps.  They were created by the Act of Congress, approved July 22, 1861.  This was the act calling for 500,000 volunteers. By the Act of Congress, approved July 2, 1862, it was enacted "That from and after the passage of this Act, Brigade Surgeons shall be known and designated as Surgeons of Volunteers, and shall be attached to the General Medical Staff, under the direction of the Surgeon-General."

During my first few days in Washington, I was busy hunting up accommodations. For a week or so, I remained at Willard's Hotel. I soon became tired of hotel life, however, and was glad to find for myself two rooms at 255 G Street, a convenient neighborhood. These were on the second floor, parlor and bedroom, and were very comfortable. My meals I continued to take at the hotel. I was now officially stationed in the Surgeon-General's office, and had a nice little office to myself, with book shelves and pigeon holes and unlimited official stationery, and the services of an orderly. I soon began to grow into official importance (imaginary, of course), and to assume all the manners and pompous behavior,* which was considered the proper thing in a well-fed, well-paid, bureau officer.

At this time, I was busy arranging in my mind the plan of my future "Surgical History of the War." It seemed to me then that my best course was to preface the professional matter with a sort of semi-historical or semi-military account or history of the military movements. I hoped thus to convey some idea of the circumstances attending and influencing the medical and surgical treatment of our sick and wounded, to describe the condition of the soldier during each campaign, his

---

*In reading the manuscript of this volume, Dr. Mitchell, the life-long friend of the subject of these memoirs, interpolated after the word "pompous," an old friend's kindly and illuminating comment in the form of two penciled words, "Oh never."—Ed.

physical surroundings, his marchings, his state of health, the general character of the action in which he might have been wounded, the character of the field hospitals and transportation, in fact, the hygienic conditions of the soldiers, as far as I could ascertain them, so that future readers might learn something of the men in health as well as in disease.

I did not suppose that I ever could really carry out this idea, but my intention was to do my best. The reports of wounds, in the early part of the war, were meager in the extreme. *"Vulnus Sclopeticum* or Gunshot wound" was the one great comprehensive category in which all gunshot injuries were embraced. No classification was attempted, and in fact, little, if any, real information of a precise character was furnished. The evils of the system were soon discovered, and before long attempts were made to create a better system of reports, with the returns of wounded and sick, to which I shall have occasion to refer frequently hereafter.

My duties on the Medical Examining Board, convened at Washington, were somewhat confusing, but not yet onerous. We met daily at 10 o'clock in a big room, just where Pennsylvania Avenue turns, for the examination of candidates for the position of Surgeon of Volunteers. I was the President of the Board, Dr. Clymer was the second in rank, and Dr. Warren Webster was the recorder or secretary. We had a long table covered with papers, and one or two fierce-looking orderlies. Of course, we were all in full uniform. Our examination was chiefly written. The candidates were furnished with plenty of paper, pens and ink, and then passed the time as comfortably as they could until three o'clock, in answering our questions. A great many came before us. Some were well prepared; some were not.

Quite a number failed to pass, until finally we were indirectly informed by the Secretary of War, the "dreadful Mr. Stanton," that he wanted more doctors, "and that if we didn't pass more, our Board would be broken up." So under this cogent military reasoning, our standard was lowered, and more surgeons were obtained. I think our system of examination was not altogether perfect, for after-observation convinced me that many men who passed high in our examination did not prove very efficient military surgeons, while some who did not do so very well before us, proved themselves afterwards able and satisfactory officers, professionally and otherwise.

On the 3rd of July, 1862, I received an order from the Surgeon-General, Dr. Wm. A. Hammond, to accompany him to Fortress Monroe. The Army of the Potomac under General McClellan had advanced against Richmond, and then, crossing the Chickahominy River, had fallen back to the James River, and had encamped "in safety" at what was known as Harrison's Landing or Bar. It had reached this point, June 30 and July 1, 1862, and vigorous efforts were being made to re-establish the organization, and to repair the losses caused by the Seven Days' Battle, during which severe battles had taken place at Fair Oaks, Gaines' Mill, White Oak Swamp, Charles' City Crossroads, Ellerson's Mill, Malvern Hill and elsewhere. In fact, the whole line of retreat from the Chickahominy to the James River had been a scene of struggle and bloodshed.

The Surgeon-Generals' party, Dr. Hammond, Dr. Meredith, Dr. Clymer, and some others, whom I have forgotten, started from Washington for Baltimore. We were all in an ambulance, a two-horse dearborn wagon employed in the army and much used around the various military bureaus in Washington. I very well recol-

lect the fun we all had when we picked up one of our
party, Surgeon Meredith, U. S. V., at the door of a
fashionable boarding-house in Washington. The ambulance had just moved off, when his young wife appeared on the doorsteps, and waving a silk umbrella
over her head, excitedly shouted, "My dear, my dear,
you have forgotten your umbrella! Take it, take it, it
may rain before you get back!" Poor lady, it was long
before she heard the last of it.

After reaching Baltimore, a pleasant sail down the
Chesapeake Bay brought us to Fortress Monroe in the
early morning, where we landed and breakfasted at the
Hygiea Hotel, which seemed full of officers and officers'
wives. Here we spent some hours, and I had an opportunity of going inside the fort, and examining the case-
mates.

Fortress Monroe, a stonework of great size, was, I
believe the largest work of defence in the country. It
had a great number of heavy guns in position, and was
supposed to be almost impregnable, if fully manned and
properly defended. Leaving Monroe, we took boat and
sailed up the James River, passing the scene of the terrible fight between the rebel ram *Merrimac* and the U. S.
fleet on the 8th of March, 1862.

As we steamed up the James, the tops of the masts
of the *Cumberland* and *Congress* could be seen above
the water. We stopped at Jamestown, and I had a
good opportunity to examine the old church and churchyard. This church, is, I believe, the oldest Episcopal
Church in this country. It is, or rather was, rich in
old tombstones with quaint inscriptions. These had
been in remarkably good preservation until the advent
of our troops, when many of them were wantonly de-
faced. I often wondered why the old churches and

yards in England had suffered in the Cromwellian period, but as I looked at the sacrilegious devastation of the old Jamestown grave stones, I felt that the answer lay before me.

On our way up, we passed under Fort Powhatan, a fort of the enemy, high on the bluff, on the right bank of the river. This fort was constantly, or rather, at intervals, occupied by a light battery, who made a target of our passing vessels. The steamer in front of us was fired at, and the one behind us, but somehow or other we escaped. I hardly like to confess how unpleasantly, or let me say at once, how cowardly, I felt, as we neared that fort. It seemed so threatening, so dominating, so high above us, and the embrasures in the bank seemed so near. I was walking with a few friends on the deck. As we approached, one or two of them slipped down in the cabin; one I noticed changed his promenade to what might be called the "off" side of the boat. I felt terribly like going below, but I thought to myself, "Here I am in full uniform, glorious in bright buttons," for I was dressed as became a Surgeon-General's companion, and had on a brand new coat. "And here are soldiers on board, who can't go below, or get out of the way, and they will think me a coward, and so I must stay." So stay I did, and walked up and down the deck, and tried to look careless and indifferent; but, oh, how I did watch that fort to detect grey coats or the glimmer of steel and bronze, and how glad I was, when we got far, far away from Powhatan, out of range and past the turn of the river.

Before long, we reached the landing at "Harrison's Landing." We disembarked, and the Surgeon-General's party went up to General McClellan's headquarters, which were pitched in a wood, not very far from the river. Here we found the Medical Director of the Army of the Potomac. When we first arrived at Harrison's, everything was in a good deal of confusion. The army, which had arrived from the Chickahominy in a disordered and shattered condition, was being reorganized and the troops were resting, and were being gathered into their proper commands.

My own particular duties at this time were ornamental rather than useful. Drs. Clymer, Le Conte, and I were attached to the staff of the Surgeon-General, and with him, we went from point to point, inspecting here and there, and, in a general way supported the dignity of our chief. By General McClellan, I was personally kindly received, on the score of my cousinship, and my present comforts were looked after by Arthur McClellan, his brother, who was an aide on his staff. At our first interview, the General asked me a great many questions in regard to General Grant, his habits, his surroundings, his marchings and battles. I spoke very freely to him, and told him a great many things, which, although they were strictly true, he seemed scarcely to credit, especially the matters which concerned the Donelson and Shiloh fights. He repeated his questions, but I knew what I was talking about, and I stuck to my statements. The tent next to General McClellan's was assigned to me, during the few days I stayed at his headquarters. It was the one occupied by his father-in-law, General Marcy, who was just then away from headquarters. On my first night's stay, General McClellan's assistant adjutant, General Seth Williams, came and shared the tent with me. He repeated George's questions, and asked a great many more of the same character. He admitted that my answers surprised him greatly, and I know that I told him much about Grant that he had never heard before. I heard afterwards from some one intimate with General McClellan, that he hardly knew what to make of my statements. I remember that on the next day, my cousin Arthur McClellan said to someone in my hearing that the army was now safe, and I knew that generally around head-quarters, a good deal of satisfaction was being expressed at the changed state of affairs.

During these three or four days, great efforts were being made to remove the wounded and disabled from the army. Some had previously been sent north from the Pamunkey River, and those who safely reached Harrison's Landing were hastily sent northward by the numerous and well-fitted transports and hospital ships, which were arriving daily. A great contrast existed, however, on the vessels intended for the transportation of the sick and wounded in the west and in the east, and struck me forcibly. In the west, the hospital boats were absolutely under the control of the Medical Department. They were boats for the sick and for none others, and were kept clean and in proper condition. In the east, on the contrary, they carried the sick and injured soldiers from the Army of the Potomac, but on their return trips, they were laden with stores, men or prisoners, and often when again used for hospital transportation, were filthy and unsuited for the purpose. This was, I believe, afterwards remedied, but at this time, the hospital transportations were defective, although from no fault of the Medical Department. Things were then in great confusion, and no one knew what to expect. A longer war was felt to be certain, and the first confidence of the North had been shaken. The Army of the Potomac was, however, safely entrenched, and with twenty-one gunboats in the river!

# CHAPTER XIV

## THE SURGEON-GENERAL'S OFFICE

On the 6th of July, I received orders to return to Washington, and arrived there on the 7th, and at once resumed my regular office duties, collecting material for the army surgical history, preparing new forms of reports of sick and wounded, and attending to the work of the examining medical board, which was in session in the latter part of July of this year. This board consisted of Surgeon Lewis A. Edward, U. S. A., Surgeon J. H. Brinton, U. S. Vols., and Assistant Surgeon J. J. Woodward and M. J. Asch, U. S. Army.

The weather during this summer was very warm, and the Washington climate did not agree with me very well. I often remembered what old Dr. McDougal had told me, "When you go to Washington, look out for your liver."

About July 23rd, General Halleck arrived from the West, and was appointed Commander-in-Chief. He was quite gracious to me, although I did not see very much of him. He lived on Georgetown Heights.

On the first of August, 1862, I was directed by the Surgeon-General to arrange all specimens of morbid anatomy, both medical and surgical, which might have accumulated. These were to constitute the Army Medical Museum. The foundations of this museum had for some time been contemplated. Thus in Circular No. 2, it is directed as follows:

"Circular No. 2.

Surgeon General's Office,

Washington, D. C., May 21, 1862.

As it is proposed to establish in Washington, an Army Medical Museum, medical officers are directed diligently to collect and to forward to the office of the Surgeon General, all specimens of morbid anatomy, surgical and medical, which may be regarded as valuable; together with projectiles and foreign bodies removed, and such other matters as may prove of interest in the study of military medicine or surgery. These objects should be accompanied by short explanatory notes. Each specimen in the collection will have appended the name of the Medical Officer by whom it was prepared.

WILLIAM A. HAMMOND,

Surgeon General."

The order to me to arrange the Museum was as follows:

"Surgeon General's Office,

Washington, Aug. 1, 1862.

Sir:—

You are hereby directed to collect and properly arrange in the "Military Medical Museum" all specimens of morbid anatomy, both medical and surgical, which may have accumulated since the commencement of the Rebellion in the various U. S. hospitals, or which may have been retained by any of the Medical officers of the Army. You will also take efficient measures for the procuring hereafter of all specimens of surgical and medical interest that shall be afforded in the practice of the different hospitals. Should any medical officer of the Army decline or neglect to furnish such preparations for the

Museum, you will report the name of such officer to this office.

Very Respty. Yr. Obdt. Servt.,

WILLIAM A. HAMMOND,

Surg. Genl.

Dr. Brinton,

Surgn. U. S. Vols."

In connection with this matter of the Army Medical Museum, it may be well for me to state just what I had to do with it. The first idea of an "Army Medical Museum" originated with Surgeon-General Hammond, and was by him communicated to the officers of the Army in Circular No. 2, which I have given. I told him, when I first saw him, that I had collected a good many bone specimens in the West, some of which I had lost, and some of which I brought home (now in my collection of gunshot wounds of bone). The order of August 1st, to me, was the first step towards really putting this notion of an Army Museum into shape, and was a most welcome duty. My whole heart was in the Museum, and I felt that if the medical officers in the field, and those in charge of hospitals, could only be fairly interested, its growth would be rapid, and the future good of such a grand national cabinet would be immense. By it the results of the surgery of this war would be preserved for all time, and the education of future generations of military surgeons would be greatly assisted.

To help me in my work, hospital steward Schafhert and his son were assigned to duty with me. The elder Schafhert was an admirable bone cleaner and working anatomist. He had for a long time worked at the

University of Pennsylvania under Dr. Leidy, and was an adept in preparing and mounting specimens for a museum. We at once went to work. I obtained for him amputated arms and legs from the Washington hospitals, and afterwards from those in the neighborhood; these he cleaned, prepared and mounted, and very soon the first specimens, the initial preparations of our new museum were ready, and made their official appearance on the top of my desk, and on the shelves put up for the purpose in my rooms in the Surgeon-General's office, at first downstairs, and afterwards in the second-story room of the office on Pennsylvania Avenue, looking towards Riggs Bank. This room I afterwards relinquished to Medical Inspector General Perley, and was moved with my museum possessions into one or two of the small rooms of a second-story back building, on Pennsylvania Avenue, below the War Department, where quarters were assigned to Dr. Woodward and myself, then actually pushing on our medical and surgical histories of the war and compiling our reports of sick and wounded, a work demanding the services of many clerks.

Before long Mr. Corcoran's art building, which had been fitted up by him for a picture gallery, was seized or occupied by the Government and turned over to the Medical Department for the Museum, and a small appropriation (of $5,000 I think, and afterwards $10,000) was passed by Congress for the support and extension of the museum.

Corcoran's building was turned over to the Medical Department, June 1, 1867. The following were the orders, which may convey some idea of the manner of doing things in those days:

"SPECIAL ORDER NO. 116.

Headquarters, Mily. Dist. of Washington,<br>
Washington, D. C., May 22, 1863.

(Extract)

11.   The School House situated on H Street North between 13th and 14th Streets, owned by Mr. Corcoran is hereby taken possession of by the Government of the United States, and turned over to the Medical Department for the use of the Army Medical Museum.

By command of

MAJOR GENL. HITCHCOCK,<br>
JNO. J. SHERBORNE,<br>
Asst. Adjt. Gen.

Surg. Genl. Hammond."

"Surgeon General's Office,<br>
Washington City, D. C.,<br>
June 1, 1863.

Sir:—

The building known as Corcoran's School House near Dr. Gurley's Church, together with its outbuildings thereto, having been turned over to this department by order of Secretary of War, you will take charge thereof, and·make such alterations and repairs as may be necessary to fit it for the purpose of the army Medical Museum.   You will, however, avoid all useless alterations or expense.

Very respy. Yr. Obd. Servt.,

JOSEPH R. SMITH,<br>
Acting Surg. Genl.

Surgeon J. H. Brinton,
    Surgeon General's Office,
        Washington, D. C."

"War Dept. Washington City,
Sept. 1, 1863.
(Copy)

Col. J. H. Barnes,
  Medl. Inspector Genl.,
    Washington, D. C.

Colonel:—

The Secretary of War authorizes the transfer of the specimens from the room of the Surgeon General's Office, to the Museum newly selected.

Very respy. Yr. Obd. Servt.

(Signed) JAS. A. HARDIE,
  Asst. Adjt. Genl.

A true copy to
  Joseph K. Barnes,
    Medl. Inspector Genl."

From the above it will be seen that the museum specimens remained at the office of the Surgeon General under my immediate care (except medical specimens proper, under Assistant General Woodward's care), from the inception of the museum. I removed them to the Corcoran building, and was responsible for them and for the growth of the Museum during my stay in Washington.

Schafhert and his son who prepared the specimens were borne on the Surgeon General's roster of employees as hospital stewards, while soldiers, and men from the invalid corps, were detached as servants and additional helpers and orderlies. In the meantime, with the funds appropriated, I was enabled under the instructions of the Surgeon-General to fit up good cases for the rapidly growing collection. The doors locked with bronze hands, which slid bolts at top and bottom, modeled after the hands in the cases of my home office, originally belonging to Mr. George H. Boker, and bought by me from Dr. Chas. S. Boker, long after the war. These cases were gradually extended, until, before I left Washington in October, 1864, galleries had been erected, and the room or hall completely filled. The Museum, after Mr. Lincoln's assassination, was moved to Ford's Theater, and not long ago, I saw my old cases, altered, yet the same, still standing in the Army Museum, containing so many of the specimens once so familiar.

One of the first additions to the Museum, was an "Assistant Curator," I being then also officially curator, who should superintend the work on the specimens, and the recording of their histories, which was diligently done by clerks appointed from the Surgeon-General's office. Dr. Wm. Moss, who had entered the corps of Surgeon of Volunteers, was the first assistant curator, and on his resignation from the army, after his marriage, he was succeeded by my old student, Dr. Brinton Stone, who had become an Assistant Surgeon. Thus the Museum was cared for.

Any account of the Museum would be incomplete without some description of how the specimens were obtained, and gathered up, and by what system they passed from their original possessors to the Museum. First of all, the man had to be shot, or injured, to be taken to the hospital for examination, and in a case for operation, to be operated upon. If all this were taking place in a city hospital, or a permanent general hospital, the bones of a part removed would usually be partially cleaned, and then with a wooden tag and carved number attached, would be packed away in a keg, containing alcohol, whiskey, or sometimes salt and water.

186 Personal Memoirs of John H. Brinton

Then, when a sufficient number of specimens had accumulated, the keg would be sent to Washington and turned over to the Army Museum, where the preparations of the specimens would be finished, so that they could take their place upon the shelves. The memoranda or histories of these specimens would in the meantime have been forwarded to the Surgeon-General's Office, and after having been fitted to objects and their truthfulness assured, would be entered in the books of *Histories of Specimens,* preserved in the Museum, and under the care of the Assistant Curator.

One of the chief difficulties at this time, was that of procuring truthful and full histories of the specimens. When these were derived from hospitals, where the patient had been under observation, it was possible to obtain a history of the case, especially where the medical officer in charge of the hospital or bed felt a true professional interest in furnishing reliable data, and in contributing what he could to the common stock of surgical knowledge. It was one of my main objects in visiting the various hospitals, and generally the military medical centers, to develop as far as I could this interest in the Museum, to make its objects and tendencies known, and to lead all medical men, from the highest to the lowest, to know and be convinced that the formation, and foundation, of a great National Surgical and Medical Museum, was not for the collection of curiosities, but for the accumulation of objects and data of lasting scientific interest, which might in the future serve to instruct generations of students, and thus in time be productive of real use.

Many of our Army Surgeons entered into the scheme of the Museum with great zeal and earnestness, but some few there were, and these mostly the least educated, who failed to see its importance. But in the course of time a belief in the importance and value of the growing Museum spread throughout the army, and an active and faithful co-operation was elicited from the medical staff generally. The publication of the first catalogue in January exerted a good effect, and the opening of the Museum to the public, and especially to medical visitors, was not without its influence.

In the case of field hospitals, after great battles, it was at first difficult to get our system to work. The number of operations was so great, the medical force (I mean the intelligent skilled force), was comparatively so weak, and overworked, that it seemed at first almost impossible to obtain from them the preparations we desired. It was hard enough to be worked day and night in those great surgical emergencies, accompanying fierce and protracted battles, and it really seemed unjust to expect the rough preparation, necessary to preserve for the Museum, the mutilated limbs. These were usually buried in heaps. To overcome all these difficulties and to set an example, I visited frequently our battle-fields, as soon as the information was telegraphed to Washington. I then saw not only a great deal of active surgery, but I had the opportunity of showing practically to the operating surgeons, and to their assistant staffs, what it was that we really wanted, and how their part could be accomplished with the least amount of labor, and in the most satisfactory manner. Many and many a putrid heap have I had dug out of trenches where they had been buried, in the supposition of an everlasting rest, and ghoul-like work have I done, amid surrounding gatherings of wondering surgeons, and scarcely less wondering doctors. But all saw that I was in earnest and my example was infectious. By going thus from corps hospital to corps hospital, a real interest was excited as to the Museum work, and an active co-operation was eventually established.

Early in January, 1863, I published under Dr. Hammond's order, a small catalogue of the Army Museum up to that time, showing a collection of 1,349 objects, of which 988 were surgical, 106 medical and 133 extracted projectiles. This catalogue was as accurate as I could then make it. Its real object was to give credit to all medical officers contributing to the Museum. In fact, it did a great deal more; large numbers of preparations had accumulated in the Museum, the donors of which were not known. Very many specimens I had brought there from the battle-fields, collected by myself. These I put into the first catalogue, assigning them to such medical officers, as I could call to mind, and especially to those whom I knew to be lukewarm in Museum interests. The effect of the procedure was good.

Once established, the Museum was rapidly enlarged and extended. A section of models was established, of ambulances and litter, of horse and mule transportation of wounded, or transportation by railway and by boat, of hospital wagons and tents for the field, of tent hospitals, great and small, and of large general hospitals. All these were shown as found in different sections of the country, in the West and East, in the front, and in the rear of active operations.

The machinery to carry on the Museum was very simple. A full photographic outfit and the employment of a corps of artists was also ordered about this time, and did notable service in illustrating the museum specimens. Artists were obtained by enlistment as hospital stewards, and were assigned to duty in the Surgeon-

General's office at the best pay a headquarters' detail could give. I had at this time a topographical artist to draw the maps for the history of the war, one or two water colorists, who would also paint in oil rapidly if required, and the bone-preparers, the Schafherts, father and son. At a later period, just before I left the Surgeon-General's office, the services of one or two photographers were obtained, and a studio and workroom was established at the Army Museum building.

At this time the drafts ordered by the President had the effect of causing high local bounties to be ordered by the various counties and towns, throughout the "loyal" North. Thus a good artist could escape the hardships of a draft, pocket a large bounty, and insure a safe duty at high pay, by securing a place as "constructive" hospital steward in the Surgeon-General's office. To secure such talent, I was sent by the Surgeon-General to Philadelphia and New York, and by hunting around, I was so fortunate as to secure the men I wanted, after some little trial, and change. They were nearly all Germans, and although somewhat difficult to manage, and perhaps a little obstinate, discharged their duty faithfully.

As soon as the Museum was fairly established in its home, it began to attract attention. The public came to see the bones, attracted by a new sensation. Then, too, it often happened that officers and soldiers who had lost a limb by amputation would come to look up its resting place, in some sense its last resting place. I remember once seeing a florid-looking officer, a Colonel, I think, with a slight limp, busily hunting up a leg bone with a certain number, in the glass case. He evidently found what he wanted, and suddenly turning to a buxom-looking young woman at the other end of the room, he called to her in great glee, "Come here, Julia, come here,—here it is, my leg, No. ——, and nicely fixed up, too." And the daughter examined the specimen with much interest and apparent satisfaction. It was indeed, a nice, white shiny, varnishy preparation. I thought at the time that it would be very doubtful if the gentleman's remaining bones would ever make so creditable an appearance.

On another occasion, a soldier, a private, came, examined the Museum, and with the help of the Assistant Curator, found his amputated limb. It seemed to him his own property and he demanded it noisily and pertinaciously. He was deaf to reason, and was only silenced by the question of the Curator, "For how long did you enlist, for three years of the war?" The answer was, "For the war." "The United States Government is entitled to all of you, until the expiration of the specified time. I dare not give a part of you up before. Come, *then,* and you can have the rest of you, but not before." He went away silently, wiser, but not convinced.

So you see that even dry bones may be regarded from different points of view. Remember Mr. Dickens's immortal friends "Mr. Wegg," and "Mr. Venus."

I can recall many other strange scenes which occurred in the course of my search for specimens. In one case, I was informed of a remarkable injury of a lower extremity. The man had died with the limb on and had been carefully buried by his comrades. For some reason or other, that specimen was worth having, but his comrades had announced their determination to prevent the doctors from having it. However, I thought I would try what I could do, so I visited his mess mates, explained my object, dwelt upon the glory of a patriot having *part* of his body at least under the special guard of his country, spoke of the desire of the Surgeon-General to have that bone, with all such similar arguments I could adduce. My arguments were conclusive; the comrades of the dead soldier solemnly decided that I should have that bone for the good of the country, and in a body they marched out and dug up the body. I gravely extracted the bone and carried it off carefully; the spokesman of the party remarking gravely "that John would have given it to me himself, had he been aᵇle to express his opinion."

The preservation of these articles coming from so many sources, demanded a large supply of alcohol. Upon official application, it was ordered by the Secretary of War that all liquor confiscated by the Provost Marshal in the District of Columbia should be turned over to the Museum for anatomical purposes. As a result of this order, an enormous amount of alcoholic beverages was poured into the Museum, everything from champagne to the commonest rum. Our side lot was piled with kegs, bottles, demijohns and cases, to say nothing of an infinite variety of tins, made so as to fit unperceived on the body, and thus permit the wearer to smuggle liquor into camp. Of all this supply, Shafhert took charge. When the whiskey was strong enough for preservative purposes, he kept it in package; when it was not, it went into the still. This, under Schafhert's watchful care, ran incessantly, and furnished the Museum with a large amount of very fair alcohol, not only for putting up our specimens, but for furnishing the various depots in the Army where fresh specimens were being collected, so that they could be kept from decomposition, and reach the Museum in good condition. Our still was a success, occasionally it blew up, but never did any active harm. It was also used for the redistillation of sulphuric ether for cleaning bones, but this was a somewhat risky process. It was not very long before this transit of whiskey and alcoholic liquors was detected by the railroad men and military guards stationed on the railroad over which my kegs and barrels passed. I soon found that the barrels leaked, and much less whiskey reached the collectors in the army than was sent from the Museum in Washington. A process of tapping had been practised, and a careful investigation showed that the packages had been bored into, the contents sampled, and the holes plugged. This had evidently been repeated over and over again on a single trip, so I determined to take the matter in hand. A tempting and attractive barrel was selected, and filled with a fair article of whiskey. Into this I placed some tartar emetic and the keg started on its travels from Acquia Creek Station. Shortly afterwards I had occasion to pass over the road when I found from the various officers that a day or two previously a good many of the employees of the railroad had suffered from some stomach disturbance, nausea and vomiting. They said it was the water, of course. I had not put in too much tartar and emetic, just enough to act. After this, the barrels of the Army Museum were religiously respected, and ceased to leak. Years and years ago, but some time after this incident, I was making a small purchase from a sedate and respectable dealer in my own city. On hearing my name, he showed unusual interest in his new customer, inquired if I had served in the old war, if I had ever been stationed at Washington. Had I ever marched over the Acquia Creek railroad? Had I ever had anything to do with the Army Museum? Had I ever sent whiskey barrels over the road? And then he asked gently if any leakage had occurred? Was there ever any complaint? And then he admitted that he had heard that by a gimlet and pipe stem, a successful tapping of those barrels had been made. He seemed rather to admire the ingenuity shown. He admitted that on one or two occasions the whiskey was pronounced very bad.

Among our various lots of complicated liquor, occasionally we would get some very fine samples. I remember a lot of cherry brandy that I set aside for a special purpose. I was often sent at short notice to the Army of the Potomac with orders to reach certain points or headquarters far remote from the railroad terminus. It was difficult to procure a horse at these times, often impossible, and I was at the mercy of the quartermaster, who was not always obliging to a strange medical officer. Now the 5th Regular Cavalry was serving in this army. It was a most gallant and favorite command, and was usually near headquarters, which, most often, was my objective point. Somehow or other an understanding arose between their officers and myself that on my request at any time a trooper would be sent down to me as a guide, with a horse for myself to use during my stay, also an extra horse for luggage, which was understood to be a small keg of cherry-brandy. This tacit understanding soon became a fixed arrangement; it did me great good, and I trust did them no harm, and I am sure greatly facilitated public business.

During my stay in Washington, the Museum was greatly on my mind, and I did all I could to assist its growth and to unite the co-operation of all the medical officers I could reach. At first, it was looked upon somewhat doubtfully; many regarded it as a joke almost, but as time went on, it obtained a fine hold on the medical, official and congressional mind, and appropriations were annually made to it by Congress. The scope of the Museum, too, was enlarged. It was made to include models of nearly everything connected with military medicine,—thus, models of ambulances, litters, hospital cars, hospital knapsacks, medicine chests, operating-tables, and all the paraphernalia of field hospitals were obtained, as also full sets of bayonets, swords, projectiles of all kinds, field ammunition, and small arm projectiles, of which not less than eighty varieties were used during the war. These, when arranged, were not only ornamental to the hall of the Museum, but were calculated to be of great use in the study of gunshot and other wounds.

This Museum, which as I have stated, originated in the brain of Surgeon-General Hammond, became a success, and led up to much which was scarcely anticipated at its inception, such as a photographic gallery, and a bureau of art, in which colorists were employed for the reproduction of the various volumes of medicine and surgery, which afterwards for so many years were constantly issuing from the office of the Surgeon-General. At the formation of the Museum, the work was entirely in my hands, but as specimens of a medical sort began to arrive, that division of the undertaking fell to Assistant Surgeon J. J. Woodward, U. S. A., a man of acquirements, energy and quickness. He was, moreover, an excellent artist and microscopist. The remainder of the work, that which pertained to the surgery of the war was in my department.

# CHAPTER XV

The greater part of August, 1862, was spent by me in museum work, getting ready fixtures, etc., and on the 23rd I went to Philadelphia in discharge of these duties.

On the 26th of August, I received the following, sending me to Alexandria:

"Surgeon General's Office,
Washington, August 26th, 1862.

Sir:—

The Surgeon General directs that you report without delay to Surgeon J. Campbell, U. S. A. Medical Director, Military District of Washington, for duty in Alexandria, Va.

The duties to which you are especially assigned are those of Medical Director of Transportation, to inspect the means of transportation for sick and wounded soldiers, and supervise the arrangements made for their transportation to and from Alexandria and to and from the hospitals in that place. You will act as efficiently as may be in your power in conjunction with Surgeon Summers, U. S. A., to carry out the orders, which he has already received for the expansion of hospital accommodations in Alexandria. In performing your duties as Medical Director of Transportation, you will put yourself in communication with Medical Inspector General Parley, now with the Army of Virginia, and also with the necessary officers of the Quartermaster's Department.

Very respectfully Yr. Obdt. Servt.

By order of the Surgeon General,

JOS. R. SMITH,
Surgeon, U. S. A.

Dr. J. H. Brinton, Surg. of Vols."

It was just at this time that the series of battles were being fought between the army under General Pope and the Army of Northern Virginia, under General Lee. The Army of the Potomac had been withdrawn from Harrison's Landing on the James to Acquia Creek and to Alexandria, and the greater portion of it for the time, passed under the command of General Pope in conjunction with his own Army of Virginia, which had hastily been gathered together by the order of the President, June 27th, 1862. With these joint forces, General Pope had met, and had endeavored to hold in check, the Southern Army moving northward from Richmond under the direct command of General R. E. Lee. The fighting had continued during the latter days of August, during which the battles at Bristow, Manassas, Groveton, Chantilly, and elsewhere had occurred. These battles were often generally designated as the "Second Manassas" or "Second Bull-Run." As a whole the result was greatly against the United States troops, Pope with his command being gradually forced backwards to the fortifications of Washington.

At the time I arrived in Alexandria, the greatest confusion prevailed, vast numbers of wounded had found their way back to Alexandria, and the hospitals were filled to overflowing. Transportation to and from the battle-fields via Fairfax Station was deficient. I at once put myself in touch with the railroad men, and as many of the wounded as possible were brought in.

The battle-grounds were occupied by the enemy, and access to our captured hospitals was in a general way cut off. Finally, Medical Inspector Coolidge was allowed to pass within the enemy's lines, with certain supplies. Dr. Coolidge had, in ante-war times, been on terms of acquaintance with General Lee, and he made strenuous efforts to have such help as was possible, rendered to our wounded. Unfortunately, just at this time, a spirit of irritation existed among the Southern leaders, brought about possibly by unwise actions and orders of General Pope. The Confederate government had retaliated and issued orders, declaring that he or his commissioned officers were not entitled to be considered as prisoners of war, etc. The ordinary humane considerations as to the wounded were therefore unfortunately disturbed, and it became hence a matter of difficulty to render very efficient aid to our own wounded, who had been left on the field.

Our surgeons, it is true, had remained with their injured, but their medical supplies had been captured and largely used. In truth, one cannot blame the Confederate medical officers for laying hands on these hospital supplies, of which their own sick and wounded were so much in need. At last, by persistency and by personal influence, Medical Inspector Coolidge did succeed in obtaining from the Southern commander, an amelioration of the strictness of their order which for a while pressed so heavily upon our wounded of the "Second Bull Run."

From the reasons which I have thus given, it can

be understood that few, if any, regular ambulance trains were at first permitted to be run to the field. Those who came were those who could see to their own transportation, and it was astonishing how many could do this under the spur of capture and imprisonment by the enemy.

My work in preparation for, and the reception of, our poor fellows was incessant, and we were very short-handed. I see from my letters that for three nights and two days I could not lie down, but was on my feet, receiving and distributing the wounded as they arrived. The work was incessant and required some judgment and discretion in its performance. The boat transportation to Washington was miserably insufficient, nearly all the steamers were busy in bringing troops up the Potomac, and scarcely any were at the disposal of the Medical Department. I was particularly cautioned as to the character of the cases to be sent to Washington, and was instructed to see to this myself, which I did to the best of my ability,—and some queer characters of soldiers I met.

I remember as I stood at the gangway of a boat, passing the wounded on, that a queer, drunken, jolly Irish infantryman staggered up to me:

"And doesn't his honor, the Major, want a good guard to keep all these spalpeens off." His arm had been taken off at the shoulder joint, as I saw. "And, who are you?" I said. "Sure," he answered, "a poor Irishman, who had his arm cut off at Fairfax this morning, and who's walked all the way in with his gun and his knapsack, and who's managed to git a little drunk, as your honor sees, but who can all the same stand a good guard." So I put him on board for Washington.

It is almost impossible to convey an idea of the confusion and demoralization of everyone at and near Washington at that time. All had failed and defeat was everywhere; there seemed to be no one who could be trusted, no one who could make headway against our Southern enemy. From a military point of view, there seemed to be little hope. And such odd things were being done. One little trick of our Secretary of War, Mr. Stanton, I will refer to.

Whenever we were badly beaten and when popular feeling was dissatisfied, Stanton was in the habit, at his own instance, of issuing or peremptorily directing the issuing of, an appeal to the North, in the first place for lint and bandages, and secondly, for surgeons and nurses. As a natural result, the Surgeon-General's office would be flooded with boxes of linen scrappings and home-made bandages, which would be piled away in the stables and yards, or sent off where really not wanted, inasmuch as the articles themselves were usually not in shape or condition for issuance to hospitals, already usually fully stocked. Then, too, both doctors and nurses were most often of little use. Most were not competent; they were untrained, did not know what to do, or how to take care of soldiers,—still less could they take care of themselves. As for the women, sanitarians or nurse corps, they were terrible,—helpless, irritable and unhappy; each one thinking herself of much importance, and acting under the direct orders of the Secretary of War, and very often indeed they had seen him before starting. What to do with these poor women was indeed a problem. They would sit in your office, if you happened to be a Medical Director, by the hour at the time, each one with an enamelled leather bag between her feet, waiting to be sent somewhere, anywhere!

And the doctors were often not much better. Poor fellows, how sorry at times I have been for them. They would come down from their comfortable homes, full of desire to be useful, and it would be so hard to find real work for them. I remember particularly one gentleman from Philadelphia, coming to report to me at that dreary wharf at Alexandria, where I stood so long, and was so tired. He wanted to see some surgery that day and then to go back that evening to Washington. Surgery, I had none to show him, and for transportation, I could only show him a written order, forbidding me to allow a single civilian to leave Alexandria on a hospital boat, so great was the demand for sick transportation. However, I did break that order in his case and gave him food and transportation, and he has been at heart my enemy ever since. He thought I had neglected and had failed to appreciate him that day at Alexandria.

The town of Alexandria at that time was in a most defenseless condition. At first, the smallest force of the enemy could have captured it. Later, the troops of General Franklin's division or corps, arrived from the Army of the Potomac, and moved outwards on the Fairfax road, General McClellan's headquarters were for a short time in the town, and I saw something of the officers of his staff. There seemed then to be a very bitter feeling prevalent, antagonistic to General Pope, in fact, it almost appeared as if some were rather glad that he was being beaten, and there did not seem to be much activity in pushing forward to his assistance, nor much desire to do so. In the course of a few days, the transportation of wounded arranged itself, and I then was actively and pleasantly employed in assisting

Surgeon Sumners, U. S. A., in professional work at the Mansion House Hospital and elsewhere.

At this place one morning, a curious rumor passed around. It was that General Halleck had declared himself "Dictator," and that the army at Washington was satisfied that it should be so. As for those who were staying at Alexandria, or who were passing through, all seemed satisfied. I merely mention this idle rumor to show into what a state of doubt and want of confidence general opinion had lapsed. Halleck was often spoken of as the "Tycoon," but why, I cannot tell. He seemed big, he had a big head and a big hat, and was credited with brains.

It was generally supposed at this time that General Lee would advance northward, and try to pass through Pennsylvania and New Jersey toward New York on that campaign of invasion which he afterwards attempted and in which he failed. I for one believed that we were in a most perilous condition, and I see from my letters that I wrote to my Mother and sisters that, as they were at North Conway in New Hampshire, they had better stay there until matters should clear up a little, telling them, too, that if things got blacker, I would write what to do with our papers.

On the 9th of September, I returned to Washington to resume my work at the office.

# CHAPTER XVI

From the 9th to the 16th of September, 1862, I remained in Washington, busy at my office work, and
daily visiting the hospitals which were being established.
In fact, during my entire stay in Washington, I made
it a rule to see as much as possible of the work going
on in the hospitals. Later, when large hospitals were
established in every direction and readily accessible, I
made it a point to visit one hospital a day, especially
when the injured were being brought in from the front.

During this week, the Southern forces under General
Lee marched northward, fording the Potomac, and began the "Invasion of Maryland." On September 2,
1862, General McClellan was placed in command of all
troops near Washington and intended for the defence
of the Capital. His reinstatement was received by the
troops with the greatest enthusiasm, and the reorganization of the previously almost disintegrated Army of the
Potomac took place in the most miraculous manner.
The army crystallized instantly, as it were, and became
once more an efficient force. Then ensued a rapid pur-
suit of Lee, who had reached Frederick, the capital of
Maryland, which town, on General McClellan's approach, he evacuated, and entrenched his command on
and along South Mountain, and during the night encamped behind Antietam Creek. On the 15th of September, General McClellan advanced with his whole

army, which he drew up on the left bank of the creek, close to the southern lines. The 16th was spent in reconnoissance, and on the 17th was fought the famous battle of Antietam, as a result of which General Lee was driven across the Potomac back into Virginia. On the 18th of September, I received the following order:

> "Washington City, D. C.
> Sept. 18, 1862.

Sir:—

You will proceed without delay to Frederick, Md., to superintend the selection of specimens for the Pathological Museum, connected with this office. All medical officers are hereby ordered to give you any aid in their power to further this object.

> Very respectfully yr. obt. Servt.
> By order of the Surgeon General,
> (Signed)   JOS. R. SMITH,
> Surgeon, U. S. A.

Dr. J. H. Brinton,
  Surgeon of Volunteers, etc."

Most of the orders from the Surgeon-General, which were given me, sending me to the army in the field, were in this shape. The object was that I might be entirely untrammeled, and that I might visit any headquarters or hospitals, and yet be at perfect liberty to go or come as I wished, procuring material for the national collection, or literary material to be used in the preparation of the *Surgical History of the War*. Not infrequently, I received important verbal orders, the execution of which was the prime object of my being sent, as where, with an apparent "specimen" order, I was instructed to find out the loss after a battle, the extent of which a general commanding was not always desirous should reach the ears of a Secretary of War. An example or two of this I will give hereafter.

Immediately on the receipt of the last order I started for Frederick, Maryland. On reaching Monocacy, a few miles east from Frederick, Maryland, we found that the bridge over the stream had been destroyed by the enemy. We were consequently delayed here for some time, but finally reached Frederick. The largest of the hospitals here was under the care of Dr. Weit, U. S. A., afterwards so distinguished as a surgeon in New York, and here I saw much surgery, and met also my old friend Dr. Hewitt, whom I knew so well in the West.

I also met here the Surgeon-General, who had come down from Washington, bringing with him the Deputy Inspector General of the British Army, afterwards Sir William Muir, holding a position corresponding to that of our Surgeon-General. He had served long in the East and in China, and was a thorough soldier, and a very jolly old boy. He was as round as a barrel, with a fine bronzed soldierly face, quick in his manner, observant, and possessed evidently of a thorough military professional knowledge. By the Surgeon-General I was ordered to go forward to the headquarters,—"the front." This, I accordingly did, in an ambulance. Reaching Middletown on the South Mountain slope, I found a large number of wounded, who were being most efficiently cared for under the general supervision of my old friend Dr. William Thomson, U. S. A., an Assistant Surgeon. Hospitals had been improvised and the best done that was possible. I made a very short stay at this hospital depot, as I had learned that fighting on a large scale had been going on at the front at or near Antietam Creek. Pushing on, I arrived at the field of

Antietam. I reached there on the morning of the 19th of September, and was busily engaged for several days in visiting the various field hospitals. Of these there were very many.

During the battle, the Surgeons of the different divisions established their field hospitals in the farm houses with their barns and out-buildings scattered over the field of battle, which extends some six miles irregularly along Antietam Creek, at a distance, roughly, of three miles from the Potomac River, in some places a little more. As soon after the fighting as was possible, the wounded who were scattered over the vast area embraced by the battle-field and the space between it and the Potomac River, over which the Confederates retreated, were taken charge of. Those who were able to bear transportation were sent back to Frederick, and the great general hospitals in the rear. Those who could not bear transportation were gathered into the large general hospitals, which had been established, one upon the right near Keedysville, the Antietam Hospital, and another upon the left, the Locust Spring Hospital. The Confederate wounded who had been left in the neighborhood of Sharpsburg, and on the Antietam or eastern side of the Potomac, were also brought back with the surgeons left by their own people for their care. It was a long time before the vicinity of the Antietam battle-ground was entirely freed from the wounded, but in a word it may be said that those treated in hospital tents in the open air did well, better indeed than had they been placed in crowded city hospitals. The season of the year, the temperature, and the superb hospital organization were all in their favor.*

*For a map of the battlefield of Antietam and an excellent description of the surgical surroundings of the action, see Medl. and Surg.

During my visit to the field of Antietam, I had ample opportunity of visiting the many little gatherings of wounded, which had formed at the numerous farmhouses, over and adjoining the battlefield area. It was wonderful indeed to see how well the poor fellows were getting along. In many places, outhouses, barns, and stables were occupied by those most seriously injured, while those less seriously wounded lay upon the ground, sheltered quite satisfactorily by portions of tents, stretched blankets, boughs of trees, straw thatchings, loose boards or fence rails. The best of them would look after the cooking, and the water supply from streams or neighboring springs. They took care of each other, seeing to physical wants, and by cheerfulness and bravery, sustaining the spirits of those who might be dependent. Surgical aid was available from adjacent and more elaborately equipped hospitals, but as above described, a mere temporary refuge and help was made practicable, until these wounded could be moved backwards to organized field hospitals. The weather, fortunately, was clear, dry and moderate; so that in fact, there was much less suffering from exposure than is usually observed after great battles.

History of the Rebellion, Part I, Surg. V. Volume, Appended Documents, page 96, Antietam Campaign. By the way, I may add that this map and nearly all the other field hospital maps, etc., of great battles in that book, except the extreme southern campaigns, were prepared under my direction when stationed in the Surgeon-General's office in Washington. They were modified and reduced by an artist named Pohléos, from the topographical maps, and the position of the hospitals I usually had located by any medical inspectors or other medical officers, who might know the ground well. My name does not appear in any of this work, but it was designed by me, and much of it executed under my direct superintendence. Some was done by my successor after my departure from Washington.

In one of these little farm hospitals, I learned of the death of my cousin, Harrison White. He had enlisted as a private in Company B of the 28th Pennsylvania Volunteer Infantry Regiment, and had won the respect of his comrades by his good behavior. During the battle of Antietam, his regiment was heavily engaged, and his company wavering, Harrison sprang in front of his comrades, calling them to advance and crying, "Sergeant, let's show them the way." He fell, ten paces in front of them, mortally wounded. He lived, I think, until the next day, and was buried near the fence in the rear of a garden. His grave was shown to me, and I gathered some leaves and grass, and sent them to his Mother, with what information I could learn of his gallant death. It seemed to me a singular circumstance that one of the two first cousins should die a private in the ranks of the army commanded by the other.

During my stay at Antietam, I had an excellent chance of examining the battle-ground, and of studying more fully many incidents which I previously noticed elsewhere. Chief of these was the battlefield rigidity, the "instantaneous rigor," or rather the "rigor of instantaneous death." My observations on these subjects were published in Hay's *American Journal of the Medical Sciences,* page 87, January, 1870, and were largely noticed, and republished in the European medical journals. The most conspicuous and famed portion of the Antietam field was the "cornfield," and "sunken road" nearby. In this cornfield, which was fought over and over again, the fighting had been very fierce, and the musketry very hot. Dead bodies were everywhere, and one could scarcely walk without stumbling on one. I see that I have stated in print that in an area, fifty or sixty yards square, I counted forty dead bodies.

"Many of these," I said, "lay in extraordinary attitudes, some with their arms raised rigidly in the air, some with their legs drawn up and fixed. In not a few, the trunk was curved forward and fixed. These attitudes, in a word, were not those of the relaxation of death, but were rather, of a seemingly active character, dependent apparently upon a final muscular action at the last moment of life, in the spasm of which the muscles set and remained rigid and inflexible. The death in the majority of cases had resulted from chest wounds; in fewer instances, from shots through the head and abdomen. The latter were accompanied by considerable hemorrhage, as was evident from the pools of dark-colored blood by the side of the bodies. These examinations were made about thirty-six hours after death, and also later.

In the "sunken road" or "bloody lane," in which a strong stand was made, and the ground fiercely contested, I also noticed the body of a Southern soldier, of middle-age, of whom I speak in my report: "The body was in a semi-erect posture. One of the feet rested firmly on the ground, while the knee of the other leg, slightly fixed, pressed against the bank of earth, forming the side of a road. One arm extended was stretched forward, the hand resting upon the low breast work of fence rails, thrown up to protect the trench. His musket with ramrod halfway down, had dropped from his hand, and lay on the ground beside him. This soldier had evidently been killed while loading, and in the act of rising to his feet, probably for the purpose of observation, a ball had passed directly through the center of his head, and had emerged posteriorly."

In many similar instances, which I observed, the recipient of the death wound had been acting on the defensive and was actually kneeling at the time. I have, however, seen the same thing, although more rarely, in one who at the last moment of life had been in motion, progressing forward. I have also seen the same rigor in animals, and notably in the instance of a dead battery horse, killed on the road near Burnside's Bridge in the same battle. A bullet had passed directly through his forehead and he had remained on his knees, his head curved in air, semi-erect, rigid and unsupported. Two other horses killed at the same moment, lay on their back and side, the usual attitude of dead animals. The posture of the one to which I have particularly referred was very striking, and full of grace. He seemed an immense figure of black and bronze, with parts of the dead harness still lying loosely upon him. It was scarcely possible to believe him dead.

When I first passed over Antietam field, the scene was a busy one. Men were actively engaged in collecting the wounded, ambulances were hurrying to the rear, many of the slightly wounded were staggering hospital-wards, and burial parties were busy digging long burial trenches. The evidences of the battle were everywhere, bullet marks on corn, twigs, and fences, trees shattered in their trunks, and the dead scattered far and wide. In a day or so, visitors and the friends of the injured thronged to the field.

During my stay in Keedysville, the central hospital point, I was ordered by the Surgeon-General to ride to the Potomac to see the field hospitals of the enemy. This I did, and found them scattered along the Potomac River, in the rear of a position which they had held. At one of these hospitals, the one near to Sharpsburg, I found an old student of Dr. DaCosta and myself. His name was Dr. Dennis, and he had been attached to Stonewall Jackson's command. From him I learned many interesting facts, and began to appreciate that there are always two parties in a campaign or battle,— you, and your opponents, and also this fact which General Grant has so well brought out in his personal memoirs,—that, although you may feel frightened at your position, you must always bear in mind that sometimes your opponent is as frightened as yourself; this, apropos of the fact, that while the Union forces were trembling in their boots at Stonewall Jackson's boldness, his troops were disturbed lest their very boldness might lead to their being cornered and caught. Dr. Dennis told me, "Doctor, if you had only been a little sharper, you might have had us all."

When near the Potomac, I wandered along the cliffs above the Maryland bank. There, I met an officer of an infantry regiment, tall, thin and very wet. "How do you do, Doctor?" said he. "Very well," said I, "but I don't recollect you; who are you?" "Why," he replied, "don't you know me? I have sold you many a book. I used to be a salesman at Lindsay & Blakiston's medical bookstore in Philadelphia, and if I hadn't been a —— fool, I would have been there yet." He seemed so upset, that I inquired into particulars, when he told me that he held a Lieutenant's commission in the 118th Pennsylvania Infantry, which had been raised by the exertions of the merchants of the Philadelphia Corn Exchange; that his regiment had been ordered over the river to see if any of the rebels remained there, and had found them and had been subjected to a terrific fire from a Southern brigade, who suddenly appeared from behind a tow path, or natural defence of the ground, and were driven back to the northern side of the river in the greatest confusion, and with heavy loss. "So, here I am," added the speaker, "but many of my company have been left on the ground behind."

General Lee made a narrow escape with his army after the battle of Antietam. Had General McClellan advanced, the Southern troops would in all probability have in good part been captured. As I was passing over the field, on this very morning, I met a young United States officer, moving forward alone. I spoke to him, some commonplace of the fight; "Ah," said he, "if General McClellan could only realize how in every hour's delay, he is losing a lifetime of glory."

I often wondered at General McClellan's unexplained inactivity after Antietam, but within a month of this writing I was told by General Ruggles, a patient of mine, that he had seen a dispatch of Halleck to McClellan, or had been told of it by McClellan, in which General Halleck positively directed McClellan not to advance, or make any offensive demonstration, but to remain quiet, and hold his own, and above all things to remember that any incautious attempt to follow, or to flank Lee, would uncover Washington, and risk the safety of the President, the Capitol, and the Nation. I have no doubt from the positiveness of General Ruggles' assertion, from his official position, and his intimacy with General McClellan, that his statement to me embodied the truth.

The Surgeon-General and his guest, Deputy Inspector-General Muir of the British Army, spent some little time at Keedysville, in the rear of McClellan's headquarters. The village hotel was kept by a very clever fellow, who had an exceedingly attractive little wife, at least so the British Inspector thought, for he insisted on paying special attentions to her, much as would have been his manner to a British barmaid. A division of our troops marched past, at the time, and I recall the inspector leaning out of the hotel window with his arm around the hostess's waist, much to the husband's chagrin, and to the evident astonishment of the young woman, who saw that no indelicacy was meant, but still felt that the custom was as yet foreign to Maryland good manners. But the Briton stuck to his post with soldier-like pertinacity.

It was just at this time that the regimental bands had been diminished in number, and in many cases discontinued. Our men marched past well, but still a little languidly, for they were tired, and I recall Muir saying to me, "It may be more economical, and perhaps it may be wise, to stop the music, but then a little strain would make the men step up, and make their heels come forward"; and I must say, I thought so too.

Taking it all in all, the struggle at Antietam was a typical battle, fought in the open; it was typical also as showing how the Americans fight, no matter where from. Every foot of ground was fiercely contested, and when either party gave way, it was before a crushing force of men or fire. It was a fight of which neither of the contesting armies need be ashamed; but each with truth, might be proud of the other.

By the 26th of September, 1862, I had returned to Washington and set myself busily at my proper work, the *Surgical History of the War,* and the collection of material for the Museum.

# CHAPTER XVII

After the battle of Antietam, the Army of the Potomac remained on the north side of the Potomac, and then crossed into Virginia towards the end of October. On the 7th of November, General McClellan was relieved from his command which was then assumed by General Burnside. On the 17th of November the army marched for Fredericksburg, and by the 20th, a large force had reached Falmouth on the north bank of the river, directly opposite to Fredericksburg. By the 10th of December, the entire army was concentrated on the north bank of the Rappahannock. During this night, and the following day, boats were placed in position and with the pontoon bridges thus formed under a heavy fire of the enemy, the army crossed the river, occupying the greater portion of the city, while that part farthest from the river remained in the enemy's hands.

On the 13th, the fierce fight of the "First Fredericksburg" occurred. General Burnside with all his force, having crossed the Rappahannock and occupied the town, advanced against General Lee, who had marched his forces along the hills on the southwest of the town. In spite of the most heroic efforts, the assault failed completely, the United States troops were repulsed and fell back to their position, as occupied on the morning of Saturday the 13th of December, 1862.

A report of what was going on at the army front reached Washington while the battle was raging, and on that evening, I was despatched with the Surgeon-General to army headquarters. I reached there on the morning of the 14th, Sunday, and immediately crossed on the pontoon bridge. The court-house, churches and other large buildings were occupied temporarily as hospitals. Very many of the wounded had already, that is during the night of the 13th and the morning of the 14th, been sent across the bridge to their respective corps and division hospitals, on the high ground lately occupied by the army in the rear at Falmouth, and along the Acquia Creek and railroad. Here, I ought to state that Acquia Creek landing on the Potomac River, about ten miles from Fredericksburg, was a base of supplies for the army, and that a railroad connected the two points. If I remember rightly, the road at this time was under the able supervision of Mr. Frank Thomson.* Communication with Washington and transportation for the wounded, and for military purposes, was thus comparatively easy, and very great numbers of wounded were readily, and in comparative comfort, carried to the hospitals at Washington, or to points farther north. Large tent hospitals had also been established at Acquia Creek and at Potomac Creek, at or near the railroad crossing.

My duty at Fredericksburg, at this time, was to help in every way those who were caring for the wounded, and at the same time to look after the interests of the Museum. Dr. Moss, who was then assistant curator of the Museum, had accompanied me, and was very busy gathering up specimens to be taken up to Washington for preparation and preservation. The court

*Afterwards President of the Pennsylvania Railroad.

house hospital was in the centre of the town. The operating-table was placed in the court-room and a great many operations were performed. During the afternoon, if I remember rightly, of Monday the 15th, all operations were discontinued and the hospital appointments were removed. Very shortly after this was done, a shell exploded in the court-room, just where the operating-table had stood, and everything was turned topsy-turvy. Fortunately no one was in the room at the time. Had this occurred the day before, or in the morning, while the operations were going on, a good many of us would have come to grief.

It must be remembered that all of the time during which we occupied Fredericksburg, the town, in one sense, was at the mercy of the enemy. It was completely at the mercy of the heavy guns, planted above and below the town; at least I heard they were heavy guns and at all events they were efficient batteries.* The pontoon bridge was completely under their fire.

Occasionally a shell or two would be fired into the town or at the steeples of the churches, or at the bridge, but in the main we were allowed a quiet possession. The scene was a busy one, the town was full of our soldiers, many bivouacked in the streets and yards and grounds, ambulances were moving to and fro, and a long trail of wounded were constantly passing toward the bridge. I slept my first night in the basement lecture or Sunday-school room of a church in the centre of

*The Confederate Artillery at Fredericksburg was very efficient and that portion commanding the city was commanded by that great artillerist General E. P. Alexander, who stated to Lee before the battle opened that he could with his guns "Rake those fields as with a fine tooth comb and that a chicken crossing them could not live."—E. T. S.

the town. It had a tall steeple, and this had been occupied by one or two men of our signal corps. When I say occupied, I mean that a rope had been thrown over the apex of the steeple, and that a man or two had been drawn up and sat there, high in the air, indicating by the movements of little flags what they saw within the enemy's lines, or conveying orders by telegraph to our commanders. Finally, their movements were observed by the enemy, and their perch became at once a target. It was a nice shot, but finally the Southern cannoneers got the range and one of their shot passed directly through the steeple, just above the attachment of the ropes, which held up the eyrie of the signal men. Evidently the latter dreaded the next shot, for they descended with great rapidity and skill, to the great delight of the onlooking soldiers below. So they escaped, but the Southerners became, and continued suspicious of the steeple, and every now and then turned their attention towards it.

Early, very early in the morning, I was awakened from my comfortable nap in the basement (I had arranged two benches with great dexterity as a bed), by a crashing sound, and a general jar and concussion. I went into the yard to see what had happened, and found some soldiers looking up at the steeple. They pointed out to me with great glee, how another shell, a big one, had also gone through the steeple, not quite so high up.

And here I saw a good example of a soldier's recklessness or stupidity. A squad were about getting their breakfast, and the man whose duty it was to light the fire had just found a nice piece of pine board, the top of a box. Desiring to split this, he had set upright an unexploded percussion shell, twelve inches long, with a brass screw percussion point upwards. I caught him in the very act of raising his board, to bring it down with all his force. I pushed him over, to his great surprise and indignation. Had I been a moment later, and the shell a live one, which I believe it was, this history might never have been written. A somewhat similar instance occurred after Antietam. Two soldiers walking in the turnpike found a shell, which had been fired. One said to the other, "John, there are two kinds of shell; one goes off by a fuse like a fire-cracker, and the other explodes when it strikes its point; that's what they call a percussion shell; I'll show you this one." And then he held it carefully point downwards and dropped it on the turnpike bed. It *was* a percussion shell,—did explode,—and but one mangled man was left to tell this anecdote.

I remember my breakfast on that morning. Dr. Moss and I had found a little flour and we chartered an old negro woman whom we had discovered hidden away in the cellar of an old mansion house, to make us some cakes. "Lor, Massa, flour a'int no good widout them oder things"; but we persisted, and such a dismal mess! I have never eaten any cake since without thinking of this. Later we saw a solitary rooster stalking along. We were very hungry, and ideas of spring chicken flitted through our brain. We consulted dear old Dr. Cuyler, who happened to be with us. "He (the chicken), *might* do," he said. So we started a darkey boy after him, for he was a wary chicken, but the darkey caught him and killed him, and we later tried to eat him, but our failure was dismal. He might have lived in the time of the Revolution.

In passing through Fredericksburg, I was much struck by the real effect of the cannonade. Both before and during the placing of the pontoons, the town had been subjected to a heavy plunging artillery fire from many of our guns, placed on the elevated northern bank of the river, Stafford Heights. The shot had gone everywhere, and had struck many buildings, and yet, save the presence of the shot holes, there did not seem to have been a very great amount of damage done. The buildings were still standing. There had not been much injury by fire. Interiors had been somewhat disturbed, but considering all the circumstances of the cannon fire, there did not seem to be a great deal to show for it. I saw one queer sight, of a room, a small one, in which a shell had burst in a feather-bed just after its occupant had risen and left the room. The effect of the explosion was extraordinary, the entire surface of the room, walls and ceiling alike were coated or plastered with adherent feathers; one could not but wonder how and why they stuck.

It was difficult for me at that time to understand why the town, when we were in it, was not more heavily bombarded, and why the pontoon bridge was not destroyed. The position of the commanding batteries was such, that it would have been an easy matter to have rendered the passage of the bridge by us difficult and dangerous. It may be, however, that the enemy, confident in their position, wished to have as many of the United States troops as possible on the south side of the river, and courted an assault, in the confidence of the impregnability of their position, a series of slopes, leading up to steep hills, defended by strong works and heavy batteries. They unquestionably had every reason to resist and repulse an assault, and I suppose that they believed that in the event of another unsuccessful effort on our part, and a retreat in confusion, they would be able to capture or destroy our entire force. I went out toward our picket lines, to see the field, and I know that from what I saw, and from what I was told, I was very much impressed with the enemy's strength, and with our weakness of position. It did not seem to me a military possibility for an attacking force to be able to make headway against a brave enemy, so favorably located, and I think that at that time our men felt so too.

I recall a funny incident, illustrative of the peculiar humor of the American soldier. The bridge of boats between Fredericksburg and Falmouth was guarded on the Falmouth side by sentries to prevent unauthorized passage. On the afternoon of the battle, a straggler hastily crossing was halted by the sentry on the friendly bank, and informed that he could not pass without permit or orders. "Not pass! Not pass!" exclaimed the astonished man. "Indeed, you must let me pass, I must get across, for I assure you that I am the most demoralized man in the whole of the Army of the Potomac."

The American soldier, or let me say, the American citizen volunteer, is a reasoning sort of animal; he knows just as well as his commander, and sometimes better, when he can advance, and when he can fall back; in other words, when he can win, or when he must lose. More than one battle in our war was "the men's fight."

As I saw our troops in front of Fredericksburg, there was little shelter for them, except in their distance from the enemy's guns, and our advance lines and pickets were flat on the ground, covered by such scanty protection as they could scrape together, yet exposed to the fire of the enemy from their well-constructed rifle pits, on higher ground. As a consequence of the supine position, some of our men received strange ranging wounds, with remote and singular points of entrance and exit.

In consequence, too, of the openness of the battle-ground, and of its exposed position, it had been a difficult matter to remove the wounded, and yet so admirably had the ambulance department, and the field hospital been arranged by the skill and forethought of the Medical Director of the Army of the Potomac, Surgeon J. Letterman, U. S. A., and so efficient were the medical officers and the attendants, that during the night following the battle, all of the wounded were taken off the field of battle and carried to the near hospitals. This demanded great bravery and determination on the part of the ambulance corps, since every movement had to be made in the dark, a glimmer of light sufficing to draw the enemy's fire. By the night of the 14th (Sunday), most of the serious operations and dressings had been performed. During that night, it was whispered that on the 15th (Monday) all of the wounded would be removed, as it was the intention to withdraw the army away from the town to the northern bank of the river. On the afternoon of the 15th, I encountered Dr. Moss, my assistant, bringing with him an immense number of surgical specimens for the Museum, some of these in boxes, which we sneaked over in the wagons; the remainder were carried in great bags on the backs of one or two very black negroes. Just as we reached the northern bank, one or two shots passed over the bridge, Dr. Moss, who was somewhat philosophically inclined, remarking, "What a blessed escape, for what a wretched ending it would have been to one's life, to have been swept into the river on an ignominious retreat, holding onto a bag of bones." I know that we made very good time on that bridge, and I felt greatly relieved as I climbed the river bank on the crooked road near the Lacy House.* On the night of the 15th of December (Monday) the army was withdrawn from Fredericksburg to its old position. I might add that after the wounded were brought away from the town, the city was carefully searched by medical officers, to see that none were left behind.

From this time, and during the next ten days, the disabled were sent as rapidly as possible on the railroad to Acquia Creek, and thence by boats to the general hospital at Washington and elsewhere. I do not think too much praise can be accorded Medical Director Letterman and his assistants for the wonderful manner in which the wounded in this battle were removed, cared for, and transported northwards.

For a day or two, I remained at the headquarters of the army, living at the hospital. Here I saw a great deal of surgery and had many pleasant experiences. I remember when I first went there, and before I had arranged my means and quarters of living, meeting one who at that time was regarded as a great philanthropist. In my judgment he was a great humbug and hypocrite and did not afterwards turn out very well. However, when I met him, he welcomed me warmly after his way, "So glad to see you, so glad, and how are you?" "Hungry," said I, "very hungry." "How fortunate, how very fortunate!" he added, "I have brought down

---

*This fine old residence, a long low mansion situated on the Stafford Hills just across the Rappahannock, was better known as "Chatham," and, if I correctly remember, was frequently visited by both Washington and Lee. On account of its associations, Lee instructed his artillery not to damage it. I saw one good sized solid shot imbedded in the back wall near the roof when I visited the old place in 1903.—E. T. S.

two fine turkeys." Here I felt myself warming up. "Two fine turkeys, for Willie Averill's dinner, but I've left them in Washington. Good-bye, take care of yourself."

Somewhere around this time, Dr. Hammond, the Surgeon-General visited at the headquarters' camp. I think I then saw him at his best. His troubles had not yet come upon him. Big, burly and genial, proud of his high position in the army, full of professional feeling, and anxious to develop good feeling in the medical corps, he looked and acted the Surgeon-General. He took also a great professional interest in the cases before him, and insisted upon operating himself, doing one or two operations fairly well, notably an elbow excision. He was, moreover, well pleased with the medical arrangements, the hospital organizations, and the ambulance corps.

I returned to Washington about the 19th of December, and was immediately at my old work. Specimens were now accumulating at the Museum. Very soon after my arrival, I sent Dr. Moss down to the army for more. By this time, the surgeons generally were becoming interested in the Museum project, and were taking pains to get and preserve what they could for the collection.

# CHAPTER XVIII

I have not yet spoken of the Medical Inspectors. The grade of Medical Inspector was established by the Act of April 16, 1862. These officers were to be eight in number, each with the rank, pay, and emoluments of a Lieutenant-Colonel of Cavalry. There was also to be a Medical Inspector-General with the rank and pay of Colonel. For this office, Dr. Perly, who was some congressman's relative or friend had been selected. I at first thought I would have been one of the Medical Inspectors, but the appointments were made by political influence and not according to the standing of the man upon the roll of surgeons of their respective Staff Corps. About this time, Dr. Hammond told me that he would nominate me for one of the positions, but I declined, not being willing to enter into any political struggle, and being well satisfied with what I had already acquired.

I had now begun to make a few valuable friends in Washington. If I remember rightly my first start in this direction was through Dr. Coolidge, who was appointed one of the new Medical Inspectors. He was a surgeon in the old army and had seen a good deal of service. He was a man of culture, of good heart, and of a most kind and gentle manner. I grew to know Dr. Coolidge well, and in fact, late in the war, I became intimate with him. After I left the army, he was stationed in Philadelphia, and when he was sent away, he left with me many of his books for safe-keeping. Dying, shortly afterwards, these volumes were sent to my old friend, his widow, who at that time was living in New England. Among the books was a complete set of United States Army Registers, back to and including revolutionary times. But two complete sets were in existence, this one of Dr. Coolidge's and one belonging to the late General Folten, Engineers Corps, U. S. A. In the War of 1812, when the British burned the Government buildings at Washington, all the official registers were burned. As far as known, these two sets were the only private complete ones. After Dr. Coolidge's death, I notified the Surgeon-General's library of the existence of this complete register. Dr. Coolidge's wife had been a Miss Morris, one of a navy family, and it was her brother, Lieutenant George M. Morris, who commanded the *Cumberland*, in the absence of Captain Radford, when she was sunk with her flag flying, at Hampton Roads, by the rebel *Merrimac*, March 8, 1862. Mrs. Coolidge was very kind to me, and presented me to the family of Captain Wilkes, so well known in the "Trent" affair, and thus I was introduced by one person to another, until I had formed a very pleasant circle of acquaintances, among the old Washington people, who antedated the political people of the day,—but all this took time.

I had hoped to be able to spend my Christmas at home this year of 1862, but affairs at Washington were so urgent, that I was not able to do so. So I spent my holiday season at Washington, feeling lonely enough, for I had been away from home for two Christmases; the week passed, however, and then came New Year's Day. New Year's Day at Washington was the day of the year, the gala day. Everyone, every official, feels it his duty to dress up in his finest toggery, and to pay his respects to the President of the United States, and from him downwards to all chiefs of lesser magnitude. First of all, the members of the diplomatic body go in state and full dress to pay their respects, then in turn comes the army and navy in full dress, then the civil service, and so on, and last of all, the general public. And this was the state programme. Let me speak of my own department, *"quorum pars (minima) fui."*

At ten o'clock or thereabouts, we officials of the Surgeon-General's office, met at the office in full, big full uniform, sword, belt and sash, and if one had them, cocked hat and epaulets, although, as these were war times, the cocked hat and epaulets might be dispensed with. However, we made quite a show and followed our chief, meeting the officers from the War Department, and officers in garrison, and in fact, officers in general, and in we filed, the General commanding the army leading, and solemnly we marched past the President, as he stood, long, lanky and plain-looking, in the big room (I think the east room) of the White House. I do not think that it crossed my mind that never man had greater work to do, or did it better, or left a nobler name to after ages. He bowed to each one of us as we passed, and then we dispersed for a little while through the rooms. The scene was a brilliant one, shining uniforms were everywhere, and there was a certain quaintness to an American eye in the strange court dresses of the diplomatic corps, who had lingered to see the military and navy reception.

On the 4th of February, I was sent down hurriedly to visit the general hospital at Annapolis, Maryland, to report upon the cases of hospital gangrene said to be there. I accordingly went, and found that a number of such cases had occurred.*

They were all Union soldiers who had been wounded, and had fallen into the enemy's hands, and had recently been exchanged, and brought up by steamers from City Point, Va. Many of them had been confined in the wretched Libby Prison and were filthy and almost starved. They had, however, begun to improve as soon as they arrived north, and were placed under healthy and more favorable surroundings. A great deal has been said about these cases by the different civil commissions, who were often disposed to find fault unjustly with the medical department of the army, and to arrogate to themselves credit to which they were not entitled. In the latter part of the month of February, I was again sent down to Annapolis on the same errand, and found that proper and satisfactory arrangements had

* ORDER.

"Surg. Genl. Office,
Washington, February 4, 1862.

Sir:

Reliable information has been received at this office that hospital gangrene is prevailing to a considerable extent at the Genl. Hospt. at Annapolis, Md. You will, on this, immediately proceed to that city, and inquire into the origin of the affection in question, and the means which have been adopted for its treatment, and for checking its progress, making in your report such suggestions as may seem proper. You will confer with the Surgeon in charge on these points. You are hereby authorized to call upon the Surgeon in charge for such present and future reports, as in your opinion may tend to elucidate the whole subject. I have the honor to be,

Very respfty,

W. A. Hammond,
Surgn. Genl.

To Surgeon J. H. Brinton, U. S. V.
Washington, D. C."

been made for all hospital gangrene cases, which were
doing well.

On March 28, 1863, I received an order to investigate
hospital gangrene in Louisville and Nashville. I immediately started for Louisville, and on arriving there
on the evening of April 2nd, I went to the Galt House,
a hotel filled to overflowing with officers and military
personages. I then called upon Dr. Middleton Goldsmith and found him to be a man of extraordinary
attainments and energy. He had at that time many
cases of hospital gangrene under his care. The hospital
impressed me most favorably. It was very large and
seemed to be managed in an original manner, and to
be replete with all kinds of ingenious devices. I was
particularly struck with the manner of making coffee.
The water percolated through a series of large tanks,
the first one being placed near the ceiling, and the last
one on the floor. The entire strength of the coffee was
by these means extracted, and none was wasted. Dr.
Goldsmith was, I believe, the first who used bromine
in the treatment of hospital gangrene, and sloughing
sores. Its effect, when thoroughly applied, seemed to
me at the time almost marvellous. It acted locally
to check the spreading gangrene, and the constitutional
symptoms at once underwent a change for the better.
I saw one case of a man with hospital gangrene, extending on the right leg from the hip to the ankle, the
tissues having been eaten away to great depth. The
man was etherized, and the bromine (pure) most thoroughly applied, and rubbed into every point. His constitutional state was very low, and he seemed very
feeble. On the morrow when I saw him, he was
propped up in bed in a semi-sitting posture, and presented a marvellous change. He was in good spirits

and hopeful, his only complaint was that he had not had enough to eat at breakfast.

The victims of this disease were horrible creatures to look at. Starvation, disease and exposure had done their worst, and contributed to the development of this horrid hospital gangrene,—the "pourriture de l'hospital" so familiar to Larrey, and so well described by Hennen, in his account of the Peninsular War, and which was especially observed at the siege of Badajos. The cases of gangrene at Louisville resembled strongly those which I had seen at Annapolis, Md., only they seemed to be worse; they probably had been exposed more in the prison pens of the South, and had been subjected to a prolonged land transportation.

At Louisville, Dr. Goldsmith was very kind to me, and took me around to see every person and everything to be seen, and thus my stay in Louisville was made very pleasant. After remaining a few days in this city, and after having fully inspected the gangrene cases, I determined in virtue of my discretionary orders, to go to Nashville, and examine the condition of affairs there. The Louisville and Nashville Railroad was at that time a military road. It was strongly guarded by troops at intervals of a few miles, but it was at all times exposed to guerrilla incursions; it was passable but not safe. Nashville itself was thoroughly garrisoned.

I made my start accordingly on a fine morning, but had a narrow escape on my way. I was standing on the rear platform of a car, smoking, when suddenly I observed the car behind, which was coupled to that on which I stood, jumping from side to side in a strange manner. Instinctively, I backed against the car door, and staggered within; as I did so the platform of my car disappeared and with the rear car attached to it, rolled down the bank. I pulled the bell rope, the train stopped and slowly backed to the place of the accident. We then found that the car at fault had jumped the track at a cattle guard (a sort of gridiron of logs at road crossings to keep cattle off the track) had rolled down the embankment, and was lying wheels upward on the slope. Most of the passengers (military) had been thrown out and scattered around. One of these, Surgeon James Bryant, U. S. Vols., occupied a very peculiar position. He was apparently planted head downwards in the dirt of the embankment, and there he stayed. I will not say stood, for his heels were upright in the air, a sort of inverted pillar, unconscious, or at all events, greatly dazed. Fortunately when they picked him up he was found not to be very seriously hurt.

I ran back on the train to Louisville, with one or two of the injured, and on the next train started again for Nashville. Morgan, or some other guerilla leader, threatened the road at this time, and made travelling somewhat precarious. As we went down, we learned at one station (I think it was a place called Elizabeth), that a band of guerillas had just passed, pushing on to a point three or four miles ahead to a place or road crossing, eminently eligible for ambushing and stopping a train, and that our train was their object. So it was a race for this point. We put on all speed, and passed the critical road crossing as the band of mounted irregulars appeared on the road over the top of the hills. The railroad speed was good, faster than I would care to travel often.

As I approached the bridge at Nashville over the Cumberland River, it presented a very military appearance, heavily stockaded, looped for musketry, and pro-

vided with cannon in embrasures. Arrived in the city,
I went to the prominent hotel, and spent the succeeding
two days in visiting the hospitals and carrying out my
instructions. I was kindly taken care of by Surgeon
Thurston, U. S. Vols. Nashville at this time as a garrison town presented a busy appearance, contrasting
strongly with the same town, as I had seen it on the
first day of its occupancy by General Nelson, when I
had gone up with General Grant after the capture of
Fort Donelson. Then, it seemed a deserted city, all
doors were closed and windows barred, shops were shut
and scarcely anyone was in the streets. Fear was everywhere, and it seemed as if those in town sat in dread
of an expected massacre. While at Nashville, I took
the opportunity of going down to Murfreesboro. Here
a battle had been fought about January 1, 1863, General Rosecrans commanding the Union forces. The
fight is known as the battle of Stone River, and the
Union success (or rather the salvation of the army),
was in some measure owing to the good conduct of the
forces under General Sheridan. In passing along the
street of the town, I met Sheridan, whom I had not
seen since I left him at camp at general headquarters
before Corinth in 1862. He was then only a Captain
in the quartermaster's department, but now, when I
met him at Murfreesboro, he had achieved the rank of
Brigadier-General, with a favorable and spreading reputation. He was very kind in manner to me, and I was
glad to have seen him. At this time, at our meeting in
Murfreesboro, General Sheridan, speaking of himself,
said to me, "Doctor, a pretty rapid rise, isn't it? Three
(or four) from a Captain, to a Brigadier-General, and
I mean to deserve it, too."

About the 12th of April I reached Washington, hav-

ing returned by way of Philadelphia, of course. After
making my report of my trip, and of hospital gangrene,
and its treatment in the West by bromine, I busied
myself with my office duties until the early part of
May, when I received an order to proceed to the headquarters of the Army of the Potomac, and report to
Surgeon Letterman, for special duty connected with
pathological specimens, and thereafter to return to my
duties in Washington.

So on the 5th of May I left with my hospital stewards. Stanch was a German water-color painter. He
had enlisted, tempted by the bounty, or to avoid the
draft, and had immediately been detailed on this special
duty as water colorist at the Surgeon-General's office.
Schafhirt was the bone artist, the son of Schafhirt who
prepared the specimens at the Museum, and who had
originally been an assistant or workman in the dissecting room of the University of Pennsylvania. Stanch's
duty was to paint sketches of such wounds and injuries as I might indicate, while Schafhirt was to assist
me in the collection of specimens for the Army Museum,
that is, to bring away the bones fractured by gunshot,
or cannon projectiles, mostly obtained from the amputated limbs, which accumulated at the operating-tables
in the various hospitals, general, division, corps or field,
which I might visit.

At first I had experienced much difficulty in obtaining
the necessary permission from surgeons, but by this time
they had become interested, and were anxious to furnish all they could to the national collection. As the
preparations were finished, or rather the limbs, etc., I
had them roughly cleaned (most often I was obliged to
do this myself), and then I had them placed in barrels,

with liquor, and so sent or took them with me to Washington.

Before I left, rumors of a decided victory for the Union army had been rife in Washington. On the boat to Acquia Creek, I met and traveled with my old friend, Dr. Thomson, then Assistant Surgeon. We noticed as we approached Acquia Creek, the depot of the railroad and the camp in Fredericksburg, that all the indications were that our army had suffered reverses. On the same train with us were the President, Mr. Lincoln; and General Halleck, the General Chief of the Army. My impression was that they were in an empty baggage car in which two wooden chairs had been placed for them. This visit was unexpected and they were on their way to headquarters to see for themselves what had happened. They were provided with a special ambulance from the station, and started campward. Dr. Thomson and I also went up in an ambulance of the Medical Department. The distance, only a mile or so, was soon passed over, but we arrived long before the great dignitaries. When they did get out, Mr. Lincoln's tall silk hat was creased by knocking against the top of the vehicle as if he had sat upon it. Their delay was caused by having been brought by a much longer wagon route, so as to furnish time for some slight moral cleansing of the headquarters' camp—at least, so we were told.

The battle of Chancellorsville had been fought and the Union Army had again retreated to the Falmouth side of the river. We, in other words, had suffered a defeat, but the enemy had sustained an irreparable loss in the death of Stonewall Jackson, who was wounded on the 2nd of May and died about a week afterward. I think he was their ablest general and, with his fall, fell the Southern cause.

Having finished my work at the hospitals and having collected what specimens I could and seen what surgery I was able, I returned to Washington, leaving my men to do some further work. The impression on my mind was that Chancellorsville was a disaster to us and that Hooker was hardly able to conduct the Army of the Potomac on a successful career. I ought to say here that Jackson's wounds and expected death seemed to cause no elation in our army. All recognized how dangerous an enemy he was, how honorable and brave, how swift in his movements, how hard a striker, in fact, how great a military genius. Yet with all this, the feeling of the Northern army was one of pity, I might also say of regret, that so great a soldier was passing away.

At Washington I busied myself with my office work until the 21st of May, 1863, when I received the following order:

"S. G. O. Washington, D. C.
May 21, 1863.

Sir:—

You will proceed immediately to the Army of the Potomac and visit the different Corps of hospitals on special duty connected with the collection of pathological specimens. Having accomplished this, you will return to this city, and resume your present duties.

Very respfy. yr. Obt. Servt.

By order of the Surgeon General,

Jos. R. Smith,
Surgeon, U. S. A.

Surgeon J. H. Brinton, U. S. V.,
Washington, D. C."

On the back of this order, I have pencilled, "Order in reality to ascertain the number of casualties at Chancellorsville which had been concealed," and this endorsement tells the truth, which I will here explain. Chancellorsville, as we all know, was not a success, and was attended with a frightful, and at the date of this order, an unknown loss, or at all events, a loss which had not yet become known at Washington, and it was said that General Hooker, in command of the Army of the Potomac, had given orders, or let me say, had instructed all chiefs, to wit, the Chief Quartermaster, the Chief Commissary of Subsistence, and the Medical Director, to withhold from Washington all reports or information which would tend to disclose the Chancellorsville loss. But the nation, and the press, and the Secretary of War, Mr. Stanton, wished to know the loss as accurately as it could be computed or ascertained. The Secretary of War therefore desired that an officer should be sent from the Surgeon-General's office, who should as far as possible obtain this information, and I was detailed for this duty, under the foregoing fictitious order, with full verbal instructions.

It so happened that Surgeon Letterman, the Medical Director of the Army of the Potomac, had at this time come up to Washington, and on this very evening on which I was to start, was dining with Surgeon-General Hammond in H Street. Hearing this, and thinking that the information desired could be readily procured from him, I called at (Doctor) General Hammond's and sent up a note with my card, asking if under the circumstances of the Medical Director being in Washington then and there, I should still start for the army in the field to "collect pathological specimens." Dr. Hammond scribbled on the paper for me to start at once, and to collect all the specimens I could, "as he could collect none from the Medical Director."

I understood, and immediately took boat to Acquia Creek, and procuring there a sorry old sorrel horse, started the following day for the army headquarters, stopping at Potomac Creek, and at all the general and corps hospitals, etc., where the wounded had been carried, or where information concerning them would accumulate. I thus made a very complete search, and obtained data which, taken with the memoranda of the transporting officers, by railroad and boat, would give a closely approximate number of the bulk of wounded. In battles of the same general magnitude and description, the ratio of killed to wounded is always about the same, say one to every four or five wounded, according to the nature and circumstances of the action, whether fought in the open, or under cover, etc. This, the military statistican easily learns, and with fixed ratios can readily guess closely at the number of wounded, dead, and missing, and thus at a general loss, as well as at the number of men engaged, on one or both sides. Indeed, I may go further, and assert, strange as it may seem, that given a correct statement of any one class of wounds, say of the arm, or body or leg, the major facts of losses, and the forces of the combatants may be figured out, providing the statistics are not French, in which wounds of the back are given at a suspicious minimum, with a relative high ratio of anterior wounds.

As a fact, I was able to report the loss of our forces at Chancellorsville at about 23,000.

# CHAPTER XIX

After the battle of Chancellorsville, matters remained stationary with the Army of the Potomac. It was "all quiet along the Potomac." In the latter part of May and early part of June, however, it became evident that General Lee was preparing to move. At Washington, rumors to this effect were abroad. One cannot tell how such rumors arise or become known. They always did, however, and no matter what secrecy was observed, a note of premonition would sound in Washington. Perhaps it would arise from among the Southern sympathizers at the capital, and perhaps then gossip would take wings, and the cackle of the Southern wives of Northern or loyal men or officers would assume a shape. At all events, it became an open secret that an invasion of the North would be attempted.

Just before the battle of Gettysburg, a number of officers of the English army, stationed in Quebec, I think, visited Washington on a professional military trip to see the American mode of warfare. They belonged to the Scots Fusiliers. I was detailed to show them the workings of our Medical Department, and enjoyed that duty greatly. One of them was named Moncrieff. I paid them every attention I could, and when they returned to Canada, I sent them a keg of Virginia tobacco, a courtesy which they returned by forwarding me a number of British blue books. They had some doubt of American valor, but meeting one of them after the Battle of Gettysburg, he told me that he had seen quite enough of our fighting, for he had looked on from a hilltop at Pickett's charge, and had seen the brigade advance and retire. In fact, I heard it said that at one time in the cannonade near Meade's headquarters, they were not unwilling to stand behind a stone chimney, which, as it was not "their funeral," was quite the proper thing to do. I found these officers to be well educated, intelligent, fine fellows.

During the march of the Southern forces north, I was in Washington at my office work, fitting up the Museum, and serving on this board and that—a general utility person in the office.

The movement of the Army of Northern Virginia northwards towards and into Pennsylvania created a very great excitement and fear. Everything was uncertain, and it was not easy to divine the object of the enemy, nor to foretell how far he would go. There was a general feeling of doubt as to the ability of the Army of the Potomac to overtake him or to stop his progress. In Washington little that was certain was known; all was rumor and vague rumor. One thing, however, was certain,—the enemy had captured Chambersburg, York, Carlisle, and even threatened Harrisburg itself. The Army of the Potomac was doing its best, but it was not supposed at that moment to be in a very efficient condition, and the community in general had not a very strong faith in the capability of its leaders.

Philadelphia was in a great state of alarm. That city was supposed to be the objective point of the enemy. Its wealth, resources, and accumulation of manufactures and supplies marked it as a most valuable prize to the Confederates. Its capture would enrich them, would

furnish their army with food and supplies, would inter-
rupt the mails, transit and transportation. Unless the
Army of the Potomac could reach and bar the progress
of the Southern force, it really did not seem as if the
occupation of Philadelphia could be prevented. The
enemy were almost at Harrisburg. Viewed from my
standpoint at Washington, the occupation of Philadelphia seemed quite possible. To my mind, however,
I believed that Lee would scarcely leave the Army of
the Potomac behind him, and that he would more likely
fight near Harrisburg, and give us the chance, the only
chance of salvation. Under the same circumstances,
Grant would have struck for Philadelphia. It requires
a great man, a great soldier, to depart from conven-
tional rule, and by audacity to win success. The highest military ability is shown in the power to conduct
an offensive campaign. Defensive generals, if I may
use such an expression, are many in number; they are
the outcome of the schools. Offensive generals, on the
contrary, are very scarce; the world's history shows but
few in a century, and each one of them is a genius,
governed by his own laws. That cause which is upheld
by the greatest offensive talent will, *ceteris paribus,*
dominate, and, in the long run, win. The South had
two offensive generals, Stonewall Jackson and Joseph
E. Johnston; possibly Longstreet might be added to the
list. Of these the first was killed; the second from
official distrust or envy, was trammelled and suppressed.
The third was a lesser light. The North had Grant,
Sheridan and Sherman. The balance of offensive military power was in their favor.

I have not yet spoken of General Lee or General
McClellan. I regard them both as grand examples of
defensive soldiers. The defensive warfare of both was

as perfect as the circumstances would allow. When they undertook offensive campaigns, or when offensive operations were forced upon them, it was evident that some idea of defense was always in their mind, latent, and unrecognized, perhaps, but still there. With Grant, it was different, his whole notion was offense, and his idea of strategy was to push on and attack the enemy. He thought little or nothing of his rear; that could or must take care of itself; his endeavor was to keep his opponent busy by his repeated blows in front. The worst part of General Grant's command was in the rear; his most solid, compact and efficient was his front.

Before the war broke out, I had done a good deal of reading on military matters, the history of Napoleon's wars and Marlborough's, and Cromwell's campaigns, etc. Among other books, I had dabbled in Jomini's volumes on the *Art of War,* and I remember on one occasion when I was with Grant on the Tennessee River, asking him what he thought of Jomini. "Doctor," he said, "I have never read it carefully; the art of war is simple enough; find out where your enemy is, get at him as soon as you can, and strike him as hard as you can, and keep moving on." When I asked him at Fort Donelson what was to prevent the enemy from attacking and capturing his rear, he replied, "He is not thinking of that, we'll keep the front busy."

When Philadelphia was threatened, and as soon as I became convinced that its occupation was possible, if not probable, I became greatly disturbed about the welfare of my Mother and sisters, and the safety of our home. All of my letters to my mother at that time are filled with advice what to do. I counselled her to draw money out of the bank, and then as soon as Harrisburg should be occupied, or our own city otherwise threatened, to go north to the White Mountains, taking with her in separate trunks our important papers, such as the estate books, and a number of unrecorded deeds of old lots, and our title papers generally, and our index of deeds, etc. Then, whatever happened, we would be comparatively safe; we would have our deeds, and the land could not be burned or destroyed.

As it happened, the immediate necessity of the family hurrying away did not arise; our city was not captured, and our records lay in their accustomed dust safely through the eventful summer of 1863.

Immediately after the battle of Gettysburg, I was ordered by the Surgeon-General to go there on special duty. There was, then, two or three days after the fight, some difficulty in reaching Gettysburg from the south, the Washington side. The railroad had been cut in a good many places, and the enemy was retreating across the Maryland line in the direction of the Potomac. There was much delay, and the transportation was rough. I remember going, I think, from Hanover Junction, in the night, in a box-car, in which were one or two horses loose, untied. I slept in the straw on the floor perfectly safe. It was wonderful to see the instinct of the poor brutes. How careful they were of their feet, and how they seemed to try not to tread on anyone, or injure them with their hoofs. And here, by the way, I may say that the horse has the greatest dread of the prone human figure. You cannot make him tread on the body of a man, or upon that of a dead horse or mule. I have tried to make a horse do this, by the spur at Jefferson City, Mo., in 1864, but have never succeeded. He will shy off fiercely and widely, and if forcibly and persistently spurred on, he will leap the dreaded object. The inanimate prone body, he appears to hold in more horror than the living, but it may be said that he will not approach these, if he can get around them. A cavalry major, serving in the West, once told me that on one occasion, just prior to entering action, he was riding with one or two squadrons rapidly down a narrow lane, being about to debouch in the open, when his horse tumbled or fell, throwing him to the ground in the very roadbed of the lane. To him, death seemed inevitable, for he thought he would be crushed and trodden by the horses' feet. He closed his eyes in horror, when after a few seconds, finding that he continued unhurt, he opened his eyes and saw to his amazement that each horse on approaching him at full speed, deliberately and dexterously jumped, so as to clear him, and leave him unharmed. The entire force thus passed over him, the only injury he received being a slight scratch on the hand, owing to an involuntary motion he made during one of the horse's leaps. This peculiarity of the horse is not known to everyone, and certainly was not known to the poet Campbell when he wrote:

"Their hoof-beaten bosoms are trod to the plain!"

In this box-car going from Hanover Junction, I met my old friend Dr. Ellerslie Wallace, in search of the body of a friend, the husband of a connection of my own, who had been killed in the battle. Arrived at Gettysburg, I found quarters, I think, at the Medical Purveyor's, and busied myself for several days in visiting the hospitals in the town, in the churches and public buildings, and also the large field hospitals which had been organized outside of the town. These hospitals were generally in good condition, and accommodated large numbers of wounded. A good many of the enemy's wounded were gathered into one hospital under the care of their surgeons. As I approached this hospital, operations were being performed at the operating tent under the trees, and from the peculiar manner in which the amputating knife was held, I recognized one of my old students. He was about to amputate a limb, and was drawing the knife in the peculiar manner which I had been in the habit of teaching, and which I had been taught by the military surgeon, Dienstl, in the dissecting and operating room in the military hospitals at Vienna. I was very warmly received by the Confederate surgeon, and his friends, a very good set of fellows, whom I was glad to meet with. Professional brotherhood is, I think, the strongest bond in the world, and my whole experience in our war convinced me more and more of this.

In my rides during these days, I had ample opportunities of seeing the field of battle, and of forming an idea of the fierceness of the struggle. In one of my rides on an old white horse, somewhere, I think in the direction of Cemetery Hill, I tried to ride across a slough or marsh of soft black mud. It was treacherous, and my horse sank slowly and steadily until his legs were buried and his body even began to sink. He could not in spite of all his struggles get out, and I began to have serious apprehensions as to the outcome for horse and man. I sank, too, but fortunately being near the shore, I scrambled to dry and firm land, and by pulling on my bridle, managed to extricate the beast. He was a white horse no longer, for he had floundered on his side and looked as if he had received a coat of tar. For myself, I was in pitiable plight; nothing was left for me save to reach my quarters, and go to bed while my clothes were being washed and cleaned and dried, for I had no others.

The town of Gettysburg was filled with hospitals and stores for the wounded, surgeons and their assistants, who were coming to see a real battle-ground, newspaper men in abundance, and a crowd of Sanitary and Christian Commissioners, who wandered about everywhere, and kept remarkably good tables at the houses which they regarded as their headquarters. Crowds of citizens were there from neighboring country and town, and many from Philadelphia. Some of these came under pretext of seeing friends, but many more drawn by curiosity. A great many were in search of relics or "trophies," as they called them, from the battlefield; shot, shell, bayonets, guns, and every sort of military portable property. The gathering and taking away of such objects was strictly forbidden by military proclamation, all articles being regarded as belonging for the time being to the military authorities and under their care. Finally, it was decided to put a stop to this "trophy" business. Guards were instructed to arrest purloiners, and take away the articles; but even this did not answer, stolen articles were concealed in the clothes and packages. The Provost Marshal (whom I knew, a Captain Smith, a relative of General Halleck's), then determined to put an end to the practice, and therefore ordered the arrest and detention of all persons found with contraband articles in their possession. This order gave much annoyance to visitors, who still attempted to evade it. So the Provost Marshal resorted to the rather summary process of sending delinquents, or those disobeying his orders, out to the field of battle, to assist in burying dead horses,—not a pleasant duty. This gave rise to trouble at once, and to threats of exceeding fierceness. I saw one squad about to start on march for the field, five or six miles on a hot July morning,—in which was a loquacious gentleman, of portly presence, who had been caught with a U. S. musket, as a battle trophy, in his hands; deep was his wrath and eloquent his protest and fierce his threats at sending him, "a gentleman and a member of the legislature of this state" to do such disgusting work. He promised to have all concerned in issuing the orders dismissed, but he had to make the march all the same, and at least go through the formality of "burying dead horses."

This energetic treatment put a stop to the practice of looting arms. Whether it was worth the trouble and hard feeling excited, I hardly know. It was almost incredible, however, to what an extent this trophy mania had spread. One farmer near the field absolutely concealed a six-pound gun, letting it down into his well.

The battle-ground occupied the farms which lay beyond the town for miles. A good many of the farmers were Germans,—I'm afraid of a low type and mean, sordid disposition. Their great object in this life, seemed to be to hoard money, and their behavior toward our troops and our wounded soldiers, was often mean beyond belief. As an instance, I might relate this case. As I was riding along the country road, I met a shabby buggy driven by a mean-looking German, and carrying two wounded soldiers. Noticing that the bandage on one of them was too tight, and had caused much swelling, I stopped the vehicle and learned this story. They had been wounded on the farm (one of considerable size, 176 acres) belonging to their driver, the owner of the buggy. They had been there for a day or two and were anxious to reach the field hospital of their command, some distance. They could not walk, and their host (if such a term can be used), finally consented to take them to the hospital, as I saw he was doing, if they would give him a silver watch, and such trifles as they carried on their person, for pay.  I wrote a little note, stating the facts, and directed them all to the Provost Marshal's guard, not far behind me.  I afterwards had the satisfaction of learning that the horse and buggy and shabby driver, had the opportunity of affording gratuitous transportation for a week to the sick and wounded under the supervision of the Marshal's Guard, and that the watch, etc., were returned to their original owners.  I could only hope that the lesson of forced patriotism would prove lasting.

As usual after battles, many of the killed were buried in trenches or pits.  One of my men on this occasion took from the body of a Southern soldier, a breast plate of soft steel, in two halves, intended to be worn under the coat or vest.  One ball had struck it and indented or bent it without perforation.  Another, if I remember rightly, had passed through in the region of the liver, causing the death of the wearer.  I think the breastplate bore the imprint "Ames Manufacturing Company."  This cuirass was placed in the Army Museum, and I suppose is there now.  It was the only example of defensive armor I met with during the war.

I have spoken of the burials *en masse*.  Many of the bodies, however, were buried singly where it was possible.  In visiting the hospitals I entered one in the suburbs of the town, which I was informed was much exposed at one time during the battle of the crossfire of the respective sharp shooters, or outlying pickets of the two armies.  In the churchyard, at one corner of the church building, I observed a number of new made graves, arranged with the greatest precision, each one of them being provided with a head board and foot board, made of shingles, the former bearing the name, rank, company and regiment of the man beneath. The head boards were exactly alike, the lines for the inscription and the styles for the lettering being alike in all cases. These men, I was told, were buried at a time when the hospital was directly in the line of cross fire on both sides, and the sepulture was directed by a medical officer. Struck with the remarkable adherence, in all these cases, to the regulations and customs of the army service, I inquired of the hospital steward, my informant, "Was this medical officer tall and thin, in exact uniform, and did he expose himself during the burial," "Yes, sir, and he read the service for the dead, the burial service over them?" "Was his name Bache?" I asked, feeling instinctively that such military rigidity could only be found in that family. "Yes, sir,"—and then I knew that my old friend, Surgeon Thos. H. Bache, U. S. Vols. must be the officer indicated,—and it was so. The Army Regulations had been scrupulously complied with.

Our loss at Gettysburg was heavy but as the battle was fought on our land, and as we remained masters of the field, we had every opportunity for the care of the wounded in large hospitals, and for their proper transportation. 'My duty at this time was twofold, first to render what help I could surgically, and secondly, to collect specimens and histories for the Museum. I was able to gather much for the Museum, and for the most part the medical officers were anxious to further me in my endeavors to carry out my Washington instructions. By the 16th or 17th of July, I had returned to Washington, and resumed my office duties.

# CHAPTER XX

OF THINGS MEDICAL AND MILITARY AT WASHINGTON

I spent the entire summer of 1863 at Peter Place on Georgetown Heights, which I have already described. The place, beautiful as it was, with the remains of former grandeur, was essentially southern in its tone. The family to which it had belonged, were all in the southern service, and its associations and surroundings were especially "Secesh." My friend Scull, of the Subsistence Department, and I had rooms in an outlying building, which I rather think was intended for the domestics in bygone times.

I will not say that we boarded at Peter Place. "Boarder" is almost a vulgar word, not in consonance with the stateliness of the Mansion; we simply slept there in the aforesaid wing, and "took our meals" in the dining-room with the big folding windows down to the ground, looking out on the high portico; we ate quietly and demurely, not talking much, never alluding to the war or army, or battles or marches. Uniform was not worn; we were simply citizens, enjoying the cool air of Georgetown Heights. The compensation was managed by Scull, who prided himself on his delicacy, the exact amount of our indebtedness (in clean notes) being placed in a note envelope, with the compliments of Majors Scull and Brinton, and handed to the waiter. An equally refined acknowledgment of its receipt would reach us the next day by the black Mercury.

With all its formality and absurdities, Peter Place was a delightful spot on these summer evenings, and I thoroughly enjoyed sitting under the trees, and smoking a pipe or cigar after dinner. The rides around Georgetown, too, were very pretty. General Halleck lived in a large house, not very far from where I was staying. He used to walk in and out to the War Department every day. I often met him and exchanged greetings, and once or twice walked with him, but he was not very companionable and was undoubtedly an overestimated man.

In the latter part of August, 1863, I served again as President of the Army Medical Board, for the examination of candidates for admission into the corps of Surgeons of Volunteers, the former "Brigade Surgeons." This was the same board on which I had served when I first came to Washington. As I have explained, the discharge of its functions was a somewhat delicate one, owing to the fact that medical officers were so badly wanted, and that pressure would be brought upon the board to relax its standard of qualifications. On one occasion, not long after I came to Washington when I was the presiding officer of the Board, we were examining a curious creature from Kansas, who was an applicant for the appointment of Brigade Surgeon. He was a man of more than middle age, apparently self educated, and evidently had been through many vicissitudes in life. At that time, each candidate was obliged to file a short written autobiography, and his began in this way: "My first recollections of myself are that I was found as a little baby, on an emigrant trail on the prairie. Since that time, I have done a little of everything. My qualifications are various. I can do almost anything, from scalping an Indian, up and down. I hope if I know enough, that you'll pass me, gentlemen."

This person was a friend of the then well known and eccentric Senator from Kansas, "Jim" Lane, who did the Board the honor of a visit, and after a self introduction, said "I'm Senator Lane, Jim Lane of Kansas, and I'm interested in this Board. I've a friend before it, and what I want to know is this, are you a passing Board or a rejecting Board?" We assured him we would do the best we could in his friend's case, and fortunately we were able to act up to his wishes without strain of conscience. His friend, whose knowledge of the English language and spelling was undoubtedly limited, was nevertheless singularly well up in the practical parts of the profession; he had lived all his life in the West and practiced there, and so he passed the Board with a recommendation to the Secretary of War that "he be assigned to duty in Kansas." He really proved to be one of the most practical men in the service.

In November of 1863, I served upon a Board of Medical Directors to consider the defects of the existing system of reports of sick and wounded, and to devise some means for a more efficient and accurate system of hospital registration; and here I might say a few words on the defects of the hospital registers, and on the difficulties encountered in the early part of the war in obtaining accurate reports and accounts of the wounded.

As I have stated, when the war broke out the only return or description of gunshot wounds was that under the heading of *"vulnus scloperticum"* on the general sick report, furnished by the medical officers on duty in every command, and at every post and hospital, and which were, of course, entirely vague and too indefinite to convey any accurate intelligence as to the extent and character of an injury. As soon as I was assigned to the preparation of the Surgical History of the War, I tried to help matters by subdividing the gunshot wounds into various classifications; but this did not answer much better, as duplication was apt to occur from the constant removal of wounded from one hospital to another, as from a small field hospital to a division or corps field general hospital, and thence to a city hospital, and thence perhaps to state hospitals in the neighborhood of the patient's home.

Some other system of registration and report was evidently necessary. At Antietam I met Deputy Inspector General Muir, of the British Service, whose experience with sick and wounded had been large. I told him the difficulties we labored under in obtaining accurate statistics. He then suggested to me the adoption of something like the British medical descriptive paper, a blank which is filled up when the wounded man comes under treatment, and which then goes with him, and accompanies him in all his transportation, and which in case of death or recovery is then forwarded to the central medical bureau, which in our case would be the Surgeon General's Office. This plan seemed feasible, and it was determined to give it a trial. I was accordingly ordered to have printed 100,000 of these medical descriptive lists, adapted to our service. These were then distributed, and Medical Directors were requested to endeavor to have them filled up by the medical officers at hospitals under their control. Perfect in theory, and well adapted for wars where the wounded were comparatively few, and the medical force numerous, this system of registration of sick and wounded failed utterly with us. Our medical officers were overworked by the enormous numbers of our wounded, and the exigencies of the time demanded a too continuous and rapid transportation of wounded from the front to northern hospitals. The notice of transportation, too, was too short; at all events this system did not work. It failed, and in consequence a Board was convened, under the following order:

"Surg. Genl. Office, Washington City, D. C.
Nov. 6, 1863.

A Board of Officers to consist of Surgeons J. H. Brinton, J. A. Sidell, U. S. V.; Assistant Surgeons Roberts Bartholow, J. J. Woodward, and Wm. Thomson, U. S. A., will assemble at the Surgeon General's Office on Monday, November 9th, or as soon thereafter as practicable to consider and report upon proposed modifications, in registers and returns for sick and wounded, and the diet table prescribed for the U. S. General Hospitals.

By order Acting Surgeon General,
(Signed) "C. H. Crane,"
Surgeon, U. S. A.

Surgeon J. H. Brinton, U. S. V.
Surgeon General's Office."

The action of this Board was the adoption of the form of registers which continued in use until the end of the war, on which every case was minutely entered, in whatever hospital the man might be. A comparison of the registers was necessary to prevent duplication, and for this purpose a large clerical force was maintained in the Surgeon General's Office. The blanks for these reports were printed in Philadelphia by J. B. Lippincott

& Co., and I had the pleasure of running on to order them. Dr. John Neill, then a Surgeon, U. S. V., had the after-superintendence. They proved a success.

Once or twice during the summer and autumn of 1863, I had the opportunity of visiting Philadelphia. In fact, Dr. Hammond, when in full power, had told me that when the business of the office and army affairs were not very demanding or urgent, I might slip on to Philadelphia, and stay over Sunday, provided I would be in my place in the office by nine o'clock on Monday morning. Of course, on these clandestine visits home, I wore a civilian's dress, with nothing about me which could possibly indicate my military functions.

Somewhat later than this, I had occasion to employ a government detective to hunt up a deserter, who, acting as my orderly, had stolen nearly all my decent clothing. He was a clever scoundrel, and while acting as my body servant or valet, had drawn my attention to many necessary repairs on my outer clothing. At the same time he pointed out some defects on my linen, and flannel underwear. He kindly offered to have all defects remedied, and the mending, generally, thoroughly done. He knew a nice German seamstress. The laundrying he hardly thought was up to the grade of my linen, so he had that attended to also at a very moderate rate, carefully and in a proper businesslike spirit; he even brought me back six cents change. My silk (civilian's) hat he had ironed, and all my shoes neatly cobbled. I was quite nicely fitted out, as good as new, and then when all was complete, he disappeared, and with him all my clothing and toilet apparatus, and even my tooth brush. He left me nothing save what I had on, not even an extra handkerchief, and he went away on a rainy day, and I had a bad cold. *Such* a desertion of his colors was not to be tolerated by the United States Government, and I was directed to put the case in the hands of the Provost Marshal's Department, and to have him arrested at any cost, as desertion from a Bureau of the War Department could not be overlooked. So one or two U. S. detectives were placed at my beck and call, but nothing was accomplished. He was seen in bad company in New York, but he evidently had some recognition of the detective, and he escaped by good running. The last we knew of him, he had found his way safely to Canada.

To return to the detective service, I learned from one of its members that all outgoing trains from Washington were watched, to stop unauthorized flitting of officers. "Do you ever find any transgressing in that respect?" I asked. "Yes, Doctor," he replied, "we often do. For example, we see that nearly every Saturday evening, you go to your home in Philadelphia, and return every Monday morning by the night train, but our orders are not to stop you, as it is all right."

The autumn and winter of 1863, and the early months of 1864, were passed by me very pleasantly in Washington. I had my daily routine of office work, some leisure in the afternoons, and in the evening, time for social amusements. At all ordinary times, I was at the Surgeon-General's about nine o'clock in the morning. There I attended to my duties proper, until about one o'clock. Then I usually lunched simply at Wormley's restaurant, a glass of wine and a slice of cold meat was all I took. My friends, Scull and Moss, usually lunched at the same time and place. Then after lunch, I would drop in at the Museum building, look after the running of Museum matters, then take my horse, visit some one of the many hospitals in and around Washington, and later in the afternoon, ride with my friends. The rides around Washington were pretty, and on pleasant afternoons, nothing could be more pleasant than a gallop out Seventh or Fourteenth Street, or in the lanes leading from Georgetown Heights. When I first went to Washington, I bought a sorrel horse but I'm afraid he was not of very good breeding, for his sole accomplishment was a canter, easy, but not very stylish. I afterwards became somewhat ashamed of him, and bought another beast,—one of great style. He was raised somewhere in western New York, of "Royal George" ancestry, whatever that may be. He was quite large and very handsome. I paid four hundred dollars for him, and was told he was a bargain. He had been brought to Washington, intended as a present for the officer inspecting the purchase of horses—in other words a bribe horse. The gift being rejected, he was to be sold for what he would bring, and I foolishly bought him, tempted by his beauty. But "handsome is as handsome does," and this brute was an incarnate fiend. After owning him a short time, I felt that I could safely and honestly warrant him to possess every vice, trick and bad habit which any horse could inherit from mischievous ancestors, or develop by innate wickedness. He would bite, kick, bolt, shy, rear, plunge back (in a sudden and startling manner), buck-jump (artistically), take the bit in his teeth and run, plunge his head down obstinately, and then raise it and strike his rider's nose in a wonderful fashion. He understood all about spurs, and if he felt them he would bite at the leg. You couldn't ride him without strong leathers, and he had a strange horror of boastful riders. He would throw a jockey or groom without hesitation. I once allowed a Hungarian, who had served for years in the Austrian service, and two terms of enlistment in the U. S. Cavalry, to mount him. The beast eyed him on his approach, and laid back his ears, but permitted the man quietly to mount him. The next moment the horse was in the air, and there was a strange and complicated movement of his forelegs, and he then stood quiet and riderless. The Hungarian had been shot from the saddle, and fortunately landed on a pile of manure in the corner of the yard. And yet this beast let me ride him in comparative quiet, only backing and bolting now and then, and then, too, in no very vicious spirit. I was afraid of him, and he knew it, and he seemed content to let matters rest on that basis. I kept him until I left Washington. With difficulty, he was sold to a cabman, and ran away with the carriage and injured his mate. A milkman bought him, and he broke the wagon and spilled the milk. Finally, he was sold for fifty dollars to the street car company. I heard no further particulars of his adventures, except in a general way that he lived up to his previous bad reputation.

In the summer of 1863, I had a visit from my cousin, Charles Coxe. He had gone into the service a boy, was now maturing into a good cavalry officer, and was a very manly fellow. The more I saw of him in the war, the more I thought of him.

In the early part of September I moved into Washington from Georgetown. Changes were occurring in the Surgeon-General's Office. Dr. Hammond, or as we used to say General Hammond (the Surgeon-General had the rank of Brigadier General), had gotten into trouble with Mr. Stanton, the Secretary of War, and had been sent off south *in partibus oripedium* on a sort of inspecting tour, banished from Washington, and I may say here, that he never returned to his official duties at the capital. He was hardly treated, for he was not guilty of any wrongdoing; he simply could not get along with the Secretary, and, so to speak, ran his head against the wall. His case dragged on, he was tried by Court Martial and cashiered. Court Martials sound well, but often do injustice, especially if packed, or when desirous of finding in accordance with higher authority. At the time of the sitting of the Court Martial, I was lunching every day at Wormley's restaurant. One morning, as one of the members of the Court came in to take his luncheon, some one present said, "How are you, General, this morning?" "Sir," said the General, "I have been fast asleep all the morning in my chair at that damned Hammond court martial. I did not hear a word." And he was a prominent member of the court.

The finding was foregone. The disabilities of the sentence were years afterwards annulled by Act of Congress, and General Hammond restored to the Army, and placed on the retired list as Brig.-Surg.-Gen. retired, 27th Aug. 1879, without pay or allowance under act of March 15, 1878.

# CHAPTER XXI

## NO ARMY MEDICAL SCHOOL—METROPOLITAN CLUB

Here I must say something about one of the great disappointments of my life. It was connected with a proposed Army Medical School, like the British School at Netley. It had been an idea of Surgeon-General Hammond's in the plenitude of his power, and at the time when he was most enthusiastic, and it seemed to me then, and to all of the medical officers of the old army, who were consulted, that the scheme was a good one, to found a medical school, the professors of which should be medical officers in the army, and the object of which should be the instruction of graduates-in-medicine, that is, doctors in the medical branches of military medicine and surgery, and in the customs of the service. It was intended to teach them how soldiers should be looked after in health, on marches, in camp, how they should be treated when sick or wounded, how cared for in hospitals or in the field, and how properly transported. All of this knowledge was usually obtained only by actual service and by bungling experience. Now, if this experience could only be imparted to the young medical man about to begin his military life, much would be gained in point of time, in efficiency of service, and in care of the soldier. Our experience in the early part of the war taught us, and I speak very positively of myself, how hard it was for a medical man who had just donned his uniform, to learn the mysteries of ob-

257

taining food from the subsistence department, or of stores and transportation from the quartermaster, how to obtain an ambulance, or to find horses, or to procure forage, how even to obtain medicines from the purveyor, and how to take care of them when received, how to draw a hospital tent, how to pitch it, how to keep it standing and comfortable for the sick.

Then, too, it was an art very different from that known to the doctor of civil life to treat a sick or wounded soldier, to make the best of opportunities, to cure rapidly, and to return him well and fit for duty to his command at the earliest moment. These and thousands of other matters, it should be the function of the military Medical School through experienced instructors, to teach the young surgeon or medical cadet, or even the hospital steward.

To assist in this end the Army Museum, with its unrivalled collection of specimens of pathological anatomy, of every sort of medical appliances, suitable for military life, of models of camps, tents, hospitals and transportation by land and water, could have been turned to good account under a wise administration.

As I have said, the foundation of such a school had been a favorite project of Surgeon-General Hammond, and under his general instructions, I had fitted up the rooms beneath the main hall of the Museum (Corcoran's Building) for teaching purposes. There was a charming lecture room, with sloping seats, a couple of convenient little retiring rooms or laboratories, a good stage to speak from, and a well constructed lecture and revolving table. The illustrations, in lavish profusion, were in the main hall above, and everything was ready for the first military medical course of the United States Army for the session of 1863-64. It wanted but the authorization of the scheme by the Secretary of War, and the appointment of the lecturers or professors.

These had in truth been selected. There was Coolidge of the regular army, an old officer, to teach the customs of the service and military medical ethics; Surgeon Sidell, U. S. V., as a teacher of chemical surgery; and Assistant Surgeon William Thomson, since famous as an oculist, and Assistant Surgeon J. J. Woodward, U. S. A., on military medicine; and also Roberts Bartholow of world-wide reputation, and several others, whose names have escaped me. Gunshot injuries had been assigned to me; my pictures were painted in gorgeous style, and even my introductory remarks had been jotted down.

In the meantime, Surgeon-General Hammond had been sent away, and Acting Surgeon Barnes reigned in his stead. As Curator of the Museum, I reported to him the forward state of preparation. The Secretary of War was to be informed. He was told by Mr. Barnes. He said he would "decide the matter and speak of it to-morrow." On the morrow, about nine o'clock, on his drive from his home to the war office, he stopped at the Museum Building, descended from his carriage, ran hastily through the Museum rooms, looked angrily at the dear little lecture room, stamped his foot, growled, "Ugh," drove to his office, sent for Acting Surgeon General Barnes and said sharply to him, "Are these lectures to be given in the evenings?" To an affirmative reply, he growled, "They will go to the theatre and neglect their duties. It shan't be," and thus was the end of a favorite plan for doing some good for the Medical Corps of the Army, and for disseminating a more correct and general knowledge of military medicine and surgery.

Sometime in the winter of 1863-64, I became a member of the newly established Metropolitan Club, and in a short time I was appointed one of the governors. This club then was the only one in Washington, and had acquired the house lately ocupied by Baron Gerault, the Minister from Prussia. Many of the high officers of Government, secretaries of the cabinet and men of inferior grade, auditors and the like, joined it, also many of the diplomatic corps, especially the younger members and attachés. It was a pleasant place to dine, to smoke, to play billiards, and spend an evening. There, too, one met many men prominent in Washington life, some from their individuality, and some from the public positions they held. I recall thus to my mind, Messrs. Nicolay and John Hay, the private secretaries of President Lincoln, Mr. Chase, the Secretary of the Treasury, popularly known as "Old Greenbacks," Secretary McCullough, and Mr. Chas. Sumner.

McCullough I met often. He belonged to a social club, to which I was often invited, and which met at members' houses,—I think on Saturday evening. On one occasion I was late, and as I entered, Mr. McCullough said to me, "Doctor, you are just in time to decide an important question, we are voting as to which design for an engraving for a greenback we shall select. We are evenly divided,—now which do you choose? Give your casting vote." I did so and I think I voted for "Columbus landing" or something of that sort, and so the choice was made. I never saw these notes afterwards without a feeling of sponsorial affection.

For some time my seat at table was next to Charles Sumner, who struck me as a dreadful pedant, always reading proof between soup and fish, and speaking

French, bad French, to the diplomats at table, who usually spoke English perfectly.

This club was a dangerous place for an officer of the army, and I came to grief from too open an expression of opinion, as I shall explain when I come to speak of why I left Washington.

In November, 1863, I remember an old squib or publication called the "New Gospel of Peace," a burlesque, if I remember rightly, on the peace movements,—a Copperhead program that the enemies of the government were starting at this time. In the "New Gospel" a good deal is said of the exploits and character of one "Ulysses, surnamed Unculpsalm." It attracted considerable attention at its first appearance, and I sent a copy of it to General Grant. The idea of making him Lieutenant General, reviving Scott's rank, was at this time much talked of, and was in fact done in the early part of March, 1864, General Grant, then in command of the Armies, being appointed by the President and confirmed by the Senate as Lieutenant General, March 10th, 1864.

At this time, I had an ambulance to take me from place to place. All understrappers, like myself, had every convenience, ambulance and other concomitants of military luxury, pertaining to official life. In reality, bureau officers and attachés had more attendants in waiting than even the President himself, or at all events, than Mr. Lincoln had. I remember very well that Mr. Nicolay told me at the club that President Lincoln was very badly off for personal attendance. He only had one or two civil attendants or messengers in his hall. He was so conscientious that he would not allow soldiers to be detailed for his personal service. The men he employed were overworked, and often he had difficulty in dispatching really important public business.

Nicolay told me that he had not even stationery enough for the office work.

During the winter of 1863-64, the Army of the Potomac was quiet. At Washington, military affairs seemed at a standstill, gaiety was at its height, society had by this time become more settled, and, as it were, had crystallized. The old "before the war" society had disappeared, or shrunk into the background. Before and at the outbreak of the war, "society" at the capital was Southern in tone. This society then represented the wealth and culture of the city. The war came,—the most active Southern sympathizers went South, and joined formally the Confederate cause. A few of the old people remained in quiet and comparative obscurity, but always on the lookout for news, and probably sending much useful intelligence to friends at the South. Some of these people regarded themselves as neutral, but I am sure that in feeling and sympathy they clung to the South, and to their former traditions.

Under the excitement of the war, strangers from the loyal states flocked to Washington, and soon formed for themselves a new society. These newcomers were composed of the fresh republicans and their friends, military officers, stationed at and around Washington, and their families in part, and government officials of all grades, at first a somewhat motley lot. Then, there was a constant tide of contractors of all sorts, people seeking to make money.

Thus constituted, the general society of Washington was at first somewhat peculiar. It was smart, quick, bright, but it was wanting in homogeneity, and the old-fashioned indolence and polish. By degrees, as time elapsed, it became less evanescent and changing, and more settled and systematized. But still there remained

in feeling, if not in fact, two circles,—one, the society
of Washington, the centers being the White House, the
houses of the cabinet officers, and the diplomatic man-
sions; the other, a circle of old-fashioned people, very
quiet and nice and hospitable to well-introduced strangers, but silent on the events of the day. If by any
chance, they expressed an opinion, it was very tender
in their judgment of the South, and strong in their
admiration of General Lee, and "President Davis."

By good luck, I was fortunate to have the entrée
everywhere, thanks to the kindness of a sister-in-law of
a friend, a woman of bright disposition and handsome
person, clever, and well bred, who knew everyone, and
went everywhere, and who just at that time was glad
to have an escort. She left my cards everywhere, and
at once I was effectually introduced. Cards of invitation
poured in on me, and I fully availed myself of my good
fortune. I remember frequently visiting at the White
House. The young ladies prominent in society would
fix on an evening, and with a sacred few, call, half infor-
mally, on Mrs. Lincoln. The ladies of the cabinet gave
a good many state receptions, and oftentimes quiet little
gatherings for the young people. At the houses of Sena-
tors Morgan (of New York), Dixon (of Connecticut),
Reverdy Johnson (of Maryland), and many others, I
was a frequent visitor. Commodore Wilkes, who cir-
cumnavigated the world, and afterwards came to official
grief in the matter of Mason and Slidell and the *Trent*
affair, had a charming old house, where I spent many a
pleasant evening with Mr. Coolidge, and the Morris family,—the famous Morris who went down on the *Cumberland,* with the United States flag still flying at the
mast head, at Fortress Monroe. Another house at which
I visited frequently was that of Mrs. Stephen A. Douglas,

the famous beauty and widow of the western politician. She was formerly a Miss Cutts, a beautiful and clever woman, who exercised great and widespread influence by virtue of her intellect, good looks and name. It was a delightful house to visit, and one met there many prominent personages of the day, especially men in and around the government. Conversation on political topics was very free, and there was less constraint than at any house in the city to which I had access. People could and did say in her parlor things touching passing events, which they could not speak elsewhere. Usually one in Government employ had to be very careful of his words, as I afterwards found out to my cost.

# CHAPTER XXII

## THE PRESIDENT AND SOME LESSER DIGNITARIES

I daresay my readers will naturally ask what I saw of Mr. Lincoln, our President, who will go down to posterity as one of the great personages of history. Over and over again, I was presented to him on official occasions, and once I amputated at the shoulder joint, the arm of a soldier at a hospital in Washington, which the President was visiting at the time. He was greatly interested, but evidently had little fondness for surgery. At the conclusion of the operation, a younger surgeon, who had been watching me, expressed with some enthusiasm and in a voice audible to the President, his congratulations upon the operation, and I remember well being startled by the voice of the President behind my back, making the solemn inquiry, "But how about the soldier?"

When times were critical, and great battles were being fought, and news from the front scarce and undecided, it was considered safer at army headquarters in Washington not to tell the President too soon how things were going, at all events until results were certain. The President, grand character as he was, was considered just a little "leaky," and delighted to surprise his political friends and cronies with news, especially glorying in good news, but it was not always well to make public, too early, announcements, whether for good or evil. The news channel to the South was too straight and active. This Secretary Stanton and others knew, and so, from prudential reasons, President Lincoln was often kept in ignorance of what was going on. At such times, he was very restless and anxious, and more than once at critical periods, I have seen him nervously hurrying from the White House to the office of the Secretary of War, and to army headquarters and back again, in search of information for the time kept from him. On one or two occasions, he spent the best part of the day in these fruitless trips; and, strange to say, not a few of the officers on duty at the different bureaus of the War Department were aware of the circumstances.

As I have said, I passed the early part of the winter of '64 in the society of Washington, enjoying it greatly, and I may state, in anticipation, that in the latter part of March, Mrs. Grant arrived in the city. Her first experience of Washington society was, I think, at Mrs. Blair's. I believe I was the only person she knew in the room at the time, and I had the pleasure of taking her through the rooms, and of presenting very many Washington people to her. She was received with great warmth, all looking to her with curiosity to see what manner of woman the wife of so great a general might be.

On March 11th, General Grant returned to Tennessee, and took leave of the armies of the west. On the 22nd or 23rd of March he returned to Washington, staying at Willard's Hotel. He was beset by visitors and politicians. I called on him several times, but could not see him. On the 27th, he was again in Washington, I then saw him and had a long chat with him. I found him just the same man he always was, simple, unaffected, and his head unturned by the adulation he received. He treated me then as always, with simple kindness.

About the 25th of March, 1864, General Sheridan ar-

rived at Washington. I had last seen him at Murfreesboro, Tennessee. Grant had just placed him in command of the cavalry of the Army of the Potomac.
Sheridan, standing under the porch of Willard's Hotel,
said to me, "Doctor, I'm going to take the cavalry away
from the bob-tail brigadier-generals. They must do without their escorts. I intend to make the cavalry an arm
of the service."

In the early part of May, active preparations were begun by the Army of the Potomac, and Grant moved
forward on the memorable Wilderness campaign, which
ended in the capture of Richmond, the surrender of Lee,
and the overthrow of the Rebellion. On the 3rd or 4th
of May, the Army of the Potomac crossed the Rapidan,
and the terrific series of battles commenced. For forty
days men fell by the thousands, telegraphic communication from Washington with the army ceased, and at
first it was found impossible to communicate with the
wounded or to transport them to Washington or to
northern hospitals.

On the 9th of May, 1864, I received orders to go to
Fredericksburg, Virginia, and to report for surgical
duty to the Medical Director of the Army of the Potomac. On the same day, I was directed by another order
to take charge of the battle supplies placed on board the
steamers *State of Maine* and *Connecticut,* and have them
delivered at Fredericksburg, Virginia, for the use of the
wounded at that place. In giving me these orders, the
Acting Surgeon-General Barnes told me verbally, "Doctor, our losses have been enormous, the wounded are by
thousands, we don't know where they are and so far all
attempts to send them supplies have failed. Take these
supplies on board the steamers and get them forwarded
at any hazard and at any loss. If you cannot deliver

all, deliver one-half; if not that much, deliver what you can; the wounded are suffering for them, and do the best you can. The Secretary of War authorizes you through me to take possession in his name of any and all wagon trains to transport these supplies to Fredericksburg. Give what orders you please in his name for this purpose."

Accordingly, I went down with these steamers to Belle Plain on the Potomac Creek. The steamers carried an immense amount of medical supplies,—hundreds of thousands of dollars' worth. A corps of engineers and bridge builders were on board and these were directed to give me every possible support and assistance in landing the supplies, when I was to look out for myself, and to get proper protection and transportation from the army to which I was to deliver them. Arriving at Belle Plain, I found a shallow, muddy shore, no wharf, no landing. The engineers immediately built caissons or cribs of timbers, some of which they had brought with them and some of which they cut. These were sunken in the shallow water and timbers and trees stretched between so as to form a sort of roadway over which the supplies could be carried safely to land. The landing was overlooked by higher ground, and it was necessary to place guards for the protection of the precious supplies. I learned that the road from Belle Plain to Fredericksburg, ten or twelve miles distant, was infested with guerillas, and that no bridge existed at Fredericksburg. I had no force by which to send forward my supplies, and it was necessary for me to go forward myself to obtain wagons and guards. To avoid the guerillas on the road, I determined to walk along the edge of the woods at a safe distance from the road, and this I did in a pouring rain, which wet me so thoroughly that my pocket case of instruments was dissolved by the wet and the instruments huddled loose in my pocket. The inclement weather protected me from the guerillas, who were not very active just then, and arriving within a mile or two of Fredericksburg, I met a small body of cavalry, who were going to Belle Plain with a few wagons in search of quartermaster stores and ammunition. Acting under my verbal orders, I took possession of these wagons in spite of the most vehement protests and threats, and I walked back to Belle Plain, loaded up the wagon train with medical stores, and sent them forward on May 10th under Assistant Surgeon Brinton Stone with instructions to get through as many of them as possible to Fredericksburg. He was a daring, persevering man, and started without escort, but with the wagons. His train became separated in two sections, the front one of which, consisting of a very few wagons, reached Fredericksburg. The latter section, and he himself, were captured by Captain Mosby, a "guerilla," that is, an independent ranger,* with from 50 to 200 troopers, acting under his own orders, hanging on the rear of our armies, capturing scouts, peddlers, wanderers, wagon-trains, and all stragglers. He was a veritable "moss-trooper," annoying us a great deal, but never preventing any serious movement.

The wagons and contents were carried off, and Stone himself was obliged to accompany Mosby for a whole night. Mosby took a fancy to him and in the morning said, "Doctor, if you will give me your word of honor not to say for twenty-four hours where you have been,

*The command of John S. Mosby, usually denominated "Mosby's Guerillas," was as a matter of fact the 43rd Virginia Regiment of Cavalry and duly commissioned as such by the Confederate Government.—E. T. S.

who has captured you, or anything whatever that you have heard or seen, I will let you go." Stone gave the promise, a man was detailed to accompany him back to the road, and he was set free, having been provided with a rather shabby horse in place of his own fine one. He reported to me, stating in general terms what had happened, but sedulously keeping his word and not violating the parole.

The train of wagons under Assistant Surgeon Brinton Stone was followed by a train from the Sanitary Commission. On the afternoon of the same day, May 10th, I sent forward a second supply train under Surgeon Homiston, to Fredericksburg. Stone and Homiston reported back to me at Belle Plain on the 11th of May.

By this time the wagons had begun to arrive from the army containing many slightly wounded men, among others my cousin Charles Coxe, who had been wounded in the arm at Todd's Tavern. I then forwarded the supply trains as fast as I could to Fredericksburg. Additional supplies were being received from Washington and soon Sanitary and Christian Commissioners arrived in great numbers. I had no quarters for these gentlemen, and at night I was obliged to let them sleep on a canal boat filled with blankets. Lights were forbidden. Stone, whom I instructed to make them comfortable, reported to me early in the morning that he was afraid there must be a good many dead Christians in the hold of the boat, "Because," he said, "I had to close the hatch to keep the stores from being damaged." Fortunately, they had plenty of air, and slept comfortably in the blankets.

A favorite trick of the Sanitary Commission agents was to ride forward with a wagon or two under the protection of a military train until the lines of safety were reached; then as their own wagons were usually better horsed than those of the Medical Department, they would whip out from the line, pass the front, open their supplies (usually of lemons and canned fruit) and the next day's New York *Herald* or some such paper would announce that "as usual the Sanitary Commission was first on the ground to assist our wounded boys."

In a train sent forward under Stone's command, an obnoxious Sanitarian with a four-horse light wagon of lemons and crackers, asked protection and escort, to which I acceded. As they started, Stone whispered to me, "I don't think that Sanitarian will be first in Fredericksburg." He afterwards told me, with a chuckle, that unfortunately the linch-pin came out of the sanitary wheel right in the midst of a deep creek fording, and that the last he saw of the Sanitary Commissioners was that they were soused in the swollen stream. He said nobody was to blame; but the teamsters, I heard, were very merry over the mishap.

Belle Plain was now established as the depot for the army, and having arranged matters at this place, I went forward with a supply train on May 13, 1864, to Fredericksburg, which I found filled with wounded, a train of six or seven hundred wagonfuls having arrived from the front. Having reported by letter to the Medical Director of the Army of the Potomac, I wrote by the same messenger to Captain Mason of the Fifth Cavalry, asking him to send me one or two orderlies, a pack horse, and a horse for myself. The pack horse, I told him I would load with a couple of kegs of Army Museum whiskey (cherry brandy), which I had taken the precaution to bring with me. In due time, horses and men arrived, and with Kelly, the trooper, I started for

General Grant's headquarters, wherever they might be. The kegs were neatly slung on the backs of the pack horses, and Kelly assured me that they and I were anxiously awaited at headquarters.

We passed over the old battlefield, over Marye's Heights, through the old Confederate defences and out through the woods and wilderness region, in search of headquarters. It was all very lonely, nobody could be seen, and there hardly seemed to be a bird in the woods. At last, and just as we were in doubt which way we were to go, whom should I meet but my friend and distant relative, Colonel Joe Brinton of the 8th Pennsylvania Cavalry. He gave me the general bearings, and I and my trooper rode on, the road becoming more and more silent as we advanced. Finally, after two or three hours' riding, we came to a fine old deserted mansion with broken greenhouses attached. There was a little clearing in the woods here, and somehow or other, I felt that we were off our track, wandering in space as it were. The more I looked, the more and more I was convinced that we were entirely wrong, so we retraced our steps and finally after much devious wandering, we struck the trodden road, and in the afternoon, reached General Grant's headquarters, where I was kindly welcomed.

After a while, General Grant asked me to take a seat by him some twenty yards in front of his tent, as he said he wanted to talk to me. I remember that he was smoking a big pipe. He spoke to me of old times. Just then Rawlins reported to him that one or two large regiments of heavy artillery were approaching. They were the soldiers who had garrisoned the defences of Washington, and had been converted and armed as infantry and sent to the front. He pointed to them approaching on the road to the left. The General remarked, "Order them in" (the 6th New York Artillery and I think, a Massachusetts regiment); they immediately advanced under fire, and took an active part in the contest, which I have omitted to state was taking place to the left of the General's headquarters. They advanced in a line which seemed to me to melt as it went on, so fierce was the fire. As darkness fell, the firing ceased and after a while Rawlins, the Chief of Staff, approached General Grant and advised him that the details of the day's fight were coming in over the telegraph. "How does it stand," said the General; the answer was, "We have lost about" so many, "the enemy have lost" so many, mentioning a greater number. "Ah!" said the General, "then we are still gaining on them, still a little ahead."

The Staff, one or two of whom I knew, seemed somewhat surprised to see a mere Doctor and Major talking familiarly with the General. After a while, General Meade came up into headquarters to know how things were going, and General Grant explained to him very quietly and simply. General Meade's manner was also very quiet and military, but it seemed to me that he recognized the great qualities of this simple unassuming man to whom he was talking.

General Grant asked me how I reached headquarters and by what road I had come, expressing surprise that I had taken so long to make the trip from Fredericksburg there. When I told him of the big house, and the green house and trailing vines, he said to me, "Why, Doctor, you have been behind the enemy's cavalry; I wonder you ever got here."

I stayed that night at headquarters. When I went to bed there was a vast force between the spot where

I was and the enemy's lines. In the morning at day-break, when I woke, there was not a soldier to be seen. I asked Rawlins how this was. He answered, "We have moved a whole wing of the army during the night." I said, "What force is there to protect these headquarters. He replied, "Not one soul. A company of the enemy's cavalry could capture us all, but we are going away now."

I may state that the Medical Director of the Army of the Potomac, Surgeon McParlin, had assigned me by letter on the 13th of May, to duty as Medical Purveyor of the Army. I explained to the General that it was not the intention of the Surgeon-General to put me on permanent duty; that I had my work at Washington to finish. He laughed and said, "We must keep you here, so that we can get plenty of castor oil." However, he directed my order changed, so that on the morning of the 15th, I was able to return to Fredericksburg, finish up the business of the supplies, see what surgery I could, and having thus fulfilled my order of delivering the battlefield supplies, betook myself to Washington in accordance with my instructions from the Acting-Surgeon-General. On the 22nd of May, I was back at my old duties in the office.

# CHAPTER XXIII

## JAMES RIVER AND CITY POINT

On the 5th of June, 1864, I received orders from the Acting-Surgeon-General to go to White House, Virginia, and report by letter to the Medical Director of the Army of the Potomac for surgical duty with the wounded at that place. General Grant was at this time operating with two armies. One, the Army of the Potomac, with which he had crossed the Rapidan, and moved southward through the wilderness, lay northeast of Richmond, with headquarters at Cold Harbor. It was the General's evident intention to swing this army around and to the south of Richmond, cross the James River somewhere in the neighborhood of Harrison's Landing, and join and co-operate with the army of the James River, which, under Gen. B. F. Butler, had been moved to the south bank, and occupied Bermuda Hundred. With the co-operation of these two forces, General Grant then proposed to act against Petersburg and destroy the railroad lines which formed the communication between Richmond and the Army of Northern Virginia and the South. This isolated Richmond, and General Lee's Army must eventually surrender. Thus, in the end it proved, and so fell the Southern cause.

I immediately left Washington by boat for White House, ascending the Pamunkey River and arriving there, reported according to my orders, and was soon hard at work at real professional duties. There were here many wounded, and there was plenty for everyone to do.

At White House I remained several days; in the meantime the Army was moving toward the James, and preparations were being made shortly to abandon White House as a base, and the stores, supplies and wounded were generally removed, and by June 22nd, White House was abandoned as a depot. On the 14th of June, I left White House, sailed down the Pamunkey, and up the James. On the 16th, I reached Fort Powhatan, eight miles below Harrison's Landing, on the south bank of the James. Here a pontoon bridge had been laid, and columns of our army had crossed and were crossing. Several pontoons had been put down between this point and City Point, which was our chief base. The laying of these boat bridges was under the supervision of General Benham, of the Engineers. I had known him in Washington, for we had for some time taken our meals at the same table. At the time I approached the pontoon bridge, which was opened for the space of two or three boats to let steamers pass, Benham was standing at the end (the mid-stream end), of his bridge. At this time, I was in medical charge of a steamer with a long tow of canal boats having medical stores. We had to approach the cut in the bridge obliquely, and somehow or other, hampered by our long train of heavy boats, we lost our headway, and came athwart the pontoon, tearing the boats from the anchorage, and doing not a little harm in spite of our best efforts to avoid injury. Benham, who was a high-tempered man, looked upon this damage as an interference with his work. He was greatly incensed (and I don't wonder), and seeing me on the deck of the steamer, in uniform, and apparently in charge, he became fiercely enraged and excited. "Shoot him, shoot him, shoot the scoundrel," he shouted, pointing to me. I called to him by name, but he was so angry it was no use, so I prudently disappeared. Thus I left him in his rage, and passed up to my destination, City Point.

At this place, I remained on board one of the steamers, and here I may say that I was quite surprised to find several of the little stern-wheel steamers taken from our Shuylkill River where they had plied between Fairmount and Manayunk. They, with so many steam vessels, had been pressed into service, and being of light draught and easily managed, proved of great service. They had a very home-like appearance to me, and when I was temporarily in charge of them, I almost thought I was in my own house. They were used for medical storage and supplies.

General Grant's headquarters were now being established at City Point, and he lived in the little log cabin which many of my readers have so often seen in Fairmount Park near the Lemon Hill Mansion, and before one comes to the Girard Avenue Bridge.* I remember riding to the General's headquarters, but he was away, and I did not see him. About the 19th, I rode out along our lines on the left towards Petersburg, and on my way out, I passed within sight of a rebel sharpshooter, stationed up a tree, a long way off, a mile it seemed to me. He was good enough to favor me with a shot, and the ball struck the ground near me. On this

---

*This historic cabin Grant gave to George H. Stuart, who had it carefully taken apart, shipped by schooner and erected in Fairmount Park. It remained the property of G. H. Stuart's estate until formally presented to the city in 1903.—E. T. S.

ride, at a hospital, I saw a poor fellow, who while squatting on a rail, over a little stream, washing out his shirt, had been shot through both thigh bones by a Whitworth bullet or bolt (hexagonal), fired by a sharpshooter from a tree said to be nearly a measured mile and a quarter distant. The poor fellow died and the bolt is in my collection of projectiles.

There was a constant skirmishing fire kept up along our front; everywhere, one could see the white puffs of smoke. We were constantly pushing out for new positions, which, of course, our enemy resisted. This ride conveyed to me an idea of continuous fighting on a small scale. Here, too, I saw a good many negro troops, the first time I had ever seen them in the field. They looked well, but did not in these operations prove altogether satisfactory, but I shall say more of them when I come to speak of the Battle of Nashville, in December, 1864.

In the latter part of the month of June, about the 28th, I think, a cavalry raid was undertaken by the Southern forces. A large body of horse and light artillery advanced into northern Maryland, occupying Hagerstown, threatening Frederick, scouring the country, collecting forage and stores, and levying contributions of money. A general panic ensued, and the utmost consternation prevailed. The object of this raid, undoubtedly, was to threaten Washington (uncovered by General Hunter's retirement to western Virginia), and thus to force General Grant to weaken his forces in front of Richmond and Petersburg, by sending troops to the relief of Washington. But General Grant was quite equal to the occasion; he was by no means "stampeded," to use a western term; and as we shall see, while sending a few troops to the defence of the national capital, he never for a moment relaxed his death grip on Lee's army and Richmond.

After having ravaged Maryland pretty well, about the 8th of July, the Southern raiding force, some thousand strong, appeared in the neighborhood of Monocacy, some miles from Baltimore. Here General Lewis Wallace (the author since of *Ben Hur*, and other productions of merit), advanced against him with General Ricketts in command of one division of the 6th Corps. These forces, on July 9th, were defeated by the enemy, who then moved against Washington, and there made their appearance, I think on July 11th.

I can give you but a faint idea of the panic which their advent created. Washington at that time had no garrison of trained or experienced troops, either regular or volunteer. We all whistled to keep our courage up, and whistled, too, very loud. The President, had, indeed, called on several Governors of northern states for troops. These were being raised, but so far had not yet arrived. The garrison of the belt of forts surrounding Washington had been stripped of troops to reinforce the Army of the Potomac during the Wilderness campaign. These men were the heavy artillery from Massachusetts and New York chiefly, whom I had seen engaged in the fight near Anderson's house. They fought as infantry.

So at the Capitol, we kept our pens driving merrily, and the Secretary of War directed that all the orderlies, messengers, military riffraff, the invalids, veteran reserve, and indeed every man in Government employ, who could put on a uniform, or carry a musket, should turn out in defence of the capital of his country, and a sorry lot they were. They laid down their pens, and off they went to "report" for military duty. My clerks went too, from my office, but they were a mild-mannered set, and I assume they would never have hurt anybody, not even in self-defence.

In the offices, everybody tried to appear very busy, no one would admit ideas of danger, but yet everyone was at heart afraid. I learned from a very trustworthy source, that even the Secretary of War, the redoubtable Mr. Edwin M. Stanton, thought so gravely of the situation, as to send his silver and valuables aboard a gunboat. This information reached me through a clerk. In Washington, the Brotherhood of Clerks knew everything, the most secret acts, and even thoughts, of men, very high in position, men who never forgot themselves, or committed an indiscretion with their equals or superiors in station, but who with their confidential clerks, were sometimes a little leaky. My head clerk was most popular among his fellows, gentle-mannered, silent, and insinuating in manners, the very man to invite confidence, as it were. He always knew the hidden counsels of the White House, and the Secretary's office. He was proud of this information, especially when he had obtained it by ingenuity, and he always tried to post me a day in advance. He was always right. His information was reliable and not sensational, and I thus learned many a bit of gossip, military and political, and many a bit of early news. He told me the gunboat story, which he said was very private, and I daresay he was very near the truth.

I doubt if many persons in the North ever knew, or knowing, realized, the true state of insecurity in Washington. I really believe that five hundred, yes, one hundred, of Early's horses could have ridden into and through Washington, and captured whom they chose, the President or his Cabinet, or even *myself*.

On the afternoon on which the enemy appeared before Washington, I took a long ride alone, from near
Rock Creek, in the neighborhood of Georgetown, around
beyond the Seventh Street Road, passing beneath quite
a chain of earthworks and forts. We had plenty of
works, and lots of rifle trenches, or their equivalents,
but they were manned by no real troops, only messengers, convalescent patients from the hospitals, all
looking and feeling very uncomfortable, and distressed
at the idea of passing the night in the open air, and
that, too, within sight of their own boarding houses,
within touch almost of their very beds. In the earth-
forts, which were well located and strongly built, and
provided with heavy guns, a few scattered artillerymen
were stationed, mostly men from light batteries, and
occasionally a gun would be fired at the enemy, who
lay a mile or two away beyond our works. A bronze
stripping from one of these big shells, fired from a
siege gun, just above my head, fell on the ground close
by me. I picked it up, a crooked, ragged piece of
metal.

The forts, as I have said, were maintained with large
guns, siege guns, as they were called, and every precaution was taken to insure their accurate fire, the distance of all points within range being accurately calculated; these distances, and the name of the locality
were printed on the stage of each gun. Let us take a
place called Smith's House, distant one and a half
measured miles from the fort. Some such inscription
as this would be attached to the gun carriage: "Smith's
house, 1-½ miles: Elevation of gun 3 degrees: Charge
for the gun 1 lb. powder; Time fuse for shell 4 seconds."

Thus an artillery man having this information, and
knowing his business, could so train his gun, mechanic-

ally as it were, as to make very certain firing. A group of rebel and southern cavalry was standing in the middle of a road, about a mile from a fort, and exactly in front of a registered locality, Smith's house, I think it was. A young light artillery man from the West, was on duty in the fort; he trained a gun by the legends printed on the traverse, and the shell burst exactly in front of the house, and apparently in the road, scattering the group. I could not tell whether anyone was hurt, but the shot seemed marvellously well directed.

For this first day, or a part of it, the town was unprotected, but later, the 19th Corps from Louisiana, and the 6th (veteran) Corps from the Army of the Potomac arrived. These immediately went into the trenches, and soon made their presence manifest to the enemy by the lively cracks of their rifles. On the following day, early in the morning, some skirmishing took place, and the enemy finally seeing that Washington had been succored, and that any attempt to capture it could not succeed, slowly withdrew, followed by the 6th Corps, under General Wright. On the morning before they withdrew, I rode out to the scene of hostilities in company with Dr. Wm. Thomson and Dr. Wm. Norris, of Philadelphia. They were at that time both assistant surgeons in the regular army. Dr. Thomson had charge of the Douglas Hospital in Washington, and Dr. Norris was on duty under him. We rode out by Seventh Street Road, I think. The enemy were at that time in full force on the opposite hills, and their firing was brisk. Our 6th Corps troops in the trenches replied rapidly. Our presence, three mounted officers, at once attracted the enemy's attention, and we became the object of their sharpshooter's fire. They were scattered in the open fields, in front of the wooded ridges occupied by their main body. Some of their sharp-shooters had cleverly concealed and protected themselves by fence rails, piled at an angle, and they fired with most provoking deliberation. One or two shots struck the ground close by our horses' feet. For my part, I (who had seen a good deal of fighting, while my two companions had not seen any) felt quite keenly the danger of the situation. It is not at all pleasant to be a target for an enterprising and skilful marksman, who, in comparative safety, fires at his leisure. I confess I wanted to get away, especially as I had little confidence in my horse, the wicked one, who seemed to have a devilish comprehension of the situation, and evidently wanted to bolt toward the enemy. I was delighted afterwards at the conduct of a 6th Corps Sergeant, who seeing the shot and the dust from the bullets, fired by one particular "reb," came towards us, and saluting, said, "Gentlemen, foolish exposure is not bravery, you had better ride back and get under cover." How I have respected that man! I have never forgotten him, and I can see his face this minute. My comrades saw the good sense of his remarks, and we returned beyond the range of the one persevering Johnny Reb, hidden behind his rails. So we went home and dined.

Thomson, who rode out the next morning after the enemy had retired, told me that he had found the poor "reb," who had singled us out for his attentions, lying still, behind his rails, with a bullet hole through his forehead. He had been spied out, and shot, by a 6th Corps man, who could not resist the chance. Poor fellow, I absolutely felt sorry for him, although he did try to kill us. He seemed so cool and saucy, ensconced in his hiding-place, so far in advance of his friends.

So this is what I saw of Early's raid on Washington.

By the evening of the 12th of July, the enemy were all away, and Washington was as safe as ever.

In a letter to my Mother from Washington, dated July 14, 1864, I wrote: "So the siege is raised, and Johnny Reb is off. We had quite a sharp fight. Fancy dining, smoking a cigar, riding out leisurely, looking at the whole performance, within a few hundred yards, and when the fighting was over, going back to a cup of coffee. I saw all the fighting here; it was quite brisk and very exciting, bullets whizzing all around. We lost about 350 men. The New York *Herald* has just arrived; we have had none for four days. I am well as usual. Our blessed forts stood us in good stead. I sat on my horse just in front of one of them, and heard the big shells screaming twenty feet above my head. The whole affair was very curious. There was not a great deal of excitement, everybody was prepared, and a hard fight was expected. We had a good many men. The current here is against Grant, but you know I prophesied a panic against him long ago; but he will not be shaken from his course, I am sure."

The months of July and August, 1864, I spent in Washington, with the exception of one or two trips to New York and Philadelphia, on business connected with the art department of the Museum. In the latter part of the summer, a photographic bureau was added to the Museum, and I had to see to engaging the proper artists and outfit. I succeeded after much trouble in procuring an excellent artist, named Bell, and much of his work figures in the volumes of the Medical and Surgical History of the War.

And here, perhaps, it would be well to say a little about the means to which resort was had to obtain the illustrations for that great work. When I first went on duty at the Surgeon-General's office, and had committed to me the preparation of the *Surgical History of the War,* I set about finding for myself an artist. Our views at that time were not very extended, and the means at the disposal of the Surgeon-General for that purpose were rather limited. The supply of artists in Washington available for my purposes was not very great. The only person I could at first lay my hands on was a German artist, who had been on topographical duty in the War Department (his name was Pohlers), excellent in his line, but not capable of drawing and coloring from the human figure. The maps, however, which he reduced and reproduced from the larger maps of the topographical engineers were very accurate and beautiful. The positions of the field hospitals and points of medical interest were furnished by the medical officers on duty at the different actions and localities. Most of these field maps were drawn under my supervision. You will see them in the appendix to the *Medical Volume,* Part I. of the *Medical and Surgical History of the Rebellion.* They have the name, "A. Pohlers del" at the bottom. Pohlers remained on duty with me while I was in Washington, employed on map work.

E. Stauch was a German water-colorist. His work was very fine, and his coloring exquisite. He came to me in the early part of 1863, or the end of 1862. He accompanied me in several visits to the army in the field, and frequently visited the hospitals with me, especially to make pictures and sketches of the hospital gangrene cases, occurring in our troops sent north and exchanged from the Southern prisons. His colored pictures, which were done in oil, are faithfully delineated in Surgical volumes, Parts II and III, of the *Medical and Surgical History of the War.* With one or two exceptions, all of the colored pictures in the work are from the pencil and brush of Stauch. He was a most excellent artist, and when in a good humor, or well satisfied, could, and would, work well, and with tolerable rapidity. Like so many artists, however, he was capricious and irritable, and when these fits were on him, he could not be depended on. When I took him with me to the army, I always took great care of his bed and food, far more than I did of my own. I worked with him thus. I first selected the patients to be pictured on the field or in the hospital. Then the point of injury, say the wounds of entrance, were carefully painted by Stauch in oil. Next a pencil outline sketch was taken of the general locality. This work he did with great rapidity, and then when he reached Washington again, the beautiful pictures you will see in the *Surgical History* were elaborated.

I was very desirous of obtaining a full and perfect series of wounds of entrance and exit, of round bullets, and conical projectiles, freshly taken. To get these, it was necessary to have an artist well to the front, while fighting was going on. This seemed at first almost impossible, but I finally arranged it thus. When the troops under General Grant, occupied the line stretching from City Point to Petersburg, heavy fighting was of everyday occurrence. Bomb-proofs, too, had been erected, well forward, to which the wounded were carried for the first surgical attentions. In my office, a young medical officer, and acting-assistant-surgeon, named Porter (a relative of Admiral Porter), was on duty. He was a singularly brave young man, cool in danger, and always having his head about him. He suggested to me to let him go to the front with Stauch, the artist, saying that when some sharp fighting should take place, he would "run" the artist into the bombproof, and then as the wounded should come in, he (Porter) would make choice of suitable cases, and the sketches and paintings could be immediately made, with a certain knowledge of the time which elapsed since the reception of the wound. This plan was put into force—Porter, the artist, and an orderly went down to City Point, and succeeded, with some trouble, and the loss of a horse, and I think, too, at the cost of a gunshot wound to the guide, or worse, in reaching the protected casemate or proof to which the wounded were being carried. Here forty-seven oil sketches were taken, which are reproduced at pages 712 and 714 of the Part III, Surgical Volume of the Medical and Surgical History of the War. Magnificent sketches they are, and truthful. Unfortunately, one thing is wanting. Each pair of wounds of entrance and exit, or singly, if but one, should be represented in a picture, showing the precise locality and the contour of the part injured. Such a series of sketches in lead pencil, adapted for future elaborations, was in fact made by the artist at that time. On emerging from the bombproof and his perilous duty, the artist came to Washington, and leaving there the precious block of oils in the office, and stating that he had the supplementary sketches in his possession, received permission to visit his home in Philadelphia on promise to return in a day or two. Not returning, I was sent to look him up, if possible, when I learned through the death records of the Board of Health that he had died of an illness of a day or two's duration, the exact nature of which was not known, and was probably of some nervous type, the result of exposure or of mental disturbance. The key of this series of pictures was not found during my stay at Washington, and I imagine that the description in small type on page 712 has been supplied from notes rather than from pictorial representations. I may, however, be wrong in this idea. At all events, the series of wounds of entrance and exit, are not presented in the manner I had designed when my attempt to arrange for their production was made.

In 1864, my friend, Gideon Scull, was ordered from Washington by the Secretary of War. Captain Scull was much attached to Mr. Pierce Butler, of Philadelphia, who on account of his supposed Southern feeling or sympathy, was not kindly regarded by the Secretary of War, and indeed, I believe he at one time was arrested by Mr. Stanton's order. The Secretary, having learned of Mr. Scull's presence in Washington (for he was a most capable officer, and was on duty in the office of the Commissary General of Subsistence) personally ordered his detail to the West at St. Louis, with, if my memory is correct, a special direction that, once there, he should be assigned to an army in the field, for poor Scull had rheumatism, and the Secretary knew it. Scull was what was then called a "white elephant," and when I said good-bye, I remember very well that I told him, "I soon, too, will be a white elephant, and will follow you." In the end prophecy proved true.

About this time, there was a good deal of grumbling in Washington about General Grant. He had not many friends amongst the Army of Potomac men. They were all McClellan men, and insisted that Grant was only treading the same path followed by McClellan, and that his bloody victories were fruitless. They did not like him, and had no confidence in him. The Northern people, as a mass, believed in him; the Eastern, especially the troops of the Army of the Potomac, did not. I, however, could not forget his exploits in the West, and the untiring bulldog perseverance he there exhibited. In a letter to my Mother of September 8, 1864, which I quote, I wrote: "You may be sure that Grant will succeed; he cannot fail; my confidence in him is the same as ever."

# CHAPTER XXIV

About the 20th of September, 1864, I was sent to the Valley of Virginia. This was then the condition of affairs: In the latter days of July and early August, a cavalry raid had been made by the enemy across the Potomac and Maryland into Pennsylvania. The town of Chambersburg was burned, and the enemy withdrew into Virginia. At this time, General Sheridan, by Grant's order, was placed in command of a considerable force on the upper Potomac, from Harper's Ferry westward and southward. He was opposed by the southern general Early, and a good deal of manœuvring took place. On the 19th of September, 1864, occurred Sheridan's famous ride from Winchester and the attack and defeat of the enemy at Cedar Creek, and on the 23rd of the same month at Fisher's Hill, not far from the town of Woodstock. The enemy's wounded fell into Sheridan's hands, and were scattered over a large area of country. He also captured a large number of prisoners, many of whom were sent back to Winchester. The devastation of the Shenandoah Valley and the Valley of Virginia then followed, the country being rendered useless to the enemy as a base of military operations or for material supplies. In fact it was left in such a state, that to use the words of Sheridan, "A carrion crow in his flight across must either carry his rations or starve." War's stern necessity!

The following was my order:

"Surgeon General's Office, Washington City, D. C.
Sept. 20th, 1864.

Sir:

I am instructed by the Surgeon General to direct you to proceed without delay, to Winchester, Va., and take charge of the wounded at that place temporarily, reporting your arrival there by letter to the Medical Director at the Headquarters of Major General Sheridan. Surgeons McKay, Hayden, U. S. Vols.; Asst. Surgeon Carter, U. S. A.; Stone, U. S. Vols., and Acting Asst. Surgeon Porter will be ordered to report to you for duty.

Ten of the most competent Acting Asst. Surgeons on duty in Baltimore, and five from Philadelphia, are also ordered to proceed at once to Winchester, and to report to the chief Medical Officer.

Very respy. yr. obt. servt.

By order of the Surg. Genl.

(sd)   C. H. CRANE,
Surg. U. S. A.

Surg. J. H. Brinton, U. S. V.
Present."

At the time at which I received the foregoing order, the state of the road to Harper's Ferry was very uncertain. However, as the supply of medical officers at Winchester was insufficient, and as the number of wounded was unknown, although supposed to be large, the Secretary of War ordered that my special train should have the right of way, and that we should make the best time possible. We left Washington on the evening of Tuesday, the 24th of September, 1864. At the depot, Surgeons Hayden, McKay and Porter, and two or three hospital stewards, reported to me for duty.

Accordingly we started, and telegraphing from the Relay House to have all opposing trains stopped and the only track to be cleared, we went forward at high speed. Some of the Baltimore doctors joined us at the Relay, and we reached Harper's Ferry in a short time, about noon. Here, I saw the ruin of some sixty or seventy locomotives. They had been purposely run off the end of the bridge, and were then burned in one ghastly heap of ruins. I have never before or since seen such a horrible scene of wanton destruction. The entire appearance of the town was poverty-stricken and war-worn, on one day in the occupancy of one, and on the next, of the other, contending armies. All the better class of people had fled, and only a few of the poorest whites and a few of the negroes were left. The arsenal, barracks, and public buildings had long since been burned, and all air of prosperity had passed away. I saw the commanding officers of our troops there and learning that a wagon-train with escort of cavalry was about to start, joined it with my doctors.

We pushed along the well-travelled road, and passed Charlestown. I had a long wagon-train of medical supplies, and in a kind of way was commander of the party. We left Harper's Ferry at 10 A.M., September 21st, and reached Winchester at 9.30 P.M. Having a strong guard, sufficient to protect us from the guerillas who infested all roads, we felt no apprehensions. Our feelings of safety were shared by a number of settlers and camp followers, who would join our train and avail themselves of our protection. One or two of these people were peddlers. I recollect one man particularly, a Jewish peddler, with a black and red wagon. He was a cunning fellow in his way, and with his heavily laden one-horse wagon, would place himself in our front and would dawdle along, at the pace suitable to his own poor overloaded, overworked beast. Finally, on a hillside, close to a wood, his wagon became stalled in a cut in the road, and the whole train not being able to pass was brought to a standstill. This would not do, so I ordered the man to shove his cart on a bank on one side of the road, and we hurried on, despite his prayers and imprecations, at being left behind. We told him to fall in at the rear which he promised to do, but somehow he must have lagged behind, for the next day after I reached Winchester, the Captain of the first train following our wake, said to me, "Doctor, we found a peddler's wagon thrown off the bank; the peddler had his throat cut, and lay dead beneath it; the contents of the wagon had been carried off, and all we found in it was this little leather-covered portfolio," and he gave it to me, one of the cheap little portfolios soldiers liked to buy in those days, and which is now somewhere about the house as I write.

On arriving at Winchester, I assumed charge of the wounded who were coming in from the neighborhood of Woodstock, where Sheridan had defeated the enemy in one or two engagements, notably at Fisher's Hill. For a day or two, I did the best I could for them in the hotel and church hospitals where I found them, and which had been hastily extemporized. It was indeed a difficult matter to care for them. On the 25th of September, the wounded in Winchester numbered 4,201, and commissary and medical supplies had to be brought up from Harper's Ferry and Martinsburg. The railroad to these places had been destroyed, and the roads were infested with guerillas, and only practicable with strong escorts. So troublesome were these gentry, that it was not safe to ride a mile beyond our lines without a guard, and we were practically cut off from obtaining the commonest supplies from the adjacent country. However, I did the best I could for the wounded I found in the hospital, making use of everything I had, and making requisitions, and bringing up fresh mounts by wagon.

In a few hours, sanitarians and worse, sanitary and "Christian women" began to arrive. Good women-nurses were a godsend; those who would really nurse and work, do what they were told, make no pets, and give no trouble. On the other hand, the fussy female, intent on notoriety and glorying in her good works, fond of washing the faces of "our boys" and of writing letters home, glorifying herself;—she was not godsent; in fact we all regarded her as having a very different origin. One of such creatures I was blest with at Winchester. She was a friend of Mrs. Stanton, the wife of the Secretary of War, and took care to let everyone know of the fact, and boasted a good deal of her influence with the Secretary and of the information she gave him. Knowing his harshness, and ruthlessness, and impetuous injustice, I felt very much afraid of this woman for a day or two. She used to wear an india-rubber waterproof, and created discontent and disorder wherever she went. The men all saw and recognized her weakness. I remember that she made a special pet of one wretched malingerer. She followed me for hours, saying that "the poor boy would relish an omelet." I told her, "that I had no eggs, but that I thought she could get them at a farm-house, just outside the lines; if she liked I would send her there." I was much in hopes that some of Mosby's men would catch her. She was too sharp, and wouldn't go, but she left me, kindly muttering her intentions to "let her friend the Secretary of War know how badly the wounded boys were treated." I took an opportunity, too, of sending off that malingerer, without ever giving her an opportunity of saying bood-bye. His comrades understood the matter, and regarded my little joke with favor.

In taking care of all these men, being without the usual medical and sanitary (I don't mean Sanitary Commission) stores, I was obliged by pure necessity to lay violent hands on everything I could find in the town of Winchester, the property of the citizens, and here it is that I approach that all-important subject, Mrs. Washington's brass kettle. You must know that the great thing in feeding sick people is to possess the proper means of cooking, and the chief means of something to cook with, namely, pots, pans and kettles. Now, I found the newly improvised hospital at Winchester town, destitute of all culinary apparatus. I appealed to the Mayor of the place, in fact, made a requisition on him for kettles. Strange to say, it was reported to me that there were no kettles. They had all suddenly and mysteriously disappeared. Luckily, for me, as I was walking through a back alley, I spied an iron pot, which had been stuck on a paling fence to dry, just outside the kitchen door. I instantly stepped in, and proceeded to confiscate it on the spot. "What, take my only kettle," said the sour-faced, poverty-stricken woman. "Why don't you take the rich people's things, and let the poor alone?" "Why," said I, "there are no rich people, and there are no kettles in town." "None," said she, "why, there are plenty. Take Mrs. Washington's kettle, that's brass, and the best and biggest one in town. I'll show you where they keep it." I saw at once an opening. "Now," said I, "I'll tell you what

I'll do. If you tell me where all the good kettles and good cooking things are, I'll let yours alone." She jumped at the chance, and soon I knew exactly who owned the big preserving jars, and where they were. Under my friend's vigilant direction (she was a poor white), Mrs. Washington's kettle was soon playing its part in soup-making for the hospital, and more of its companions were quickly in like manner pressed into this new duty of helping to furnish good food for hated "Yankees." And strange to say, as soon as one or two kettles were seized by martial process, every woman in town seemed to be willing to tell of her neighbor to save herself. Of course, I had plenty of complaints, and visits from indignant dames, some complaining, some threatening, and some appealing to my sympathy, some even on the ground of acquaintance in their girlish days when they were in school in Philadelphia at Picots, or Mrs. Gardelle's; but somehow I survived the War of the Kettles.

After reporting by letter to Surgeon Chiselin, General Sheridan's Medical Director, I received instructions to forward the wounded north, both Union and Rebel, and to send supplies to the front as rapidly as possible. At the same time, I was to establish a large tent hospital on a plateau in the immediate vicinity of the town, near a fine spring and stream of running water. The hospital was to be of a capacity of four to five thousand beds, and to be well equipped. I therefore made, by telegraph, requisition on the Surgeon-General's office for, I think, 500 tents, each tent holding comfortably eight sick beds. I also made requisition in the same way for 500 stoves, and these, I was told, would be (and indeed were) promptly sent me, for in a few hours, the wagon-trains containing them began to arrive. To pitch 500 tents (hospital tents) was no slight matter. I was directed to call upon the post commandant at Winchester for the necessary details of men. Fortunately, I had been so long on duty at Washington that I had learned how to take a sufficiently large view of work to be done, and to be sufficiently imperious in exacting the assistance of others. I therefore, called upon the Colonel acting as a Brigadier-General in command at Winchester, telling him I wanted men to pitch tents. He was a little uppish, as behooved his dignity, but after some hesitation, he said, "Well, Doctor, I will give you a few men; how many do you want?" I wish you could have seen his astonishment when I answered, "At least five or six hundred with their full complement of officers." "Impossible," said he, "I never heard of such a demand." But I told him I made the demand, and should do so in writing, and instantly report his answer by telegraph to Washington, as I was acting by special orders from the Surgeon-General's office, direct from the War Department. His change of manner was immediate. "The men will be ready in the early morning, and the officers should have special orders"; and so it was. That night, September 24, 1864, having previously ridden over the ground and marked the boundary of the hospital to be, I put a medical officer in charge, and drew out the plan of the hospital. The tents were to be pitched free, end to end, between wooden frameworks for the attachment of the tent ropes, and with wide streets. This would have formed good wards, capable of being easily heated by stoves, and well ventilated, and containing about twenty-five patients each. I went to bed, well satisfied with my plans, leaving orders to start work at the earliest hour in the morning of the 25th of September. The surgeon in charge whom

I had selected, was a man of high scientific attainment, and I anticipated a superb hospital. In the morning, as soon as I had dispatched my necessary office work, I hurried out to see how my hospital was getting along. On reaching the ground, I found what looked to be a series of canvas tenpin alleys, long, narrow, snaky-looking constructions. My precious surgeon had, on his own responsibility, changed my plans, and pitched six hospital tents end to end in violation of every sanitary and hygienic consideration, and without ventilation, either inside or out. I was stupefied at the sight, but the mischief was done;—the tents were up and time pressed. All that I could do was to order the third and fourth of each group to be struck down, thus forming a central narrow street, and leaving the tents in groups of two. I was dreadfully mortified at the appearance, but I ordered the remaining tents to be properly pitched, despite the resulting unsymmetrical appearance which was thus given to the whole company. It was the best I could do under the circumstances. After this, the equipment of the hospital was rapidly pushed and the occupation by patients effected. To give an idea of what I did at Winchester, I insert a copy of my report to the Surgeon-General:

"Winchester, Va., Sept. 26th, 1864.
General:—

I have already forwarded you telegrams, indicating my action here. I have the honor now to report more fully. On my arrival here on the night of June 21st, I found matters in much confusion. Every exertion possible has been made by Assistant Surgeon General DuBois, U. S. A. in charge, of the hospitals, to systematize relief for the wounded, but the scanty supplies, the filthy condition of the town, and the number of the wounded, rendered the matter one of extreme difficulty. By the morning of the 22nd, all of the wounded were collected from the houses near the field, and were brought to hospitals in or near the town, and within our picket lines. On the afternoon of the 22nd, 188 hospital tents arrived by wagons. I directed these to be pitched in an eligible situation, close to a fine spring near the town, and placed Surgeon Hayden, U. S. V., in charge. 108 tents have arrived since and are being pitched,—in all 296. 104 tents, the balance of the 400 sent, were by General Sheridan's orders pitched at Sandy Hook to increase the capacity of that hospital. The supply of medicine in hospital stores has been exceedingly scanty, only eight wagon loads having as yet arrived, and these were rapidly exhausted. A train is now on the way hither. Of blankets and hospital clothing we have none. I directed Surgeon Shields, who has been appointed Purveyor of the Army, to obtain 5000 from the Quartermaster at Harper's Ferry. I also instructed him to make a requisition on the Purveyor at Baltimore for such additional supplies as he might stand in need of. Cooking apparatus, etc., I obtained on application to the Provost Marshal. Yesterday morning, the 25th instant, I sent 1200 wounded to Harper's Ferry, as the railroad to Washington was not yet opened.

I last night received instructions from the Army Headquarters to send off all light cases, Union and Rebel, to Martinsburg. Asst. Surgeon Ohhschloger has been assigned to duty in charge of transportation at that point. The severe cases I am instructed to place in the tents, and as fast as the latter become empty to transfer them to Martinsburg, the new army base.

I telegraphed you this morning, requesting that the Quartermaster's Department may be furnished with 150 wood stoves, suitable for hospital tents. The weather is becoming cold, the town is overcrowded, and I must get the wounded into the tents as soon as possible. There probably will be 1500 men who cannot be moved for some weeks.

P. S.   Since writing the foregoing, a large train of medical supplies, and also 3000 blankets have arrived.

Very respfty. yr. Obt. svt.

J. H. BRINTON,

Surg. U. S. Vols. Chf. Medl. Officer."

My time in Winchester was spent in very hard work, but the results were satisfactory to me.   I had all ready in forty-eight hours, and this was the largest hospital of the war.   I had lodging for the four or five days in a store-keeper's house.   Of course, nearly everybody was Southern in their opinions.   They hated us, but they had to put up with us, and indeed, tried their best to make out of us all the money that they could.   There was, however, some Union feeling, but I think it was confined to people of the Quaker descent, who had a good deal of the business of the place in their hands. One of these families I came to know.   Their name was, I think, Griffith, and before the war, I believe, they had been millers.   I took tea at the house, and visited there once or twice.   They were very nice people and devotedly attached to the Union.   One of the ladies told me that they had always managed to keep the national flag, and whenever the Union troops occupied Winchester, they were able to hang the Stars and Stripes from the porch.   This irritated their rebel neighbors greatly, and just as soon as the Union troops would retire, and the town again become in the possession of the Confederate forces, they would become subjected to domiciliary visits, and the house would be most rigidly searched.   But their flag was never discovered, and from what they said, it was either very securely hidden or else on the person of some of the ladies, which was most likely.

During this time, the subsistence and medical supplies of the place were very short. We had hardly enough to eat, and there was much deprivation and suffering which I hardly like to recall. We had a large number of wounded rebel prisoners, some eleven or twelve hundred, I think. These were penned up, or confined in an open square, fronting on the main street, and surrounded by a high iron railing, such as Washington Square, and the squares generally in Philadelphia used to have. These poor fellows were without covering or shelter of any kind, and what was far worse, we had scarcely any rations to give them. In fact so closely did Mosby and guerillas watch all the roads and the outskirts of the town, that neither food nor provender could be brought, save under heavy escort. We had really almost nothing, and I know one or two mornings when the Commissary of Subsistence had only two or three hundred rations in store, and they were nothing among so many. Our poor prisoners were almost starved, and I have seen them struggle almost to the death for a biscuit or crust, thrown over the iron paling by their sympathetic friends. It was a pitiable sight, heart-breaking, but we could not help it. Their wounded in the hospital fared better; they got the same food as our own; we made no distinction, and never did in my whole experience of our war.

I worked very hard at Winchester; I think I did good work, furthering the operations of the Medical Department, and preventing much suffering to the wounded of both sides. You can therefore imagine my surprise (or at least, it would have been surprise had I not been so long on duty in Washington) when

I received the following, forwarded to me from Harper's Ferry, by Doctor Blaney:

[TELEGRAM]
"Washington, D. C.,
Sept. 24-1864.
To Surgeon Blaney,
    Medl. Director.
Detail some competent Medical Officer as Acting Director at Harper's Ferry, and go forward at once to Winchester, Virginia. Relieve Surg. J. H. Brinton, U. S. Vols. of his duties there, and report your arrival by telegraph to this office.
                                J. H. BARNES,
                                        Surg. Genl.
A true copy
    Jos. V. Z. Blaney,
        Surgeon U. S. Vols.
            Chief Medl. Director,
                At Winchester, Va.
                    (and the original of the next).


                        Surgeon General's Office,
                            Washington, D. C.
                                Sept. 25th, 1864.
Surgeon J. H. Brinton,
    Winchester, Va.
    Upon the arrival of Surgeon Blaney, turn over your instructions to him, and return to Washington.
                        JOSEPH K. BARNES,
                                Surgeon General.
A true Copy
S. G. O.
Oct. 4, 1864.
                    C. H. Crane,
                        Surgeon, U. S. A."

I could hardly make this out. I rather suspected that somehow or other, I had come to grief. I had, as it were, a presentiment, but still I hurried on with preparations. I turned over my instructions to Surgeon Blaney, U. S. V., and then had to wait a few hours for an escort or guard. The Post Commandant was very kind, and said he would make some excuse and send a strong guard to Martinsburg, the next morning, and I could travel with them. Martinsburg was distant about twenty miles. In the meantime, I visited a good many cases in the houses in Winchester, among others, a Colonel from New York, who was mortally wounded, and near his end.

It became known in Winchester, the day before I started, that I was going to Washington. Several of the Southern ladies were anxious that I should carry up letters for them to their friends in the North. Among others, a lady belonging to the family of General Fauntleroy of the Confederate Army, called upon me, and begged me to take several letters to the Surgeon-General, Dr. Barnes, who had married a Miss Fauntleroy. Under the circumstances, I said I would do so, and accordingly took charge of the package, promising to put it in the hands of General Barnes myself. In former times, I had known Dr. Barnes very well, that is, soon after I came to Washington. He was then on duty as Surgeon in attendance upon officers of the regular army and their families in Washington. I used to meet him almost every day in the corridors of Willard's Hotel, and we would have long talks together. He was full of news, especially as to what was going on in the South, and as to the future dangers to Washington, which seemed not to grieve him greatly.

Surgeon Barnes was from Pennsylvania, and had

served in the Mexican War, had been quite a favorite with, and indeed, I believe, the personal medical attendant of old General Scott, who, toward the close of his life, held the grade of Lieutenant-General. During his medical attendance of the regular officers, Dr. Barnes attracted the notice of the Secretary of War, Mr. Edwin M. Stanton, who took a great fancy to him. On the 9th of February, 1863, he had been appointed Medical Inspector, with the rank of Lieutenant-Colonel; on the 10th of August, 1863, Medical Inspector-General, with the rank of Colonel. He was afterwards created Acting-Surgeon-General, and as we have seen Surgeon-General on Hammond's dismissal. So he proved himself a successful man, and the Secretary of War was his friend, and he was the Secretary's. But I had noticed from the days of our confidential and whispered chats at Willard's, when he used to talk in a very unguarded way of what was going on in the South, in proportion as he rose in rank and position, he became more and more reserved. Indeed, I fancied that since he had become Surgeon-General, he rather chafed at my presence, so that I had kept out of his way, as much as possible forgetting the past. Altogether I had tried to be as prudent as possible, remembering that new dignities change men, and that there are times when it is best that "auld acquaintance" *should* be forgot. Now all this is merely introductory to the delivery of these letters.

On the following morning, the day on which I left Winchester, I was furnished with an escort of thirty or forty mounted men, and started with one or two ambulances full of wounded, and with an ambulance wagon for myself, in which I had the pleasure of taking down a very pretty girl, in some way connected with the Griffith family of Winchester, whom I have mentioned. She was engaged to be married to a Union officer and wished to reach Philadelphia or New York to procure her trousseau. We had a very pleasant trip to Martinsburg. Our escort threw out cavalry men as flankers, who rode a couple of hundred yards on either side of our train, and not far from them, a number of guerillas rode in parallel lines, following us to within a mile of Martinsburg, but apparently not maliciously inclined; at all events, they did not fire on us. From Martinsburg, I telegraphed to the Surgeon-General:

"I have been relieved by Surgeon Blaney at Winchester on 28th. Have arrived here with train of wounded; have received no orders. Shall I return to Washington? Address me at Harper's Ferry."

I then transferred my wounded (two hundred and fifty) to Acting-Assistant Surgeon Ochschlager and reported to Gen. Thomas Neill. My ambulance, I directed to report to the post quartermaster, and then to Surgeon Blaney at Winchester. We arrived at this town toward evening, September 30, 1864, and were obliged to stay there over night. As I was walking in the main street, a gentleman came up to me, and abruptly said, "Do you know anything of Colonel ———," mentioning the name of the officer I had seen at Winchester, as I have stated above. "Yes," said I, "I saw him yesterday." "How is he?" "Dying," said I. "Oh, my God," gasped a female voice behind me, and turning, I saw a beautiful young woman to whom I was presented. She was the Colonel's wife from New York, and was trying to reach Winchester. She asked me all about him, but I had a hopeless story to tell. She was anxious to get on, but no wagon-train would leave until the morning. She would not come into the house, say what I would, but anxiously and hopelessly trod that street, hour after hour, fearing that she might miss some possible conveyance. I promised to send her on with the returning escort, but she could not rest. At last she hired an old negro, who, with a wretched vehicle, and still more wretched horse, agreed to try and get her through. I gave her a card to Mr. Mosby and his men, stating who and what she was, and begging them to let her pass. I had afterwards the satisfaction to know that she did reach Winchester unmolested, and, contrary to my expectations, in time to find her husband still living and conscious.

# CHAPTER XXV

## RELIEVED FROM DUTY IN SURGEON-GENERAL'S OFFICE

On reaching Washington, I at once saw Surgeon-General Barnes, and gave him the package of letters from his wife's family, and the private verbal messages, sent by me. He seemed quite abashed when I spoke to him about them, and I thought, looked rather sheepish. However, I did not say anything about my return, but after my interview with him, went to my own office, farther down the avenue, near the War Department. Here in my desk, I found this order:

"WAR DEPARTMENT.
Surg. Genl's Office,
September 30, 1864.

SPECIAL
ORDER
No. 324.

Recd.

Adjt. General's Office,
Washington, Sept. 29, 1864.

[Extract]

17. Surg. John H. Brinton, U. S. Vols. is hereby relieved from duty in the Surgeon General's Office, and will report in person without delay to Asst. Surgeon Genl. R. C. Wood, U. S. Army, at Louisville, Ky., for assignment to duty.

By order of the Secretary of War.

(Sd)   E. D. TOWNSEND,

Official                              Asst. Adjt. General.

E. D. Townsend,
    Asst. Adjt. Genl.
Surgeon John H. Brinton,
    Thro. Surgeon General."

This was not unexpected. I had been long enough on duty in the Surgeon-General's office to read the signs of the times, and I felt certain, from the manner of my relief at Winchester, that something was in the wind. That same day, I saw Dr. Crane, U. S. A., the Chief Medical Officer of the Surgeon-General's Office, and asked him about turning over property, etc. I also asked him what was the true cause of my being sent away, and whether there was any real cause of dissatisfaction with my duties in the Surgeon-General's office. His answer was this, "Doctor, what is General McClellan's middle name? George *Brinton* McClellan—that's all I can say," and then he told me that I would turn over all my property and duties to Dr. Otis of the Volunteer Surgeons, who would arrive from the South in a day or two.

So my literary work was thus cut short, and I was to leave Washington. At heart I was delighted; I hated the manual work of writing, and the sense of relief was immense, though I loved the Army Museum and all that belonged to it,—the trips to the front and the hospital visits,—everything in fact but the writing.

Why I was relieved from my bookmaking in Washington, which was the preparation of the *Surgical History of the War,* I have often wondered; I never knew and do not know now. It must have been from one of two causes, or from both of them combined, viz., first my literary and museum work may have been in the opinion of the Surgeon-General unsatisfactory; second, I may have been personally objectionable to the Secretary of War.

As to the first causes: I think my work, literary and otherwise, was satisfactory to the head of my department, at least Dr. Crane assured me that there was no complaint, and that they were satisfied at the office with me. I have already hinted that I had imagined my presence was disagreeable to Surgeon-General Barnes. I had known him too well, when he first came to Washington, but still I think I had been, I know at all events, I had tried to be, discreet. In Washington, in bureau life at that time, everyone had enemies. The "outs" wanted to become the "ins," and everyone who was in, *ipso facto,* became a target for the malice of his enemies. I suppose in the very nature of things, that that kind of target practice was not only justifiable, but even praiseworthy, and by some, considered patriotic.

Apropos of this, I remember well that on one occasion, Dr. Barnes, after he became Surgeon-General, called me into his private office, and standing before the open fire, said, "Doctor Brinton, I will read this note to you, and then burn it." And he read an anonymous note addressed to him, denouncing me, saying that I was a friend of the overthrown William Hammond, and a secret enemy of Dr. Barnes, and warning him against me. I looked at it, thought I recognized the style of expression as that of a rival, and handed it back to him. He dropped it in the fire, saying, "I have forgotten it," but he always afterwards seemed to regard me with suspicion, and to hold himself aloof.

As to the Secretary of War, Mr. Stanton, he did look upon me, and justly, as a friend of Dr. Hammond; the ex-Surgeon-General Hammond, in his view, was criminal, for the latter had differed in his opinion from the Secretary. Now, in my judgment, the Secretary looked upon men from his own peculiar standpoint. He was,

I think, an honest man, and patriotic, but very strong in his own convictions. Believing himself to be right, he regarded all those who differed in opinion from him as wrong thinkers, and wrong-doers, criminals, in fact, and that it was his duty as Secretary of War to punish them, when he conveniently could. Now, I not only was a friend of Hammond's, but a relative, a blood-relative of General McClellan, who, high in the esteem of the Democratic party, and a possible candidate for the presidency of the United States, was in the eyes of Mr. Stanton little less wicked than the Arch Fiend himself.

Then, too, there was someone at the Secretary's elbow, ready to point out any of my personal delinquencies. This came about in this wise.

When I was living at the Metropolitan Club, three or four weeks before that time, at our table-d'hôte, there sat opposite me an old gentleman, named Lewis, I think, from West Chester. He had some auditing appointment, and was quite a friend, and in fact a crony, of the Secretary of War. McClellan at that time was being talked of as a Presidential candidate. This man, Lewis, disliked him, and could not abuse him enough. Now political abuse of a candidate for public office is perhaps fair enough, as things go, but on one occasion this old fellow went beyond the public limits, and began to abuse my cousin George's personal character; he said he knew McClellan's character, and that he was a coward, as all his Mother's (my Aunt's) family were. This I could not permit, so I spoke out loudly before the whole table, saying I was sure that one of the family believed in personal responsibility, and then I gave him the lie direct, owning my relationship to McClellan, and warning him at his peril, never to make slanderous remarks again. He sat aghast and speechless, and I never saw him again. But Mr. Nicolay, President Lincoln's Secretary, who was present, said to me, that while I did perfectly right, he was afraid I would hear of this again, as the man was a friend of Secretary Stanton.

I never did hear of him again until, very many years afterwards, when the man was near his end, someone came to ask me professionally about his case.

One other possible cause, call it No. 3, might have been this: I saw that the end of the war was approaching, and I knew that a great many capable and trained surgeons of U. S. Volunteers would be thrown back into civil life. It occurred to me that if a certain number of them could be retained in the Regular Army, transferred, in fact, great efficiency in the Medical Department might be obtained. At the same time a corresponding number of Assistant Surgeons of the Regular Army might be promoted. So I arranged in my mind a scheme for the accomplishment of this end, which on submission seemed to be satisfactory both to the Surgeons of Volunteers (Old Brigade-Surgeons) and to the Assistant Surgeons of the Regular Army (U. S. A.). Equal numbers of each were to be transferred and promoted to the rank of Surgeon, U. S. A. Even Surgeon-General Barnes *appeared* to approve of the plan, though I suspect that in heart he did not. In effect, it would have brought in the Surgeons of my Corps (U. S. Vols.), on equal and fair terms with the Assistant Surgeon of the Regular Army. I doubt if this result was agreeable to the Surgeon-General. In fact, after the close of the war, a few of the old and experienced Surgeons of Volunteers entered the army as Assistant Surgeon, U. S. A., but at the foot of the list, so that their long service and war experience went for nothing, in the matter of their new grade and rank.

I moved in this matter, because, from my rank in my Corps, from my service, and from having been on duty in the Surgeon-General's Office, I was in some sort a representative of my Corps, and because, as I knew I should return to civil life, I had nothing to gain by reorganization. I could, therefore, with propriety, act. I was honest in my views, but I doubt if I was politic or wise.

So from what I have thus egotistically written, I think I have shown you that between Stanton, Barnes and myself, a good case was made, why I should not remain longer at Washington, and why I should again start west. So I put the best face I could on it, and began to make my preparations to depart.

In a few days, my successor, Surgeon Otis, U. S. Vols., arrived, and I then received the following order:

"Surg. General's Office,
Washington, D. C.
October 3, 1864.

Sir:

Surgeon George A. Otis, U. S. Vols., will relieve you from the charge of the Department of this Office, which you now occupy, and also from the duties of Curator of the 'Army Medical Museum.'

You will transfer to Surgeon Otis all official books, papers, records, funds, and property, of any description under your charge and he will receipt to you for those articles for which you are responsible. After turning over your property, etc., you will proceed without delay, to Louisville, Ky., and report to Assistant Surgeon Gen-

eral Wood, in compliance with Special Order No. 324,
dated War Dept. Sept. 29th, 1864.

Very respectfully yr. Obt. servt.

By order of the Surgeon General,

(Sd)   C. H. GRANE,

Surgeon, U. S. A.

Surgeon J. H. Brinton,
U. S. Volunteers,
Surgeon General's Office."

I immediately turned over my public property to my
successor, settled up my accounts, and put my papers
in order for Dr. Otis's use.  It was rather a melancholy
business, that departure, under all the circumstances, but
really I was not sorry, and longed to be far away from
Washington, out of reach of the wire-pulling and
scheming and envy of that political place.  I felt all
the time as if my very clerks were laughing at me, and
were watching me.  So, turning over my official property, and packing up my private library, and my anatomical preparations, which I had brought on from Philadelphia, to illustrate my proposed, but never given,
course on military surgery, and which I sent back to
Philadelphia, I was ready to depart.

I had been a long time in Washington, and had many
friends.  To some of these, I said good-bye, and to
one of them, Mrs. Stephen A. Douglas, I sent a picture.
I had often joked with her when officers had been sent
away from Washington under the displeasure of the
Secretary of War,—exiled in fact, for the Secretary
looked upon a detail to Louisville or St. Louis as a
banishment, quite as in Russia they regard banishment
to Siberia.  Some officers took removal from Washington as a rather hard fate, but I had often told Mrs.

Douglas that I was sure to be decapitated, but that when it came, like St. Denis (she, Mrs. Douglas, was a Catholic), I would lose my head with good grace. So I requested one of the artists of the Museum, Faber, a German of facile pencil, to make a pen-and-ink sketch of myself as St. Denis leaving the Museum, head in hand, for the region of the setting sun, with the bloody headman's sword, the unfinished work of the *Surgical History of the War,* etc.

There is an odd sequel to this picture story, which I will give in the words of Dr. Otis, my successor. A month or two afterwards, Dr. Barnes heard of the St. Denis caricature, and expressed a wish to see it. Dr. Woodward had Faber make a copy from memory. A few additions were made, as the motto by Faber, "So Woodward says, but I suspect our friend of instigating," Dr. Otis writes. Faber's picture was photographed by Dr. Otis. The original was given to the Secretary of War by Dr. Barnes. Barnes, Crane, Thomson, Billings and Otis had copies, and two were sent to me at Nashville, where I then was, and the negative destroyed.

From the motto *"Si tacuisses Philosoph Mansisses"* on the latter, you may infer that my tongue had been my enemy. Perhaps it was so, but dear me, what difference! Stanton, Lewis, Barnes, Crane, Otis and my anonymous enemy, all are long since gone, and I can laugh at the very recollection of St. Denis.

# CHAPTER XXVI

So, having finished my work at Washington and gladly shaking, as it were, the dust of the town from my feet, I left, and after a short stay at Philadelphia, reached Louisville in obedience to the War Department Order, and reported to the Assistant-Surgeon-General Wood for assignment to duty on the 15th of October, 1864. By him, and his Assistant, Surgeon J. B. Brown, I was received with the greatest kindness. I was fresh from Washington, from the Surgeon-General's Office, and had all the news and gossip of the Department at my fingers' ends.

They did not know exactly what to do with me. I had almost too much rank, and almost any assignment would disturb existing arrangements. Finally, they asked me if I would like to go to St. Louis, and report to my old friend Madison Mills, the Medical Director of the Department of the Missouri, commanded by General Rosecrans. Of course, I assented with delight. I was glad to go to St. Louis, where a rather active campaign was just beginning, and I had much respect and admiration for Surgeon Mills, U. S. A., a man of executive ability, broad views, and a very decided character. His views on all subjects were clear and strongly expressed. He had the reputation of being a man of means, acquired by fortunate speculation in land around Fort Leavenworth. My order ran thus:

"Assistant Surgeon General's Office,
Louisville, Ky., Oct. 17, 1864.

Surgeon John H. Brinton, U. S. V., having reported
to the Asst. Surgeon General in obedience to Special
Order No. 324, War Dept., Adjt. General's Office, Washington, September 29th, 1864, is assigned to duty in the
Department of the Missouri, and will report in person
without delay, to Surgeon Mad. Mills, U. S. A., Medical
Director, Department of the Missouri, St. Louis.

JOSEPH B. BROWN,
Act. Asst. Surgeon General,
U. S. Army."

I left Louisville on October 18th, and arrived in St.
Louis on the 19th, went to the Lindell Hotel, and immediately afterwards reported at the Medical Director's
Office to Surgeon Mills. My trunk not having yet
arrived, I was in civilian's clothes. I excused myself
for this breach of military decorum, at which the old
gentleman, himself in citizen's dress, grunted a signifi-
cant "Pah! Come to the office to-morrow. Look
around the town to-day." On the 21st, he gave me this
order: I was to act as Medical Director in the field
on General Rosecrans' staff in the campaign then going
on in southwest Missouri; to me a delightful detail.
The duty, however, was responsible. Rosecrans' army
was thirty or forty thousand men, and was moving light
and rapidly. He had not informed his Medical Director
exactly where he was going, or where his base would
be. Dr. Mills was quite in the dark, but this he told
me: "Doctor, reach Rosecrans, find out where he wants
his medical supplies if you can (I can't), and then establish medical depots for thirty thousand men in two or
three points; keep me advised by telegraph, all the time,

and I will see that you are supplied with medical stores
and officers wherever you want them. Be sharp, learn
all you can. Keep your subordinates well up in their
work, and let me be daily informed what is wanted, how
you are getting on, and I will support you in every way."

Nothing could be more satisfactory and liberal than
the old Doctor's instructions, and we both acted up to
them.

Having made the necessary arrangements, on the 24th
of October I left St. Louis with horse and negro servant. I went by rail as far as Hermann, which place
I reached by night. I here put my horse on the steamer
*Lillie Martin,* and stayed on board all night. On the
morning of the 25th, the steamer started up the river,
and in the afternoon about four o'clock, we reached
Jefferson City the capital of Missouri, on the Missouri
River. The river was low, and as we stuck on the
sand every now and then, I had an opportunity of admiring the ingenious mode of raising up the bow of the
boat by two poles, and then backing her off. At Jefferson City, I stayed a day and a half, appointing a
Medical Purveyor, transferring to him the stores I
brought with me, and arranging the hospital accommodation of five hundred beds in anticipation of coming
wounded. For this purpose, buildings were seized, and
hospital tents were held in readiness for pitching. When
pitched, these were to be heated by underground flues.
Furnaces and caldrons for cooking I requisitioned from
St. Louis, and I also requested additional medical officers
to be sent on. Every request I made was promptly
granted, and I was assisted in every way by the efficient action of the Medical Director, Surgeon Madison
Mills, who was at all times ready to help me. I also
perfected the telegraphic arrangements to keep up the

communications with the headquarters and St. Louis, and to obtain fresh supplies as needed.

When I finished my business at Jefferson City, I started on October 27th, by railroad, across the prairie in the direction of Sedalia, as far as Warrensburg, the railroad terminus, at which place I arrived at 4 P.M. Here, upon inquiring from the Commandant, I learned vaguely that Rosecrans was somewhere on the prairie, but exactly where, no one could tell. I also heard the pleasant information that the whole country was full of guerillas, murdering and cutting the throats of stragglers at large. Now, I had to reach headquarters, so I concluded to leave my negro servant (as guerilla bands objected to negroes, and usually gave those captured short shrift) at Warrensburg, and pushed on alone, trusting to luck to get through. But just as I was starting, I was told that a body of horse (Union forces) were encamping on the hills beyond the town. Riding out to see who they were, to my great joy I found the camp to be that of General Rosecrans and his staff. Almost the first person I saw was my old friend Scull, whom I have mentioned so often. He could scarcely believe his eyes; he thought I must be an apparition, my own ghost—to part in Pennsylvania Avenue·and to meet on a slight hill in Missouri Prairie, exactly as when I had last seen him I jokingly prophesied I would do! However, he was glad to meet me, offering me a part of his tent, and, as he explained, thus getting rid of the Provost Marshal, a Captain on the Staff, whose function it was to hang guerilla murderers and spies, and who could not help reverting to the subject afterward, especially to his mess mate and tent companion. As Scull was a delicate-minded man, despite his gloomy name, the Provost Marshal's presence distressed him.  As he put it, "I would even prefer yours," so I found quarters before even reporting to General Rosecrans.

In a few minutes General Rosecrans came out of his tent, and I was presented to him, and submitted my orders.  As Scull vouched for my being a reasonably good fellow, and a "white elephant" from Washington, the General was very nice and gave me a warm welcome.  Somehow or other, I said something about soap,—I believe in this way.  A fire had been built in front of our tents, as evening closed in.  The wind was high, and the smoke drifted in our faces, and some allusion was made to the cleaning powers of soap.  The General addressed his conversation chiefly to me, and I listened well.  He had been much interested in the manufacture of soap before entering the army (he was a West Point graduate), and once on his favorite topic he talked and talked.  The men of the staff dropped off to their tents and sleep, but still he talked, and still I listened.  But he became after that a good friend of mine, although Scull stuck to it that it was the influence of soap.

He proved a kind friend to me.  Talkative in some respects, he was close enough in others, and I had hard work to find out which way he would go, or where our medical supplies should be sent.  The course of events, however, settled themselves.  In a few hours, General Pleasanton, in charge of the cavalry arrived, having one or two of the rebel generals prisoners, and reporting that the raiding forces under the southern general, Price, "Pap Price," as he was called, had been driven out of Missouri, and had crossed the Osage River.  The campaign was thus finished, and General Rosecrans with his staff determined to return to St. Louis.  The fighting had taken place at Marais des Cygnes, and General Pleasanton's wounded, which amounted to about 360, had been sent to Kansas City for treatment, so I countermanded my orders as to supplies.

The generals we had captured, Marmaduke and Cabell, seemed good sort of fellows, and we had long talks around our camp-fires. In returning, the troops crossed the prairie by rapid marches. They had marched already thirty-five and forty miles a day, and here I may say in passing, that General Rosecrans possessed a wonderful capacity of marching men, a rare accomplishment. He would at night know where every brigade or regiment or separate command would be. He excelled, too, in making such judicious arrangements, that the artillery, baggage-trains, etc., would never be in the way of the marching foot. His line of march was never blocked.

As we, that is, headquarters, steamed across the prairie, in train from Warrensburg, we passed the marching troops. One of our generals, A. J. Smith, was greatly beloved by his men. He was an old Indian frontier soldier, and had been on continuous duty there for many years. At the time he came up to us at Warrensburg, he had just lost a favorite horse, a "single-footed racker." He said that it had been stolen and he swore "he would hang the scoundrel if he caught the thief." He sat on the back platform of the car, to see if he could discover his horse in the marching column. The men seemed to know what he was after, and as he was adored by them all for his soldierly qualities, they cheered him all along the line of march, as our train flew by. At Jefferson City, we spent the night of March 22nd on board the steamer, and in the morning started down the river, stopping for a little while at a place called Hermann on the right bank, I think, of the Mississippi. The little place had been settled by Germans, and one of them to whose house we went, grew a grape from which she made a wine, much like Assmanhauser, a wine I always liked. We drank a bottle of it with gusto. Hermann's was the only American Assmanhauser. I often thought of this wine, contrasting it in my mind most favorably with other American wines.

By November 3rd, at 8.30 P.M., we were again at St. Louis, and I settled down to do almost nothing for a month.

# CHAPTER XXVII

## ST. LOUIS

When I asked kind old Madison Mills what my duties were to be, he said, "Drop down and see me every morning, then go see the girls, and go to parties. If I have anything for you to do, I'll let you know."

On the 7th of November, I was detailed as President of an Army Medical Board, which was in session in St. Louis. The Board was in a sort of permanent session, and the duties had become almost nominal. Thus my life for a month was a life of leisure, and in order to carry out Dr. Mill's instructions, I sent home for my dress-coat and had as good a time as I could.

I lived with my friend Scull at the Lindell Hotel, dined at General Rosecrans' table, paid a visit every day to the office, rode on horseback, called on the ladies, attended to social duties, dressed carefully for dinner, and went to parties, where my dress-coat, almost a solitary one at that time in St. Louis, was derisively spoken of as a "steel-pen coat."

Society then in St. Louis was divided into two parties or sections, Union and Secesh. One dancing club, I forget which, was called the Imperial, and the other I have even forgotten the name of. I belonged to both, and went regularly, and was having, as they say, "a good time." Society in St. Louis was queer. One old gentleman by the name of Clement, a very rich man, gave a gorgeous dinner to the General and the staff. He sat at table with his hat on. He said he had a cold, and his friends seemed to think it quite the proper thing.

With all this gaiety going on, I still did some good in this month of pleasure. I saved a young girl's life, thus: A young woman in southwestern Missouri, only seventeen or eighteen years of age, had a lover in a rebel guerilla band. At his instigation, she cut down a telegraph pole, cut the wire, interpreted a most important telegram, and as a consequence of its non-transmittal, several thousand of our troops were marching at cross purposes, and an important military operation came to naught or worse. The girl was caught and admitted the charge, indeed, rather gloried in it. Rosecrans was furious and ordered her tried by a court martial of some kind, and she was condemned to be hanged. His staff and many other of the officers were dreadfully concerned, and represented to him the odium of executing a woman. But he was inexorable. He was an obstinate man, and reasoned, not illogically, that such a deed in war, by a civilian, deserved death, be the perpetrator man or woman. Nothing would move him. In despair, some of his staff and best friends consulted me, as to what I could do. I saw the poor creature in the military prison of St. Louis. She was almost half-witted. I told her what answers to give to certain of my leading questions, knowing that Rosecrans was a strict Catholic, and that under certain circumstances, he dared not hang the woman. Indeed, I told him more than one lie about her, and finally he countermanded the order of execution, when she apparently had but a few hours to live. She was chained, and it was to me a horrible sight to see a woman chained. Rosecrans told me plainly that under the circumstances, while he did not believe what I said, he would forgive me for the motive of saying it. We were all greatly relieved at the happy termination of this affair.

On December 1, 1864, Dr. Madison Mills was appointed Medical Inspector-General in place of Barnes, promoted to the Surgeon-Generalcy. The Surgeon-General wrote him of his appointment, addressing the letter in his own handwriting, "Colonel Madison Mills." I came down to the office the day the letter arrived, before the Medical Director, and recognizing the Surgeon-General's handwriting and surmising the contents of the letter, put it conspicuously on Dr. Mills's desk. The Doctor saw it, but would not touch or open it, and was quite confused when we all called him "Colonel." Finally, he opened and read it. After a while, he said to me, "You know Washington, would you take this appointment if you were I?" I replied, "If you take it, and go to Washington, in a month you will be in hot water. You are too independent to hold a post which is so nominal and useless as the Medical Inspector Generalship's now is. You will try to do something, and will come in collision with the Surgeon-General and others. You are not subservient enough for the place." He laughed, but he did accept the office, and it turned out exactly as I predicted.

In a letter of November 14, 1864, I thus wrote to Dr. DaCosta: "I have seen a great deal of Rosecrans. In fact he has taken a fancy to me, and we are quite intimate. He is a good strategist, no tactician, no administrator, a religious enthusiast, a fair chemist, and an excellent soap manufacturer. His skill in the last capacity is his peculiar pride. He will talk hour after hour on the subject; he never wearies when on his beloved hobby of soap."

On the 7th of December, 1864, I wrote to my Mother,

a letter, a portion of which I copy, and which explains itself: "Your letter catches me on the wing. Let me tell you the how and wherefore: General Rosecrans has taken quite a fancy to me, and on old Dr. Mills's being promoted recently to the Medical Inspector-Generalship, the General sent a very strong telegram to Washington, asking that I should be appointed the Medical Director of the Department. The reply from the Secretary of War was a telegram, ordering me to Louisville at once to the Assistant Surgeon-General. I shall most probably be sent to Nashville as the Director. Both the Secretary and Barnes were very savage. Although I am inconvenienced, I chuckle mightily at showing them all in Washington, that if I am a 'singed cat' there, I have made friends here. I believe Rosecrans is really attached to me."

General Rosecrans and Medical Director Mills unquestionably had meant to do me a kindness, when they telegraphed that I should be made Medical Director on Dr. Mills leaving St. Louis, but as I stated in my letter to my Mother, I afterwards learned that the Secretary of War was very much enraged at their suggestion; why, it is hard to say. The telegram he sent me, received while at an evening party, was sent by his own Assistant Adjutant-General, ordering a reply by telegraph. Under ordinary circumstances, it was strictly forbidden by War Department orders for an officer not on command, to use telegrams for Washington answers. Moreover, I was not wanted in Louisville as events showed. There was difficulty in assigning me a post. I was quite in ignorance of the cause of my relief until from Dr. Mills and General Rosecrans I learned of what had taken place, and of the Secretary's resignation.

I immediately got ready to leave, and on the 8th of December I arrived at Louisville, went to the Galt House, and at once reported to the Assistant Surgeon-General, where I was kindly received by the Assistant Surgeon-General, Colonel Wood, and the chief of his office, Surgeon Brown.

On the 9th I received an order to go to Nashville, Tennessee, and was assigned to duty as Superintendent and Director of the general hospital at that place.

The duties of this office were somewhat vague. It had been found that whenever general hospitals were grouped, it was expedient that some medical officer should be appointed, clothed with authority to act finally upon such matters as were of immediate importance to the welfare of the patients, to avoid the delay of referring matters of business to the Medical Director of the Department, often absent. In this way, requisitions could be acted upon at once and contracts with citizen physicians and nurses made without delay. Necessarily a great deal was left to the discretion and common sense of the superintendent.

In my letter home of the 14th, I state that I had arrived safely and found the City of Nashville almost in a state of partial siege. The Southern General (Hood) had moved northward, had crossed the Tennessee River, and had attacked our troops at Franklin, Tennessee, on the 30th of November. His object was to threaten, and if possible, to capture, the City of Nashville, forcing General Thomas to retreat and thus carry the campaign back to the Ohio River.

In the attack at Franklin, he had failed with heavy loss, but General Thomas had slowly withdrawn his army to Nashville in order to strengthen his forces and remount his cavalry. Thomas was a man of great prudence and slow in movement, possibly over-cautious, and hence the delay which characterized his movements.

On my arrival at Nashville, I was informed by Assistant Surgeon Dallas Bache, U. S. A., who was acting as the Director of Hospitals, that a battle was hourly expected, but that while there were a large number of hospitals organized, there were comparatively few vacant beds.

On assuming the office, I immediately directed all my efforts to extend the hospital accommodation already in existence. I therefore called upon Brigadier-General Miller, Post Commandant, to turn over to me for hospital purposes the Court House and all of the churches in the city. He immediately turned over to me all the churches, but it was considered that good reasons existed for retaining the Court House.

I encountered considerable opposition from the authorities of the Catholic Church, as they objected to having their church turned into a hospital, and said that it would desecrate its sacred character. Father Kelly visited me, and was quite in earnest in his opposition; he said that churches were respected in war. I asked him to consider the events which had taken place in the Italian War, and reminded him that all of the Catholic churches in the city of Milan and elsewhere had been seized by a Catholic Prince, the Emperor Napoleon III., and turned into hospitals. He laughed, admitted the fact, and then explained that the basement of one of the Catholic churches in Nashville was used by the Sisters as a home for the community, and that the sacred vestments had all been carried there. I told him that under those circumstances, I would place a military guard over all those portions of the building, and that no one should be allowed to intrude. This was done. I afterwards learned that these facts were reported to General Rosecrans, who was at first very angry, and demanded the name of the medical officer so offending. He was told "Surgeon Brinton." "Oh, then!" said he, "it is all right."

On the 15th and 17th of December, the battle of Nashville occurred. I saw it at first from a housetop and afterwards rode out to the line of battle four or five miles from the city. The enemy's attack was very fierce, but was repelled with great slaughter. I witnessed the fighting of the negro troops; they behaved well. Finally, the enemy was forced to retreat, and was vigorously pressed as far as the town of Franklin.

Our wounded were rapidly brought in in great numbers, and soon occupied all of our hospital accommodations and the hospital tents, which had been hastily pitched. The wounded black troops were carried to the hospital which had been especially assigned to them. The wounded rebels were also in a day or two's time brought to the rebel prison hospital. The churches which had been seized answered well as hospitals, the pews had either been boarded over or removed, and all of the church hospitals were soon filled with wounded with the exception of the Episcopal church, which was inconvenient of arrangement.

The negro hospital was in a series of four-storied warehouses, which were closely packed with wounded. All of the wounded in the hospitals were promptly and efficiently cared for, and as a rule, did well.

Some curious occurrences took place with regard to the wounded prisoners. A young lady came to my office and asked to see a wounded prisoner of high rank. I told her that sisters, mothers and wives alone were allowed to see prisoners; was she either of these? She said no, but she was willing to marry the gentleman in question, if that was the only way she could obtain permission to see him. I inquired and found that he was not badly wounded. I told her to come to see me on the following morning at a given hour. I sent for him to be brought to my office at the same hour, and so the interview was arranged, and no rule of service was broken.

In another case a Southern prisoner, wounded and of high rank, begged my permission to ride outside of our lines to visit a lady to whom he was engaged, promising me on his word of honor to return at a given hour. I told him I could not do this, but that if he would give me his word of honor that I should not be injured by his people, I would ride with him; he could then make the visit he desired, and come back with me at a given hour.

At ten o'clock, on the cold winter's night, we rode out together. We passed our pickets, and went to her father's house. My prisoner had a long interview with his lady love, while I sat in the adjoining parlor talking to the sisters, and at the hour agreed upon we remounted, rattled along the pike, passed our picket line and sentry line (I having the password of the night). Then I accompanied my friend to his hospital, and there took leave of him. No harm came of this ride, but the lady in question changed her mind, and afterwards married a Union officer. On our return, we came near being shot by our pickets of negro cavalry, whose minds work slowly, and who did not understand fully the use of a password. We rode right upon them, they challenged us fiercely, and we were obliged to dismount instantly to save ourselves from being shot.

One or two of the Confederates, wounded and prisoners in our hands, were Masons, and I received several letters from the Order in the North, authorizing me to furnish them money. Another Southern officer was of Jewish birth. One of the most prominent and wealthiest bankers in New York, Belmont, authorized me to draw on him for any amount required.

My Christmas dinner, I took at Governor Bankhead's.

My office as Medical Director in Nashville was very stylish; I had three or four sentries and an excellent corps of clerks and cavalry orderlies. Some of my clerks were quite well educated.

One day I was astonished to see an old lady descend from an old-fashioned carriage, and come into my front office, announcing herself as Mrs. Polk. She was the widow of President Polk and wished something done, which I attended to at once. I gave her my arm to see her to her carriage, having sent out word to the sentries to salute as they would a General commanding, and to fully present arms. I asked her never again to descend from her carriage, but always to send in for me, that I could never forget that she was the widow of a dead president. She seemed to be very much touched by these marks of respect, and invited me to her home.

It was an old-fashioned residence of brick with a large yard. The tomb of her late husband, President Polk, was placed in the yard in full sight of her windows. She received me with great courtesy. The company was entirely Southern in feeling. I went, of course, in uniform. One of the young ladies who had been from New York, but who was exceedingly Southern in her feelings, made a personal attack on me, and was very rude. I replied to her and told her that renegades were always more bitter than original enemies. Mrs. Polk learned, after I left, what had occurred. She reprimanded the young woman severely, saying that she would never have an officer of the United States insulted under her roof, and she forbade the offender ever to visit her home again until a sufficient explanation had been made. Mrs. Polk was the sister-in-law of the famous General-Bishop Polk. She always afterwards spoke well of me, and never forgot the respect with which she had been treated at my office.

My quarters, when I first went to Nashville, were in the part of a house which belonged to a family of strong "Secesh" propensities. I shared my rooms with Captain Jenny, an officer whom I had previously known at Shiloh. He was a graduate of the School of Topographical Engineers in Paris, was commissioned as an Engineer in our army, and rendered immense service by his knowledge of roads and their construction, corduroying and the like. He originated the idea of skyscrapers.

Here let me relate an interesting incident which did not become generally known. Jenny had charge of a pontoon train. On the day of the fight at Nashville or the day after, in a pouring rain, I met him hurrying his train of boats away on the turnpike. I asked him, "Where are you going?" He said, "God knows, where a pontoon train can do the least possible good."

When he came back a day or so afterwards, I asked him in the quiet of our chamber, "How about that pontoon train?" He said, "That is a very good story and a very great secret. After the battle, General Thomas sent for me, and told me to take my train out on the Murfreesboro pike. I said, 'General, do you mean the

Murfreesboro Pike?' because I knew that was away from the enemy. He said, 'Yes, on the Murfreesboro Pike.' I went away, but I was uneasy in my mind, for I knew that a bridge train could not be wanted where there were no rivers. I turned and went back, and again I asked him, 'General, do you mean the Murfreesboro Pike?' He seemed heavy, but aroused himself, and half-angrily said, 'Yes, the Murfreesboro Pike, go and execute your orders.'

"I went and led out my pontoon, as directed, and the next day was recalled by a messenger, when the General discovered his mistake. He had meant to say the Granny White Pike, but at the time of the battle, he had had no rest or sleep for two or three days and nights; he was sleeping heavily when aroused to give my order, was dazed, confounded the Murfreesboro with the Granny White Pike and gave me the useless order. If the train had been sent on the pike, on which it should have been sent, it could have been used at Duck River and other streams, and the probability is that the entire forces of the enemy would have been captured. As it was, they reached Franklin, slowly retreated southward and succeeded in making good their escape by crossing the Tennessee River, and thus reaching Alabama safely." *

A tolerably good public order was maintained at Nashville at this time, but the streets were very dark, badly lighted, and murder occasionally took place. I well remember how often I have walked at night through the streets with a lantern in one hand and a cocked pistol in the other, calling to those I was about to meet to keep on the other side of the street. On one or two

* See the Personal Memoirs of General Grant, Volume 2, page 386.

occasions, I heard a shot fired and learned afterwards that men had been killed.

In one instance, a sentry told me, that it was "only a damn civilian."

Toward the end of December, in order to increase the capacity of our hospitals still more, a number of houses belonging to people of Southern sentiment and affiliations were seized; some of these proved satisfactory, but as a rule the accommodation was too crowded and insufficient.

On one occasion, in the early part of my stay at Nashville, I took possession of a large circus tent for a hospital, but found that it was useless, since it was impossible to heat it in any way, and the weather was exceedingly cold.

The management of most of the hospitals was very good, but in some, it was not. There was evident rascality. I could not tell how or where the frauds were accomplished. To test the matter, knowing that the persons who furnished the hospital were men of doubtful character, I determined to make a wholesale arrest. Accordingly, one Saturday afternoon, I arrested eight or ten of the merchants, grocers, victuallers and general provision men. I had all of their books sent to my office, and spent Sunday in examining the intricacies of their accounts. I found out the secret of their frauds, which consisted in charging for more goods than were furnished, and paying the balance in money to corrupt officers, interested in the steal. These, I am happy to say, were not surgeons in charge, but were generally the lower officers, commissary sergeants and the like. All of this system was at once thoroughly broken up.

One of the medical officers in charge of Hospital No.

15 had made a large fortune in various ways, probably by falsity in his accounts, by corrupt speculation of every kind, by the purchase of condemned horses, by fattening them on government land and on government provender and re-selling them, and by many objectionable practices. His rascality was evident, in these and other ways, which I cannot state. I gave him the option of resigning in twelve hours, or of preferring charges against him. He chose the former, and the Government was well rid of a bad officer.

About this time, an event occurred which well-nigh cost me my commission. A portion of the North was at this time largely excited on the subject of negro troops. By some they were much over-estimated. One of these negrophiles was General Thomas, the Assistant Adjutant-General. Not greatly esteemed at Washington, he seized upon the negro question as a means of ingratiating himself in the estimation of his superiors. He was sent from Washington to the west by the Secretary of War with a kind of roving commission, his duty being to look after the interest of negro troops wherever they might be found. His great object was to praise the negro troops, and to find as much fault as possible wherever he thought their interest neglected.

Among other places, he visited Nashville, and inspected the negro hospitals. With one of these hospitals, No. 16, he professed himself greatly displeased. This was the warehouse hospital, several stories in height, each room or ward of which was provided with a stove of the large kind known as the "bar-room" stove. These, the negroes, in spite of directions and precautions to the contrary, kept heated red-hot; the men, too, were dirty, and to a certain degree, this could not be prevented, as it was the character of their race.

Give them what clean linen we could, what clean pillows and pillow-cases we could, they would, in a very short time, be in a filthy condition. Indeed, it seemed, strangely enough, to be a prominent idea of the negro soldiers to keep their hair thoroughly greased, and for this purpose they would steal the candles and grease of every description, and using it plentifully as a pomade, would necessarily get their beds in a filthy state. This condition of affairs General Thomas, spied, and professed himself to be very indignant with the condition of his beloved negro troops.

He sent for me in haste; I met him in the street, and he opened on me a tirade of abuse, such as no officer should have addressed to another. He did not know me personally, but I frequently had met him in Washington and knew exactly what his status in the War Department was. I attempted to explain to him the cause of trouble, but he would hear no explanation. He took the opportunity of showing his power and rank, and ended his personal abuse of me with the threat that he would telegraph to the Secretary of War, and have me dismissed from the army at once. Of course, I had nothing to say. I simply bowed to him and turned on my heel and left him.

I did not know what to do, and I knew that a complaint of any kind to the Secretary of War, concerning me, coming no matter from whom, would be instantly seized as an opportunity for dismissal.

Now it happened that there was on duty at Nashville a most excellent and gentlemanly old soldier of the regular army, General Donaldson, a man of rank, goodheartedness and kindness, and also a man of means. As he was the Chief Quartermaster, I had frequent occasion to call on him for all imaginable supplies. I had bothered him a good deal, but I knew that he believed that I was trying to do my duty, and had a certain sort of good feeling toward me. Moreover, his step-son, who had broken his nose, was a patient of mine.

I went to General Donaldson and told him of the circumstances. I told him that it was impossible to keep the negroes clean, told him of my relations with the Secretary of War, and explained to him that any report from General Thomas would be most injurious to me. I went to him because I knew that General Thomas was about to dine with him that afternoon. "Put your heart at rest," said General Donaldson to me, "I know Thomas, I understand all the circumstances, and will take great care to see that you shall not be injured in any way."

The dinner took place, and Thomas was drawn out to make his complaint, concerning me. General Donaldson told him that I was not remiss in my care of the negro troops; on the contrary, that I was a very energetic officer, and called upon him more than any other officer had done for supplies for the comfort of the negro troops. As a result, he impressed General Thomas with the idea of my efficiency in that particular direction, and so influenced him that the Adjutant-General, in making his report, stated that my services in the interest of the negro troops had been of the most valuable character, and submitted not a word of complaint.

I insert here a note which I received from General Donaldson, which shows the opinion entertained of the Adjutant-General and his efforts on behalf of the negroes:

"Nashville,
Jan. 15, 1865.

Dear Doctor:

I went to see Genl. Thomas this morning, and talked with him about the colored hospital. I took occasion to speak of you, and the result of our talk was Genl. Thomas said he would take no steps to hurt you. We all understand how this subject is regarded, and how it may be used to injure. Genl. Thomas, however, was very much incensed against a doctor by the name of ————, who is said to be much in the habit of cursing his patients.

Very truly,
J. S. DONALDSON."

I might here state as a curious fact that the negroes in this crowded hospital, with their stoves red-hot, with the wards overcrowded with men, women and children, all did remarkably well. It is true that the odor of the wards was abominable, and the cleanliness by no means what could have been wished, yet their wounds healed kindly and few intercurrent diseases occurred. The men seemed to be entirely free from pneumonia, and affections of that kind, from which the negroes are so apt to suffer. Comparatively few deaths took place, less indeed than the average number of such cases of white troops in well-ventilated hospitals.

It was decided by the War Department to build for the negro troops a large pavilion hospital on the best model, thoroughly equipped, well ventilated, and situated two or three miles from town. The negro occupants were here placed under the best hygienic conditions, viewed from the standpoint of white troops, yet the mortality was fearful. They died from pneumonia and affections of the chest very rapidly, and the results of the new hospital contrasted most unfavorably with the apparent overcrowded hospitals in which they had been placed in the city.

In the early part of my stay in Nashville, when the negro hospitals were full, a great degree of insubordination was noticed among these troops. Those who were not sick or injured insisted upon having free access to the hospital, especially when the women and children were furnished shelter in the hospital buildings. They beat down the guard, and attempted to force their way in. I was called to one of these hospitals on an occasion of this kind. The turbulent crowd gathered around the gate, and fiercely insisted upon pressing in. I stepped between them and the guard behind them, closed the gates, and ordered the guard to load with ball cartridge, and let the men see that this was done. I instructed them to fire on the first man who should attempt to pass the gates. I was asked, "Do you mean this?" I said, "Yes." The gates were opened as I went out, but not a single man attempted to pass the sentry line.

At the negro hospital No. 16, a singular event took place. In visiting the hospital, one day when I was in the office, examining some of the books, I noticed in the mirror on the wall, the Surgeon in charge stealthily creeping along the entry, in stocking feet, and placing his ear to the chink of the door in an endeavor to hear what I was saying. I detected in the books evidence of irregularity, and on thinking the matter over, I was convinced that I had seen that man before. It flashed across me all at once that long before the war, in a visit to Cherry Hill Prison at Philadelphia, at a time at which my friend, Dr. Lassiter, was the resident physician, he had asked me to see a prisoner, a counterfeiter, who was engaged in carving in ivory some peculiar models. My Surgeon-in-charge of that hospital was that man; I was sure of it. I sent for him to come to my office, and I said to him, "Doctor, I have been looking over your accounts; something is wrong; but Doctor I have seen you before at Cherry Hill Prison; I know you." He changed color, and dropped on his knees, and made me the most astonishing confession. He repeated as if reading from a paper, the numerous incidents of robbery and theft of hospital stores; thus he would say, "On such and such a day, I stole an ounce of quinine," and so he enumerated a long list of articles pilfered, extending over a considerable period of time. These articles, he confessed that he sold to Southern agents, and that they were smuggled into the Southern Confederacy. He and his father-in-law had been convicted of counterfeiting United States bank-notes. They were from Ohio, and had been imprisoned in the Eastern Penitentiary at Philadelphia. Of course, I removed him from the hospital and placed him under arrest. I notified the Assistant General and Surgeon-General and through them the Secretary of War. I at once received a telegram to place the man in the military prison, to report the case to General Thomas and to have him tried by court-martial, and in the meantime, to open all letters addressed to him and find out what I could. These orders were literally executed. The Secretary was exceedingly angry and was determined to punish him severely.

However, letters continued to arrive from his wife near Pittsburgh, Pa., who knew nothing of the events which had been occurring; pitiful heart-broken letters, begging her husband to abstain from evil courses, to commit no robberies and to desist from sending her blankets and stores which she said she was sure he could not have acquired honestly. She told him at the same time that her children were suffering for food, that she had no credit with the baker or the grocer, and that she did not know what would become of them.

Her letters were those of an honest woman, trying to do right and in great trouble of mind and body. These letters impressed me so much that I sent them to the Secretary of War with a strong appeal on behalf of the man. Finally, I was informed that I might leave him in the military prison under the idea of condign punishment to come, and I did so. The poor fellow remained in prison under the idea that he might be executed at any moment. He was still in prison when I left, and I have never heard anything more about him.

I have said already that the hospitals in Nashville numbered eighteen or twenty. Among these was one especially appropriated for small-pox patients. I had on an average a chaplain and a half for each of the ordinary hospitals, but for the small-pox hospital it was impossible to obtain the services of such an officer. One morning, I announced that I intended in two days to detail a chaplain for the small-pox hospital. In the course of the next twenty-four hours, I was visited by almost every chaplain in Nashville, each one representing to me how much good he was doing, and how injurious it would be for the cause of religion and to the Government to move him from his present position. I finally selected one of the most inefficient chaplains under my command, and detailed him, despite his protest, to the hated office. He placed his tent outside of the limits of the hospital. I found on my next visit the following morning that he was by no means over-officious in his ministrations, nor did he ever become so.

At this time, numbers of civilian refugees were pouring into Nashville from the surrounding country. They were a wretched set, uneducated, ignorant, half-barbarous, and in the most destitute state. Very many of their women and children required hospital accommodation, and for this purpose, a refugee hospital was established and eventually proved of value.

When I first entered on duty at Nashville, my detail was that of Superintendent and Director of General Hospitals. Later, in '64, I was ordered by General Thomas, commanding the Department of the Cumberland, to act as Assistant Medical Director. On the 11th of January, '65, I was ordered to perform the duties of Acting Medical Director of the Department of the Cumberland in the absence of the Medical Director in the Field, but on his return to Nashville on February 15th I was relieved from this duty, and continued to act under my first detail of duty, that of Superintendent and Director of General Hospitals.

# CHAPTER XXVIII

The Medical Director on General Thomas's Staff was Surgeon George E. Cooper. He had been the chief witness in the Court-martial of Surgeon-General Hammond, and it was especially on his testimony that Hammond had been cashiered from the army. He was a peculiar man, rough, coarse, and in a certain way honest. He hated Hammond, and at my first interview with him on my arrival at Nashville, he asked me, "Doctor, you were a friend of Hammond's, were you not?" I said, "Yes." "Do you believe him guilty or innocent?" I said, "I believe him innocent of fraud or intentional wrong-doing." He said, "I am glad you say so; I knew you were a friend of Hammond's; I asked you the question to see whether you would answer me in a straightforward manner. Now, Doctor, I will tell you, in the late trial, it was Hammond's head or mine, and I saved mine."

Cooper treated me well, dealing with me in a straightforward and honest manner, and I never received anything but kindness at his hands during my stay in Nashville.

Nashville was always strong in its Southern feeling. There was very little Union element present, and where it existed, it depended upon self-interest rather than patriotism. The lower classes were altogether "secesh."

I saw a remarkable evidence of presence of mind on

342

one occasion, and had an opportunity of witnessing the power of one soldier when on duty. A soldier had arrested two Southern men and was trying to take them to the military prison. They refused to go with him, and the surrounding crowd sympathized with them, and obstructed the soldier in his duties. Finally, he cocked his gun, stepped back one pace, brought his gun so as to cover one of the prisoners in front, and then ordered them to march straight before him. He said, "If anyone attempts to interfere with these men, or to obstruct me in the discharge of my duty, I will fire, I will kill one or two; and then you may do with me as you like."

Two or three officers, I among them, were sitting on a balcony of a restaurant, smoking, and seeing the difficulty, but not knowing what it was, hurried down to his assistance, but the trouble had subsided when we reached there. The men were marching quietly away as prisoners, in front of this solitary soldier, who understood how thoroughly to discharge his duty.

On one occasion, I received a peculiar request from the Provost Marshal. He said a negro came to his office a few days before, a servant in an old family which had left Nashville at the time it was occupied by our troops. Before going, he stated that they had taken all of their silver plate and valuable papers, had placed them in a coffin and had buried them in their lot in the cemetery. The Provost Marshal had been ordered to examine the lot and the coffin, and see whether the money was there or not. For some reason or other, he fancied that a doctor would be a protection against ghosts, or the like, and thought that it would be well to have me go with him when he made the examination. Foolishly, I consented to accompany him on this horrible ghoul-like errand. We went to the cemetery in broad daylight, the guards were placed at the gates, and we approached the vault. Now, it was not a vault in our eastern sense of the term. Nashville is built upon a rock, the soil is only a foot or two deep, and so instead of burying their bodies, they placed them upon the ground in small iron houses constructed above ground, instead of digging a vault beneath the surface. On examining the door of the vault, there were evident signs that it had been opened by force, with a crowbar or pick, within twenty-four hours. However, the Provost Marshal went on. The door was forced. There were coffins in plenty, but no evidences of posthumous disarrangements were to be seen. The negro adhered to his story. He stated that he had helped to deposit the silver in the coffin, and had helped to bring the coffin to the vault, but that things did not look as he left them.

The Provost Marshal determined to search. He insisted upon unscrewing several coffins, but the treasure was not to be found. Finally, influenced by his dislike of the work, and by my earnest solicitations, he desisted and reported at headquarters the result of his search. A great outcry was raised about this piece of vandalism, and I afterwards learned that the negro had been right in his statement, but, somewhat unguarded in the use of his tongue, he had let out his secret before the information was given to the Provost Marshal, and the parties concerned had gone the night before and removed the treasure sought for. I was very much ashamed of my part in this transaction, for which I have no excuse except that of a certain kind of morbid professional curiosity of an anatomical pathological variety.

At this time, a series of robberies occurred in my office, which baffled all my efforts at investigation.  Letters for patients in the hospital, with uncertain addresses, and oftentimes to medical officers, were sent daily to my office for distribution to the hospitals.  Repeated complaints were made that letters known to be sent were not received at their destination, especially when these letters contained drafts or money.  Investigation satisfied me that the thefts were committed in my office by some of the clerks or attendants on duty.  I had frequent interviews with officials of the Post-office Department, but all our attempts failed to detect the delinquents. We therefore placed decoy letters in the mail, containing marked bank-notes.  Those which I placed in my box myself were stolen during the night.  I determined to arrest everybody in the office, clerks, orderlies, and sentries,—and I should say that the sentries had been changed the night before, and strangers from distant commands placed on duty.  A thorough search was made of the parties interested, the carpets were torn up, and drawers, books and papers overhauled, but all in vain, the daring thieves were never discovered, and no light could be obtained as to the adroit robberies.

On the 6th of March, 1865, I received an invitation from the medical officers on duty at Nashville, asking me to give them a series of eight lectures on some points connected with the surgical history of the war.

This I was most glad to do.  I selected for my subject the flight of projectiles, and the character of the wounds they produce at the entrance and exit, always a favorite subject of mine.  The projectiles to illustrate the course, were kindly furnished to me by Major Mordecai, of the Ordnance Department, and rifle barrels were sent to show the character of the rifling, etc. Many illustrations were prepared by one of my clerks, who was a good draughtsman. These projectiles and diagrams I have still, and have often used them. The lectures were delivered in the Hall of the Masonic Building, a large room. My audience was a brilliant one, including all of the medical officers in Nashville, many of the Staff and other military officers in uniform, and others. I had two cavalry soldiers for assistants in uniform, and I lectured in full uniform. I enjoyed these lectures very much, and was only sorry that I could not give the entire course. This, however, was not possible, as the lectures were brought to a close by the acceptance at Washington of my resignation. Of this I must say a few words.

Since I had been relieved at Washington in October, 1864, and sent to the West, I had made up my mind that in view of the approaching termination of the war, my family interests at home imperatively demanded that after serving a few months more, I should send in my resignation. This, I accordingly did on February 16, 1865, in the following letters:

"Nashville, Feby. 16, 1865.

Genl:—

I have the honor hereby to tender my immediate and unconditional resignation of my commission, as Surgeon of Volunteers (formerly Brigade Surgeon, August 30th, 1861). I am led to do so by the urgent necessity which exists for my immediate presence at my home in Philadelphia, in order that I may protect the financial interests of my mother and sisters, jeopardized by unexpected circumstances, which no one but myself can properly act upon.

I hereby state that I am not indebted to the U. S., that I have no public property in my possession, except that which I am prepared to turn over to the proper officers; that I have not been absent without leave; that no charges exist affecting my pay, and that I have not been subject at any time to charges, or trial by Court-martial. I was last paid by Major A. Holt to January 31, 1865.

Very Respty,

Yr. Obt. Servt.

J.  H.  BRINTON,

Surg. U. S. V.

Brig. Genl. L. Thomas,
 Adjt. Genl. U. S. A.
  War Department, Washington, D. C."


After a delay of some weeks, I received, March 23, 1865, the following acceptance of my resignation:

"B. 162.  B. 165.

War Dept. Adjt. General's Office,

Washington, March 11, 1865.

Sir:

Your resignation has been accepted by the President of the United States, to take effect the 9th day of March, 1865, on condition that you receive no final payments until you shall have satisfied the Pay Department that you are not indebted to the United States.  I am Sir,

Very resptfy.

Yr. Obt. Servt.,

(Sd)  S. F. CHALFIN,

Asst. Adjt. Genl.

Surgeon John H. Brinton,
 U. S. Volunteers,
  Nashville, Tenn."

Presenting this order at the headquarters of General Thomas, I was relieved from duty by the accompanying order:

"Headquarters, Department of the Cumberland,
Nashville, Tenn. March 23, 1865.

SPECIAL FIELD ORDERS NO. 76

[Extract]

IV. Surgeon J. H. Brinton, U. S. V., is hereby relieved from duty in this Department, his resignation having been accepted by the War Department.

By Command of Major General Thomas,

HENRY M. CIST,
Asst. Adjt. Genl.

Surgeon J. H. Brinton,
"U. S. V."

No longer a soldier, I was now a citizen, and having turned over my official belongings to my successor in office, I prepared to return home.

I received from some of the surgeons on duty at Nashville, a number of specimens of gunshot. These they had a right to give me, as they had been notified from Washington that they need forward no more wet preparations to the Museum. I was glad to get a few, and had them barreled, and afterward took them to Philadelphia, where they now form part of my cabinet. I had also collected some shot, shell and muskets, used to illustrate my lectures at the Masonic Hall. All these, I passed home under the following orders, a permit, which I obtained without trouble, as all my friends seemed to sympathize with me in my desire to take home my military illustrations for my future lectures.

"Headquarters, Department of the Cumberland,
Office Prov. Mar. Genl.,
Nashville, March 23, 1865.
Permit is hereby granted Surgeon J. H. Brinton,
Supt. & Director of Hospitals to ship by express or
otherwise from Nashville, Tenn., to Philadelphia, Pa.,
one keg, two boxes, and one package, containing two
(2) damaged and condemned muskets and objects of
professional interest.

By command of

MAJ. GENL. THOMAS,
(Sgd)   R. M. GOODWIN,
Capt. & A. P. W. Genl."

"Headquarters, Department of the Cumberland,
March 23, 1865.
Guard and Military Conductors will pass J. H. Brin-
ton, Esq., beyond the limits of this Department.

By Order MAJ. GENL. THOMAS,

SOUTHARD HOFFMAN,
A. A. G."

I had greatly enjoyed my duty in Nashville. It had
been full of incident and new experiences. At first, I
had been overworked, but had soon gotten affairs in
good running order, and with the exception of the
Thomas incident, everything had gone along smoothly.
I had formed, too, some very pleasant acquaintances, and
among others, I greatly enjoyed the society of Surgeon
Fletcher on duty as Medical Purveyor. He was an Eng-
lishman, thoroughly educated, and a deep Shakesperean
scholar. Many and many a pleasant talk we had together,
and much I learned from him. After the war was ended,
he was in the office of the Surgeon-General at Washing-

ton, and was employed in the library of the office of the Surgeon-General, and in the preparation, with Dr. Billings, of the Index Medicus.

After taking leave of my friends at Nashville, my last official act was to order the running to Louisville of a hospital train of cars, for as the Director of Hospitals, I had charge of two or three trains, thoroughly fitted up for the conveyance of sick and wounded. On one of these, I shipped a number of invalids, with whom I went to Louisville. I was accompanied by one of my orderlies who had formed a strange attachment to me, why, I could not tell. He was as sharp as steel, and I never quite trusted him. In fact, at the time of the robbery of letters in my office, I suspected him. But odd as it may seem, the harder I was on him, the more he clung to me. Before I left, he said he would like a few days' absence, and come to Philadelphia with me. I assented and he did so, looking after my comforts with the utmost care, and paying great attention to the safety of my kegs and boxes; he behaved, indeed, as a model attendant.

We stopped in Louisville, where I saw the Assistant Surgeon-General, and afterwards stayed a day in Cincinnati. We then went straight to Philadelphia, arriving there in the latter days of March, 1865; my orderly starting for Nashville again on the same evening.

I found my Mother and sisters well. How glad I was to be with them again I cannot tell you. It seemed strange to me to be once more a civilian, to lay aside my uniform, and to feel that I was again my own master. But it was hard to discard the habits acquired in the army, and to fall again into the humdrum customs of peaceful life. The Rebellion was now in its death gasp, military operations were over in the West, and were closing in the East. On the 9th of April, 1865, General Lee surrendered the Army of Northern Virginia, and the war was practically at an end. The news was telegraphed from Washington about ten o'clock in the evening, and our city was notified by the screeching of the whistles of the fire engines and by clamor and noise of every imaginable character. The War was over. The great experiment had been made. It had been definitely proven that the United States was a Nation.

# APPENDIX

LETTERS FROM GENERALS GRANT, SHERIDAN AND ROSECRANS

# APPENDIX

NEAR CORINTH, MISS.,
May 24th, 1862.

HON. E. B. WASHBURN,
Washington, D. C.

DEAR SIR:
Permit me to introduce to your acquaintance Surgeon Brinton of the Army, a gentleman who has served on my Staff at Cairo and in the field. Dr. Brinton was with me at Belmont, Fort Henry and Fort Donelson, and as we have lived together most of the time for the last six months our acquaintance is more than transient, it has become intimate.

Any attention shown Dr. Brinton will be regarded as a personal favor to myself.

Yours truly,
U. S. GRANT.

HOLLY SPRINGS, MISSISSIPPI,
Jan. 7th, 1863.

HON. E. B. WASHBURN, M.C.,
Washington, D. C.

DEAR SIR:
Learning that additional Medical Inspectors, with the rank of Lieut. Col., are to be appointed, I want to urge the appointment of Surgeon J. H. Brinton, who is now on duty in Washington, having been selected as one to compile the Medical History of this rebellion.

I have selected you to write to on this subject because you have always shown such willingness to befriend me. I acknowledge the many obligations I am under to you and thank you from the bottom of my heart for them. I will feel further obligation if you can give this matter your attention and support.

355

Dr. Brinton has served with me and messed with me. I know him well. He is an honor to his profession and to the service both for his moral worth and attainments in and out of his profession.

Although yet but a young man you will find that Dr. Brinton has won for himself, in Philadelphia where he resides, a reputation attained by but few in the country, of any age, and by none others as young as himself.

I am now feeling great anxiety about Vicksburg. The last news from there was favorable, but I know that Kirby Smith is on his way to reinforce Johnson. My last advices from there were to the 31st. If Banks arrived about that time all is well. If he did not Sherman has had a hard time of it.

I could not reinforce from here in time, and too much territory would be exposed by doing it if I could.

Yours truly,<br>U. S. Grant.

West Point, N. Y.,<br>June 11th, 1873.

My dear Doctor:

Learning from your letter of the 9th inst. that you are a candidate for the "Professorship of Anatomy" in the Jefferson Medical College of Pa., it affords me pleasure to bear testimony to your professional skill and ability as demonstrated, in the field, in the early days of the rebellion. At Donelson particularly I always regarded the improvised arrangements for taking care of the wounded as due to your executive ability and energy, and the care taken of them—and success in bringing so many badly wounded out alive—as very largely due to your professional skill.

While I do not join in special recommendation of one friend over another for any position over which I exercise no control, yet I can say, and do say unreservedly, that I do not doubt but that if the coveted professorship should fall to you it will be filled with honor and credit to the institution, and that the directors who put you there will never have reason to regret the choice.

My kindest regards to Mrs. B.—to whose friends I once gave a favorable endorsement of you—and the children.

Very truly yours,

U. S. GRANT.

DR. J. H. BRINTON,
Phila., Pa.

CHICAGO, ILL.,
June 16th, '73.

It gives me great pleasure to acknowledge a personal acquaintance with Dr. Brinton during the War of the Rebellion. In common with all his acquaintance, I can bear testimony to his high professional standing and the zeal with which he worked in the cause of science.

His devotion to the unfortunate wounded of our Armies will always be gratefully remembered by his sincere friend,

P. H. SHERIDAN,
Lt. General U. S. A.

PHILADELPHIA, PA.,
June 9th, 1873.

MY DEAR DOCTOR:

Learning that you are to be an applicant for a medical professorship, I thought you might be gratified to have a note from me saying that during your service as Surgeon in the Dept. of Missouri under my command I formed a very high opinion of your ability and professional qualification, as evinced by my appointment of you a chief medical director of the Army in the field during the campaign against Price in 1864, the duties of which, as all others under my command, you discharged in a manner that commanded my approbation and won my personal esteem.

Wishing you a successful and happy professional career, I remain always your friend,

W. S. ROSECRANS.

DR. J. H. BRINTON,
Philadelphia, Pa.

# INDEX

359

JOHN Y. SIMON, professor of history at Southern Illinois University at Carbondale, is the editor of *The Papers of Ulysses S. Grant* and a founder of the Association for Documentary Editing. He has published more than sixty articles in such journals as *Military Affairs, Journal of American History, Ohio History, Journal of the Abraham Lincoln Association,* and *Journal of the Illinois State Historical Society.* The editor of *The Personal Memoirs of Julia Dent Grant* and the coeditor of *Ulysses S. Grant: Essays and Documents* and *The Continuing Civil War: Essays in Honor of the Civil War Round Table of Chicago,* Simon has held office in national professional associations and has served as a consultant for federal and state agencies, university and commercial presses, and other editorial projects.

JOHN S. HALLER, JR., holds a dual appointment as a professor of history at Southern Illinois University at Carbondale and a professor of medical humanities at the SIU School of Medicine, Springfield. He is the author of *Outcasts from Evolution: Scientific Attitudes of Racial Inferiority, 1859–1900; The Physician and Sexuality in Victorian America; American Medicine in Transition, 1840–1910; Farmcarts to Fords: A History of the Military Ambulance, 1790–1925; Medical Protestants: The Eclectics in American Medicine, 1825–1939;* and *Kindly Medicine: The Physio-Medicals in America, 1836–1911.* He is the author of numerous articles on the history of nineteenth-century sexuality, anthropology, medicine, and pharmacy and is the editor of *Caduceus: A Humanities Journal for Medicine and the Health Sciences.*